SHAKESPEARE'S *HAMLET*

SHAKESPEARE'S *HAMLET*

Philosophical Perspectives

Edited by Tzachi Zamir

OXFORD
UNIVERSITY PRESS

OXFORD
UNIVERSITY PRESS

Oxford University Press is a department of the University of Oxford. It furthers
the University's objective of excellence in research, scholarship, and education
by publishing worldwide. Oxford is a registered trade mark of Oxford University
Press in the UK and certain other countries.

Published in the United States of America by Oxford University Press
198 Madison Avenue, New York, NY 10016, United States of America.

© Oxford University Press 2018

CIP data is on file at the Library of Congress
ISBN 978–0–19–0–69852–2 (pbk.); 978–0–19–0–69851–5 (cloth)

1 3 5 7 9 8 6 4 2

Paperback printed by Webcom, Inc., Canada
Hardback printed by Bridgeport National Bindery, Inc., United States of America

CONTENTS

SERIES EDITOR'S FOREWORD

RICHARD ELDRIDGE

At least since Plato had Socrates criticize the poets and attempt to displace Homer as the authoritative articulator and transmitter of human experience and values, philosophy and literature have developed as partly competing, partly complementary enterprises. Both literary writers and philosophers have frequently studied and commented on each other's texts and ideas, sometimes with approval, sometimes with disapproval, in their efforts to become clearer about human life and about valuable commitments—moral, artistic, political, epistemic, metaphysical, and religious, as may be. Plato's texts themselves register the complexity and importance of these interactions in being dialogues in which both deductive argumentation and dramatic narration do central work in furthering a complex body of views.

While these relations have been widely recognized, they have also frequently been ignored or misunderstood, as academic disciplines have gone their separate ways within their modern institutional settings. Philosophy has often turned to science or mathematics as providing models of knowledge; in doing so it has often explicitly set itself against cultural entanglements and literary devices, rejecting, at least officially, the importance of plot, figuration, and imagery in favor of supposedly plain speech about the truth. Literary study has moved variously through formalism, structuralism, poststructuralism, and cultural studies, among other movements, as modes of approach to a literary text. In doing so it has understood literary texts as sample instances of images, structures, personal styles, or failures of consciousness, or it has seen the literary text as a largely fungible product, fundamentally shaped by wider pressures and patterns of consumption and expectation that affect and figure in nonliterary textual production as well. It has thus set itself against the idea that major literary texts productively and originally address philosophical problems of value and commitment precisely through their form, diction, imagery, and development, even while these works also resist claiming conclusively to solve the problems that occupy them.

These distinct academic traditions have yielded important perspectives and insights. But in the end none of them has been kind to the idea of major literary works as achievements in thinking about values and human life, often in distinctive, open, self-revising, self-critical ways. At the same time readers outside institutional settings, and often enough philosophers and literary scholars too, have turned to major literary texts precisely in order to engage with their productive, materially, and medially specific patterns and processes of thinking. These turns to literature have, however, not so far been systematically encouraged within disciplines, and they have generally occurred independently of each other.

The aim of this series is to make manifest the multiple, complex engagements with philosophical ideas and problems that lie at the hearts of major literary texts. In doing so, its volumes aim not only to help philosophers and literary scholars of various kinds to find rich affinities and provocations to further thought and work, they also aim to bridge various gaps between academic disciplines and between those disciplines and the experiences of extrainstitutional readers.

Each volume focuses on a single, undisputedly major literary text. Both philosophers with training and experience in literary study and literary scholars with training and experience in philosophy are invited to engage with themes, details, images, and incidents in the focal text, through which philosophical problems are held in view, worried at, and reformulated. Decidedly not a project simply to formulate A's philosophy of X as a finished product, merely illustrated in the text, and decidedly not a project to explain the literary work entirely by reference to external social configurations and forces, the effort is instead to track the work of open thinking in literary forms, as they lie both neighbor to and aslant from philosophy. As Walter Benjamin once wrote, "new centers of reflection are continually forming," as problems of commitment and value of all kinds take on new shapes for human agents in relation to changing historical circumstances, where reflective address remains possible. By considering how such centers of reflection are formed and expressed in and through literary works, as they engage with philosophical problems of agency, knowledge, commitment, and value, these volumes undertake to present both literature and philosophy as, at times, productive forms of reflective, medial work in relation both to each other and to social circumstances, and to show how this work is specifically undertaken and developed in distinctive and original ways in exemplary works of literary art.

Richard Eldridge
Charles and Harriett Cox McDowell Professor of Philosophy
Swarthmore College

CONTRIBUTORS

Sarah Beckwith is the Katherine Everitt Professor of English, Theater Studies and Religion at Duke University. She is the author of *Signifying God: Social Relation and Symbolic Act in the York Corpus Christi Plays* (University of Chicago Press, 2001) and *Shakespeare and the Grammar of Forgiveness* (Cornell University Press, 2011). She is an editor of the series *Re-Formations* (University of Notre Dame Press), and of the *Journal of Medieval and Early Modern Studies*. She is now at work on a book on Shakespearean tragedy and ethics, and another on versions of *The Winter's Tale.*

Sanford Budick received his A.B. from Harvard College in 1963 and Ph.D. from Yale University in 1966. Before being appointed Professor of English at the Hebrew University of Jerusalem he was Professor of English at Cornell University. At the Hebrew University he served twice as chair of the English department, was a Fellow at the Institute for Advanced Studies, and was founding director (1980–2000) of the Center for Literary Studies. He is the recipient of Guggenheim and NEH fellowships. He has written books on Dryden, on eighteenth-century poetry, on Milton, on Kant's relation to Milton, and on the

Western theory of tradition. With Geoffrey Hartman and Wolfgang Iser, he has edited collections of essays on a variety of topics in literary theory. He is currently writing about Shakespeare's plays, Wordsworth's poetry, and Milton's influence on Wordsworth.

John Gibson is Professor of Philosophy at the University of Louisville and Director of the Commonwealth Center for Humanities and Society. He publishes in aesthetics and the philosophy of literature, and he is especially concerned with connections between these areas and central issues in the philosophy of language and the philosophy of the self. Much of his recent research explores the uniqueness of the forms of meaning artworks bear and the implications this has for accounts of the cultural, ethical, and cognitive significance of art. He is the author of *Fiction and the Weave of Life* and is currently completing a new book on poetry, metaphor, and nonsense, both for Oxford University Press. He is the editor or coeditor of numerous volumes, including *The Philosophy of Poetry, Essays on Fiction, Narrative and Knowledge,* and *The Routledge Companion to Philosophy of Literature.*

Kristin Gjesdal is Associate Professor of Philosophy at Temple University and Professor II of Philosophy at the University of Oslo. She is the author of *Gadamer and the Legacy of German Idealism* (Cambridge University Press, 2009), *Herder's Hermeneutics: History, Poetry, Enlightenment* (Cambridge University Press, 2017), and a number of articles in the areas of aesthetics, hermeneutics, and nineteenth-century philosophy. Kristin Gjesdal also works in philosophy of literature, with a special emphasis on Shakespeare and Ibsen, and is the editor of *Ibsen's "Hedda Gabler": Philosophical Perspectives* (forthcoming with Oxford University Press). She is also the editor of *Key Debates in Nineteenth Century European Philosophy* (Routledge, 2016), coeditor of *The Oxford Handbook of German Philosophy in the*

Nineteenth Century (Oxford University Press, 2015) and the forth-coming *Cambridge Companion to Hermeneutics*.

David Hillman is Senior Lecturer in the Faculty of English at the University of Cambridge, and Fellow and Director of Studies at King's College, Cambridge. He is the author of *Shakespeare's Entrails: Belief, Scepticism and the Interior of the body* (Palgrave, 2007) and of *Shakespeare and Freud* in the Great Shakespeareans series (Continuum, 2012). He is the editor or coeditor of *The Cambridge Companion to the Body in Literature* (Cambridge University Press, 2014); *The Book of Interruptions* (Peter Lang, 2007), *The Body in Parts: Fantasies of Corporeality in Early Modern Europe* (Routledge, 1997), and *Authority and Representation in Early Modern Discourse* (Johns Hopkins University Press, 1996). He is currently working on a monograph, *Greetings and Partings in Shakespeare and Early Modern England*.

Paul A. Kottman is Associate Professor of Comparative Literature at the New School for Social Research. He is the author of *Love as Human Freedom* (Stanford University Press, 2017), *Tragic Conditions in Shakespeare* (Johns Hopkins University Press, 2009) and *A Politics of the Scene* (Stanford University Press, 2008). He is the coeditor (with Michael Squire) of *The Art of Hegel's Aesthetics: Hegelian Philosophy and the Perspectives of Art History* (Fink, forthcoming), and the editor of *The Insistence of Art: Aesthetic Philosophy after Early Modernity* (Fordham University Press, 2017) and *Philosophers on Shakespeare* (Stanford University Press, 2009). He is also the editor of the book series Square One: First Order Questions in the Humanities (Stanford University Press).

Joshua Landy is the Andrew B. Hammond Professor of French and Professor of Comparative Literature at Stanford University, where he codirects the Initiative in Philosophy and Literature. His books include *Philosophy as Fiction: Self, Deception, and Knowledge in Proust* (Oxford University Press, 2004), *How to Do Things with Fictions* (Oxford University Press, 2012), and (as coeditor) *The Re-enchantment of the World: Secular Magic in a Rational Age* (Stanford University Press, 2009).

David Schalkwyk is currently Academic Director of Global Shakespeare, a joint venture between Queen Mary and the University of Warwick. He was formerly Director of Research at the Folger Shakespeare Library in Washington, DC, and editor of the *Shakespeare Quarterly*. Before that he was Professor of English at the University of Cape Town, where he held the positions of Head of Department and Deputy Dean in the Faculty of the Humanities. His books include *Speech and Performance in Shakespeare's Sonnets and Plays* (Cambridge University Press, 2002), *Literature and the Touch of the Real* (University of Delaware Press, 2004), and *Shakespeare, Love and Service* (Cambridge University Press, 2008), *Hamlet's Dreams: The Robben Island Shakespeare* (Arden Shakespeare, 2013), and *The Word against the World: The Bakhtin Circle* (Skene, 2016). His latest monograph, *Shakespeare, Love and Language* is forthcoming from Cambridge University Press in 2017.

Paul Woodruff is Professor of Philosophy and Classics at the University of Texas at Austin. He has published on ancient Greek philosophy, ethics, and philosophy of theater. His recent books include *The Necessity of Theater: The Art of Watching and Being Watched* (Oxford University Press, 2008) and *The Ajax Dilemma: Justice, Fairness, and Rewards* (Oxford University Press, 2011).

Tzachi Zamir is a philosopher and a literary critic (Associate Professor of English and Comparative Literature) at the Hebrew

University of Jerusalem. Zamir is the author of *Double Vision: Moral Philosophy and Shakespearean Drama* (Princeton University Press, 2006), *Ethics and the Beast* (Princeton University Press, 2007), *Acts: Theater, Philosophy, and the Performing Self* (University of Michigan Press, 2014), and *Ascent: Philosophy and Paradise Lost*, forthcoming from Oxford University Press.

SHAKESPEARE'S *HAMLET*

Introduction

TZACHI ZAMIR

Is Hamlet a genuine philosopher or a pseudophilosopher? Does he exemplify the kind of reflectivity that interrogates experiences for their abstract underpinnings, or does he, rather, instantiate a recoiling from life into bubbles of thought, seeking escape rather than illumination? When philosophers take a close look at *Hamlet*, their different observations are likely to be rooted in how they answer these prior questions. Those for whom Hamlet is an authentic thinker will grant weight to his abstractions, probing them for insights on mortality, or on grief, or on feeling the world's richness. Those for whom Hamlet is merely toying with philosophy will look for insights in the play regarding the relationship between faux thought and pressing circumstances.

While these orientations are irreconcilable—one does or does not take the content of Hamlet's assertions seriously—let none overlook what both standpoints share: a sense of growth and of understanding something when spending time with *Hamlet*, the work. Whether growth issues from Hamlet's words or from fathoming something through his intimacy with (or his disconnection from) his words, both camps attempt to account for an overlapping intuition—that *Hamlet* extends to philosophers, in particular, an invitation to realize something. True, all great literary works promise and deliver insights. Yet something about this play—specifically, its protagonist—proves especially irresistible for philosophers. If, as Hamlet says, theater is meant to mirror back identity-related truths that bypass defensive grids, philosophers encounter in Hamlet a version of the shifts between experiencing and reflecting, shifts they are familiar with. Philosophers will be disinclined to simply equate a temper of this nature with philosophy, because in philosophy the buds of thought are expected to blossom into disciplined (defined, argued) claims. Still, Hamlet captures the spirit of a sizzling philosophical soul, a mind instinctively leaping from the particular to the general, from observation to its potentially greater significance. Hamlet also emobodies the captivating urgency of a young person's search. And it is this vitality in transiting from feeling to thinking that renders Hamlet winning. Nowhere else in Shakespeare do we find such a sympathetic portrayal of philosophizing. When his characters flatter themselves for having uttered something wise, it typically comes in the form of self-posturing (Navarre's young aristocrats, who decide to devote themselves to lofty study), or of myopic cynical self-importance (Jacques's in *As You Like It*). As for the supposed wisdom of the old, such is exposed as either ludicrously hollow (as exemplified by the stuffy Holofernes and Nathaniel, the smug academics of *Love's Labour's Lost*) or is rendered cold, aloof, and even cruel (Prospero). The "philosophy" by which the Friar attempts to sooth Romeo is unserviceable, and is immediately trashed.

When abstract insights genuinely crystalize in Shakespeare, this never results from someone setting out to reflect. It hits unexpectedly. You crawl about in a battlefield eying the corpses of the young and dead, and that gets you to understand something about the emptiness of honor. You lose your partner, and sense how his presence had infused meaning and variety into everything you saw—and that *this* is the love you had been searching for. One suspects that the idea of a detached mind preoccupied with rigorous reflection—an Aquinas, an Erasmus, a Wittgenstein—would draw amused curiosity from Shakespeare, not respect.

Hamlet differs. Even his most committed admirers will find it hard to be persuaded by his conclusions. Are all women hypocritical? Are all men untrustworthy? Do we persist in living only because we fear something worse in death? Is the sacrifice of thousands of lives justified when honor is at stake? His way of reaching such surmises— his "method," if you will—is also unimpressive. The guarded self-criticism of a mature philosophical mind is altogether missing. He appears to carelessly generalize from his own case in ways that help him cope with his predicament. He is also indifferent to his conclusions after reaching them, tossing them aside as soon as they are formulated. They do not gather up. They do not ask to be integrated. A genuinely curious mind would not be as offhand with its findings. And yet, while Hamlet is not a philosopher, there is a nonartificial quality in the manner whereby experiences spark reflections in him. Philosophers cannot but warm to this. It is the lifeblood of philosophy, the energized restlessness that gets people to philosophize to begin with. This explains why, while the thought content of Polonius's or Claudius's assertions is more defendable than Hamlet's, we remain unmoved. (Mock them if you must, but first do them the courtesy of taking a hard look at some of Hamlet's own "discoveries.")

Animating Hamlet's language when he articulates wrong thoughts is a kind of energy that makes his words pass for more than eloquence. What comes across as admirable is a struggle to think, a dislike for platitudes, a rejection of what is "common"—the word he picks on with such loathing as soon as we meet him. What elicits admiration, too, are his questions: How can things go on when a loved one has died? More specifically, under what conditions, temporal or other, can moving on after a death justifiably occur? What counts as a proper response to injustice upon realizing that whatever one does, there can be no undoing of the initial wrong, no retrieval of that which has been taken away? What do our commitments to the dead amount to? How can we continue injecting meaning into action despite the degradation of death and our own replaceability? Hamlet's is a mind that has been hurled into straits in which the most discomforting questions are faced. He misses none of the holes that gape within the sense-making grids with which he has been equipped. He cannot cast himself into the role of an avenging son, the model which so many others in and around him—Fortinbras, Laertes, Pyrrhus—adopt with such ease. He cannot reconcile himself to the ordinariness of death through the routes offered him by Claudius, by his mother, or by the gravedigger. The words he is so nimble with are, he finds, deceptive and ineffective Band-Aids.

Has such a thoroughgoing crisis been induced by grief? The temptation to conclude this, to regard *Hamlet* as a "mourning play," should not last. The more time one spends with Hamlet's hyperbolic, ultimately impersonal idealizations of his dead father, the more strained becomes the belief that some deep emotional tie has been broken. It seems less the loss itself than the bewildered anger at how life so easily resumes that shakes Hamlet's trust in the standard maps that enable life's navigating. For this to amount to the quality of rage anticipated in grief, a more lingering focus on the singularity of the person mourned for is expected. But Hamlet's father is, for him, an aloof, godlike, faultless figure, somewhat disembodied even when he was still alive. Were Hamlet primarily a mourner, one would expect emotions to play a far more central role in his experience. Yet, apart from anger and disgust, he appears to orbit about emotions, not to dwell in them. He jokingly reports that he has lost all his mirth. He tells Ophelia that he has loved her once. His suicidal thoughts do not go beyond a flirt with death. Such a judgment does not weaken if one acknowledges that the detachment he exudes throughout the play—his less than kind break from Ophelia, his belittling the deaths of Rosencrantz, Guildenstern, and Polonius—may well reflect a withdrawal from sunnier days (he was, after all, loved by so many). Nor does such a judgment alienate Hamlet from his audience, particularly not from philosophers. To experience grief not primarily through waves of feelings would draw sympathy from the latter, precisely because Hamlet's emotional distance does not devolve into cynicism or world-weariness. It is, rather, accompanied by unremitting questioning. What philosophers are looking at, and cannot but respect, is a vibrant young mind which is pained by the dearth of what passes for explanation by others, and demands a better answer. Philosoph has numerous lookalikes; cravings for superiority, for evasion, for self-import, can all masquerade as a search for wisdom. Hamlet is a neophyte version of the real thing.

Moreover, to philosophize is to pressurize one's vocabulary, its aptness, its precision. Like poetry, philosophy appeals to those who are at home in language but who also doubt it. Hamlet thrives in this ambiguity. He is as eloquent as a Cicero. But he is also aware of language's capacity to conceal complexities. Like a philosopher, he experiences a burning need to know. To begin with, the need is unphilosophical: the knowledge Hamlet is after—the cause of his father's death—is of practical import. Yet from this limited inquiry soon spiral out more abstract puzzles. The zone he enters seems anchored to his worldly circumstances only by chance. Nothing that can take place in the world—his father brought back to life, an acquittal of Claudius by discovering that the ghost is a misleading devil— will enable Hamlet to become a Laertes, a Horatio, or a Fortinbras. Forced into acquaintance with the imperfect machinery responsible for attaching meanings to things, Hamlet will not be turned away or reacculturate himself to his conventions. In this, too, he is like a philosopher.

Shunning norms, Hamlet shares the philosopher's loneliness as well. Hamlet's solitude lies in his wavering among explanatory schemes that make themselves more or less appealing, but are ultimately found to be equally useless. Shakespeare grants him the kind of stand-apart quality he gives Richard II and Lear: not only do you find yourself alone, but you also realize that loneliness was always there. For Lear and Richard, this understanding crystalizes when discovering the hypocrisy of the attachment-talk of others. Hamlet finds this, too, but rather than merely grieve for the shattered illusion, he begins searching for what is real. The solitude resembles that of Plato's released philosopher who, upon returning to the cave, is unable to communicate his findings to those who have never left it. The newly liberated philosopher and the imprisoned non-philosopher share signifiers, but the signifieds differ. Unlike Hamlet, Plato's philosopher has actually glimpsed truth, whereas Hamlet merely senses that the terms he has inherited are polluted. The miscommunication, though, is the same, as is the inability to go back to the simpler pre-reflective self. Perhaps that is why the story he asks Horatio to divulge after his death may only be communicated "more or less."

Hamlet is no philosopher. But, perhaps, more than any other character in literature, he succeeds in embodying the cue for philosophical passion.

None of the authors of the following essays perceives literature merely as a lively exemplification of a philosophical insight. Literature, more precisely, literature written for theatrical performance, is not a mere illustration of a philosophical idea. And yet, when these authors allow themselves to be stopped by a work such as *Hamlet*, claims begin to form. These claims are directed at concepts that cannot but interest a philosopher. Philosophy is both addressed and undermined by this play; philosophy's interests are satisfied, but one suspects that its standard methods are being bypassed. How to account for this duality without devaluing any of its dimensions?

The following essays may be regarded as various responses to this question. These responses—it will be pointless to deny—are often incompatible with one another: while all of them address *Hamlet* and philosophy, they differ not only in the philosophical insights being attributed to the play, but also with regard to what the very act of locating philosophy in literature means. The readers of this book are invited to consider whether this plurality is in and of itself damning (if sensitive readings support conflicting knowledge-claims attributed to the same play, something in the method as such could be off). Conversely, they may be led to think that the incompatible knowledge-claims suggest that we suffer from an engrained, overly restricted perspective on what constitutes philosophical understanding. Perhaps some concepts encompass disagreement, tension, and inner contrapuntal movements. Perhaps believing P and not P is impossible, but experiencing P and not P is not only possible, but occurs quite often. Perhaps such experiential understanding—representable and conveyable by literature— may cluster together incompatibles in uneasy conjunctions (indeed, perhaps it must do so, for such literature to be true to life's ruggedness).

All of the contributions examine knowledge and what locating it within a literary work may require. Yet readers who choose to read the chapters in sequence will encounter the more explicit engagements with this question in the earlier essays. John Gibson finds in *Hamlet* an intimation of a new way for understanding "literary knowledge"—the kind of insightfulness attributed to a literary work that bears fruits relevant for philosophy. The knowledge Gibson sees *Hamlet* as communicating is termed by him "narrative understanding," an accessing of the ways by which concepts become more than ghostly entities hovering over cultures and selves. Concepts entwine with personal and cultural "forms of life," and sensitive literary works capture and convey this. Such works communicate the interlacing between concept and emotion, between concept and circumstances, between concept and moods, feelings, and identity-claims. By providing the glue that bonds selves to cultural framings, such literature thereby offers a distinct kind of knowledge. A narrative demonstration of this kind, Gibson maintains, makes a human possibility meaningful not by establishing its truth, but by "showing that a coherent story can be told of it."

The coherence of the story should not be confused with the coherence of the unfolded possibility. Rather than insist on narrative coherence and flow, Gibson finds that *Hamlet* lingers on experiences of discontinuity and of distance from one's voice. He argues that "what is dramatized is the challenge of self-organization in the face of such [a crisis]: of our ability to arrange the moving parts of our psychological interior into a coherent self when called on to establish who we are through our actions." Hamlet's challenge, for Gibson, is to identify with an estranged voice, a voice that cannot be persuaded that the available possible commitments are compelling. His Hamlet shows "that one can generate, and identify with, a voice that functions only to express alienation from all that would otherwise make self-constitution possible: desires, thoughts, actions—the whole lot of it." In relating to Hamlet, we feel for an identity that resists identifying.

Paul Woodruff shares Gibson's interest in the distinct knowledge accessed through *Hamlet*. Yet whereas Gibson relates to the play as a species of literature, Woodruff regards it as theater. For Gibson, *Hamlet* is a work designed to be read; for Woodruff, it is a work to be watched. Such radical differences in outlook—two sensitive critics who regard the same work as belonging to altogether different aesthetic types—may or may not be the reason motivating Gibson and Woodruff to locate learning from *Hamlet* as issuing from dissimilar processes. Nevertheless, the different paths taken by Woodruff and Gibson provide the reader of this book a rewarding critical entry point into the essays: considering the relative importance that authors allot (or not) to the theatrical setting of *Hamlet* in their assessment of the relationships between the play and philosophy. Are the arguments professed with regard to the philosophical contributions of literature—say, its capacity to offer unique kinds of knowledge—exportable to the context of *performed* literature? Alternatively, perhaps the assessment of the potential contribution of a *dramatic* work to philosophy demands the forging of a new rationale? Shakespeareans may sense here the shadow of an old controversy dating back to Jonson regarding "audiences" versus "spectators": is theater to be heard or watched? To put the question in more precise terms: is theater—Shakespeare's kind—basically poetry, whose staging is redundant, or does the synergy between poetry and creative performers somehow beget an aesthetic object whose philosophical relevance is irreducible to its words, captivating as these may be? Woodruff's emphasis on "watching" suggests the latter.

Woodruff's wisdom differs from Gibson's contextual knowledge. It is an awareness that requires repetition, and is not achieved once and for all. Such wisdom often manifests itself in an acute apprehension of the narrowness of the parameters of one's capacity to understand. It is therefore humbling: "Tragic poets offer us a wisdom that is all too human, that reminds us of our limitations, our potential for error, our destiny for death—and, above all, paradoxically, of the folly of believing that one has found wisdom." Woodruff thereby overturns a staple of theories of tragedy: the notion that tragedies present and encourage self-knowledge. For Woodruff, critics such as Tolstoy, who had deprecated *Hamlet* for featuring a protagonist who has not been sufficiently thought through, miss the gold. Yes, Hamlet will not achieve self-knowledge. But sometimes that, precisely, is the point. *Hamlet* is not a play in which a hidden blueprint is revealed. What surfaces, rather, is an unfathomable core in others, in us. To acknowledge this mysteriousness rather than resist it is, sometimes, wisdom.

TZACHI ZAMIR

While Gibson and Woodruff think of "knowledge" or "wisdom" along lines of epistemic mastery—the grasping of an insight, the internalization of a realization—David Hillman's essay resists this identification. Hillman's meditation on Hamlet's sexuality refuses a metaphorical understanding of carnal knowledge. What, Hillman asks, characterizes the knowledge yielded by copulation, and should its similarity to other kinds of knowledge be taken for granted? Could Hamlet's disgust over sexuality betray a shunning of a particular knowledge? Hillman's essay locates Hamlet's skepticism in the inability to know another through sex. Rather than connect with another, what we rub our noses into is matter—the element which, on its own, leaves us no different from animals, from each other, or from our bodies once we die. Part of Hamlet's crisis, for Hillman, is caused by the eroding of his belief that erotic connections single out others for us, and that this is what is unique in the not merely reproductive sexuality that befits human beings.

Hillman's coupling of sex with knowledge exposes a tension between two contradictory insights. The first is that the sexual drive is a drive to know. The second is that sex entails a letting go of knowledge because, through intercourse, concepts, distinctions, and boundaries crumble away. Sex is thus simultaneously a wish to know and to forgo knowledge. Unlike Gibson and Woodruff, Hillman suggests a not entirely positive relationship to knowledge. Knowledge can be resisted or avoided. The roots of this idea—disowning knowledge—are traceable to Stanley Cavell's readings of Shakespeare. Cavell has called into question the manner whereby philosophy demotes acknowledgment into knowledge, transcribing interpersonal challenges as epistemological enigmas. If what lies behind Hamlet's rage and aversion is a preoccupation with the distinction between the erotic bonds that humanize as opposed to those that degrade, the play is a study in acknowledgment, in hoped-for (or avoided) moments of intimate recognition through gestures that escape routine. Hamlet's epistemological concerns—finding out whether Claudius did or did not murder his father, lauding an inner selfhood that eschews show—are but a smokescreen meant to conceal countercurrents of attraction and repulsion when envisaging contact with another, when imagining touching and allowing oneself to be touched. There emerges an intriguing point of possible disagreement among the very forms of knowledge Woodruff, Gibson, and Hillman are setting forth. The attempt to—as Gibson and Woodruff do—look for what *Hamlet* may or may not tell us about knowledge may entail reproducing the avoidance that the play dramatizes.

Paul Kottman's essay moves us from knowledge to meaning. Shakespeare's theater departs from ancient Greek conventions in its targeting of the implicit trust extended—by characters, by the audience—to processes of meaning-making. Greek tragedy relies on perspectives, narratives, explanations, and the like. Shakespeare's tragedy, by contrast, is structured around the breakdown of these elements. The point that Shakespeare's tragic protagonists reach is not chaotic. What is communicated is a crisis of meaning-making as the conventions framing a world are being undone. If the knowledge that Gibson sees *Hamlet* as imparting resides in the self's relationship to its narrative possibilities, and if, for Woodruff, it consists in facing the indelible component that escapes explanation, for Kottman, what is fathomed is the contingency of the norms and conventions which underpin lives. Kottman avoids judging this process to be a resignation to nihilism. Instead, he is interested in tracing the ways whereby characters cope with this dismal discovery. Characters experience not only the collapse of structuring assumptions, but also how this apprehension generates a more fundamental distrust in any other set of norms. When this deeper skepticism awakens, and when it is wedded to the life-affirming refusal to give up the attempt to anchor a self in a context, a mind like Hamlet's is born.

The competing claims of authenticity point to another dimension in which the next four chapters may be rewardingly compared. Lines such as "I have that within which passes show" or "To thine own self be true" are repeatedly cited in these essays. For Sanford Budick, Hamlet is struggling to maintain fidelity to a nontheatricalized being. The "that within" is not a self in the sense of a kernel of core beliefs, attitudes, emotions, and the like. Authenticity, rather, amounts to tapping into a unique temporality. There is, for Budick, an experience of time which establishes oneness with the "that within." Authenticity does not require a correspondence between outward performance and a real essence, but a being in tune with one's real time. Budick sees Shakespeare as anticipating Husserl's "bracketing" of the world, the process whereby selves step back from reality in order to reclaim it later. But Budick does not permit this to remain a phenomenologist's abstraction. He traces in *Hamlet*'s literary surface, specifically in the play's heavy reliance upon chiasmus, a foregrounding of rhetorical effects calculated to intimate an alternate temporal experience. Beyond the substantive point regarding authenticity and time, by emphasizing the linkage between poetic effects (chiasmus) and a philosophical knowledge-claim, Budick's strategy makes a claim regarding method. He is proposing that philosophy may sometimes be an experience and so its creation in a reader may require experience-establishing tools. In some cases, poetry in particular is able to provide these tools.

Unlike Budick, for Joshua Landy, the fact that the ideal of being true to oneself is delivered by the unimpressive Polonius advises against taking this idea seriously. Authenticity of that kind is, for Landy, a mirage. Landy sees Hamlet as experiencing several foundational assumptions giving way. When he can no longer follow tradition or place his trust in providence, Hamlet must find his own reasons for his acts. This could have suggested something like Polonius's model of authenticity, an aspiration to being true to one's self. But there are just too many incompatible selves that Hamlet could become, and none exhaust who he is. Upon diagnosing this very problem, John Gibson, we saw, finds a Hamlet able to give voice to his fragments while sustaining a kind of alienation from them. For Landy, Hamlet's solution is different, amounting to modeling his agency upon play-acting. Inspired by the players' visit and by their performance, Hamlet learns that it is possible to (momentarily) fully identify with a role which, in truth, constitutes only a facet of who one is. For Landy, the shallowness of Polonius's paradigm of authentic subjectivity is contrasted to Hamlet's superior model, a model able to capture a genuine dimension of authenticity (along with the possibility of living nonauthentically) while eschewing the simplified inner-outer correspondence assumed by Polonius. Hamlet's realization is that he cannot simply be an avenger. He can only act as one. It is precisely via such role-playing—the very activity that ostensibly drives a wedge between self and performance—that Hamlet's agency succeeds in becoming a realization of who he is: "It's not that Hamlet has become able to act; it's that he's become able to act in the right way. . . . it's not that Hamlet has found himself; it's that he's found a way to be true to his various selves."

For all their dissimilarities, both Landy and Budick show us a Hamlet who attains a momentary haven (harmonizing with his genuine temporality in Budick, discovering the ability to be via role-playing in Landy). David Schalkwyk's Hamlet, by contrast, is irremediably restless and cannot be mollified by these solutions. Schalkwyk's Hamlet is pained by sensing that his "interiority" is made up of language games that are linked with forms of life. The problem is that "the social world of Elsinore leaches all meaning from the language games through which intimacy can flourish." It is the collapse of meaning-establishing processes that makes it impossible for Hamlet to find even episodic comfort in role-playing or in genuine temporality. Both necessitate credible language-games which, for Hamlet, have been poisoned (Schalkwyk draws on Wittgenstein's exposure of the manner whereby the application of concepts to self or other depends upon criteria, where criteria cannot be self-validated and depend upon a social context—a corrupted one in Hamlet's case). Schalkwyk's broader claim is that it is mistaken to regard *Hamlet* as an instance in which modern interiority is born, not merely due to the historical unsoundness of the claim, but because Shakespeare's focus is more specific than "interiority" as such. For it is the interdependence of inwardness and socially governed language-games that come into play. Inner knowledge, a "that within," may indeed bypass show. But it is not insulated from the social. And when the social cannot be trusted, the emerging skepticism metastasizes. Doubt in one's world becomes doubt in oneself, in who one is, in whether or not one loves. If anything is born in *Hamlet* vis-à-vis interiority, it is the interdependence between inwardness and trust in one's context.

Sarah Beckwith's engagement with Hamlet's subjectivity differs from that of other contributors in her insistence that Hamlet's preoccupation with his identity cannot be severed from his moral concerns. Overemphasizing Hamlet's crisis risks psychologizing the genuine moral questions he struggles with. Calls to act in this way or that in response to the violence around him, strike him as interchangeable ways of missing an important point. True, whenever Hamlet works up the necessary zeal, the expected agency of an avenging son seems unavoidable. Yet as soon as he reaffirms his commitment to this ethos, the hold of this particular kind of self-scripting immediately slackens. The spoke in the wheel of revenge is, for Beckwith, Hamlet's realization that to kill his father's murderer would render him akin to Claudius and to the moral world for which Claudius stands. Hamlet's resistance to the ethical calculus governing such repayment is, accordingly, not limited to opposing revenge. It extends to a more comprehensive critical outlook on morality as such. Morality is not confined to actions, duties, obligations, and the like. It encompasses response, a manner of perceiving and registering others. More specifically, in Hamlet's case, response means love—an ability to do justice to the particularity of another. Although Hamlet ends up killing Claudius, Beckwith concludes that the play is not a revenge tragedy. Hamlet succeeds in freeing his act from the kind of framing that would have robbed it of its distinctiveness as a particular response. He achieves this when pressing circumstances drive him to subscribe to predictable heteronomous ways of action. Hamlet's delay becomes a unique love. "Doing justice" to the memory of a loved dead father is sometimes thwarted rather than fulfilled when leaping into this or that expected deed. Sometimes de-automatizing the transition from motive into action is the real manifestation of care.

Kristin Gjesdal's essay is the only one in this collection that makes its subject matter not the play, but the centuries of critical engagement with it. The strength of this entry point lies in the fact that, when contemplating a canon-defining author such as Shakespeare, to explain the greatness attributed to his creations by limiting one's perspective to the works alone is insufficient. When documented responses can be studied, what gets registered along the way are changes in the effect of the work upon sensitive readers, as well as shifts in the underlying criteria for the assessment of aesthetic merit. Gjesdal selects a particularly consequential period—later eighteenth-century Germany—in which *Hamlet* appears to reshape the very engagement with a work of art. Lessing's critique of Wincklemann enables her to trace a shift from Platonism to Aristotelianism. Rather than a "topdown" approach—checklisting a work against this or that yardstick of merits—the response to art gravitates to emphasizing conversing with a work: interpretation. Through Herder, Gjesdal exposes a tendency toward a growing centralization of the audience. Interpretative activity is not a mere unraveling of the potential inherent in a work. Nor does it consist of placing the work in dialogue with an idealized reception. To interpret is to establish connections between a work and the genuine concerns of a present audience, to show why the experience of a work matters.

A NOTE ON THE TEXT

Citations and line numbers throughout this book follow the Second Quarto included in the Arden III three-text edition of the play. When references to the Folio text have been made, such is explicitly noted by the authors, and they follow the Folio text in Arden III.

Chapter 1

On (Not) Making Oneself Known

JOHN GIBSON

All a world can do is appear.

—Joseph Massey[1]

INTRODUCTION

If you were to ask a room of educated sorts what constitutes philosophical knowledge, you would expect serious disagreement about
what the answer should be but little as to what the question itself was
asking. Ask, however, what constitutes literary knowledge and considerable confusion as to what you *mean* is likely to arise. "Philosophical
knowledge," one assumes, indicates the form of insight into the world
and human predicament philosophy attempts to produce. And while
no two philosophers will offer the same account of the nature of this
insight, most will hear the phrase as meaning, minimally, something
like "philosophy's presumed contributions to human understanding."[2]
The phrase "literary knowledge," however, is likely to ring odd in many

---

1. Joseph Massey, *Illocality* (Seattle: Wave Books, 2015), 4.
2. "Presumed" because one can be skeptical about philosophy's actual contribution.

JOHN GIBSON

ears. It is, at the very least, ambiguous. To the literal-minded, "literary knowledge" will not be taken to refer to a kind of insight at all, except for the kind literature trivially gives us: the knowledge *of* literature that comes from reading lots of poems, novels, and plays. To the more charitable-minded, however, the phrase might be taken to indicate the possibility that we can speak of literary knowledge in the same register as we speak of philosophical or, for that matter, psychological, historical, or geographical knowledge. That is, it might be taken to claim for our various practices of literary production that they can yield, collectively if not always individually, a "form of knowing": that there exist distinctly literary ways of making sense of the world and thus of presenting it as an object of understanding.[3] It is this fuller and more cognitively ambitious sense of "literary knowledge" that I explore here.[4]

Hamlet is surely not the only literary work that obliges us to think seriously about the idea of literary knowledge, but it does provide a

3. Many readers will find it bewildering that one might sincerely ask whether literature can "make sense of the world" (of course it can, surely in some manner). But if it bewilders, in academic philosophy, even in academic philosophy of literature, it is still a live question. Given our common ways of understanding the fictionality of imaginative literature, the nature of literary language, and the aesthetic and artistic concerns of art, it turns out to be remarkably difficult to explain in a theoretically satisfying manner how art engages with life. For discussion of this issue from various philosophical and disciplinary vantage-points, see Gerald L. Bruns, *On the Anarchy of Poetry and Philosophy: A Guide for the Unruly* (New York: Fordham University Press, 2006); Gaskin, Richard. *Language, Truth, and Literature: A Defence of Literary Humanism* (Oxford: Oxford University Press, 2013); Berys Gaut, *Art, Emotion and Ethics* (Oxford: Oxford University Press, 2007); John Gibson, *Fiction and the Weave of Life* (Oxford: Oxford University Press, 2007); Richard Eldridge, *Literature, Life, and Modernity* (New York: Columbia University Press, 2008); Rita Felski, *Uses of Literature* (Malden, MA: Blackwell, 2008); Andy Mousley, *Literature and the Human: Criticism, Theory, Practice* (New York: Routledge, 2013); Peter Lamarque, *The Opacity of Narrative* (London: Rowman & Littlefield, 2014); and Bernard Harrison, *What Is Fiction for? Literary Humanism Restored* (Bloomington: Indiana University Press, 2015).
4. Readers familiar with contemporary analytic aesthetics will hear in my description of literary knowledge the general problem of "aesthetic cognitivism," that is, the debate on whether works of art bear distinct forms of cognitive value (and whether they derive their aesthetic value in part from the forms of understanding they presumably articulate). For a survey of contemporary work in this debate, see John Gibson, "Cognitivism and the Arts," *Philosophy Compass* 3.4 (2008): 573–89.

site for doing so that approximates the ideal. This is not because, or just because, the history of *Hamlet* criticism has made of the work a veritable philosophical giving tree, finding in it everything from a critique of modern subjectivity to a proto-existentialist statement of the general blahness of being.[5] Nor is it because, or just because, the problems *Hamlet* presents to the critic embody nearly perfectly the great philosophical problem of literature itself, namely the problem of meaning: the sheer expanse of interpretive possibilities a complex literary work generates and the challenge of understanding how we can legitimately adjudicate among them. All these features of *Hamlet* and its reception matter, but they have come to matter because at its core *Hamlet* seems possessed of a secret. And it is this secret, whatever it precisely may be, that calls on us to make meaningful a play that very well might be about, if not quite nothing, then nothingness. Philosophers and philosophically minded critics return to *Hamlet* with such frequency because unraveling this secret promises to make sense not only of the text but also, in some manner, of ourselves. We may be disappointed when we come to learn its secret—secrets, like promises, can be empty—but the work nonetheless seems to know something and to prompt in the reader or spectator an urge to share in its knowledge. Understanding why we find that Hamlet personifies so powerfully the oppressiveness of existence, the destructive powers of thought, the limits of agency, the allure of the slacker—deciding which, exactly, is where the problem lies—goes some way in understanding how literature of any sort can seem to possess philosophical secrets.

5. Many of these critics were of course philosophers. A very incomplete list of philosophers who have had something to say about *Hamlet* includes Kant, Hegel, Marx, Schopenhauer, Kierkegaard, Nietzsche, Heidegger, Benjamin, Arendt, Foucault, and Stanley Cavell. For discussion of the philosophical reception of *Hamlet*, see Simon Critchley and Jameison Webster, *Stay, Illusion: The Hamlet Doctrine* (New York: Pantheon Books, 2013); and Andrew Cutrofello, *All for Nothing: Hamlet's Negativity* (Cambridge, MA: MIT Press, 2014).

On the reading I shall offer here, *Hamlet* engages the problem of literary knowledge on two fronts. In the most direct respect, *Hamlet* apparently produces content that is of philosophical significance: the drama of the play is in part a drama of ideas, and those ideas seem to speak directly to standing philosophical concerns regarding, by my reckoning, the nature of the self and self-knowledge. But the particular manner in which *Hamlet* reveals its content—its mode of presentation, as it were—raises questions about the nature of literary meaning itself, including the meaning of the very content that gives *Hamlet* a claim to philosophical significance. The questions it raises are not skeptical and they do not lead us to cynicism regarding all talk of literary meaning and the general idea that a work of fiction can be about something.[6] But they do require that we think very carefully about how the "words, words, words" (2.2.189) that constitute the work deliver meaning and so yield an object of understanding. If we take seriously *Hamlet*'s particular way with meaning, it will bring into relief a striking possibility for giving sense to the idea of literary knowledge.

A KIND OF LIFE

Before beginning I need to say a few brief and general words about methodology. If *Hamlet* is in part a drama of ideas, what should we expect these "ideas" to look like in their proper literary and dramatic context? What should we take ourselves to be looking for in *Hamlet*, or in any work of literature for that matter, if we hope to find something that can act as an object of "worldly" knowledge (leaving it

---

6. In setting up my discussion this way I make it clear that I approach *Hamlet* as a literary narrative, as a text, and not as a play, or even as a poem. It is by emphasizing the narrative dimension that I am best able to stage my general philosophical point.

open, for the moment, as to what constitutes such a thing)? In a very general sense, how does something of cognitive significance *appear* in a fictional narrative?

The approach I favor regards literature as apt to produce a form of *narrative* understanding. To claim that literature at times generates a distinctly narrative variety of understanding is to assert that a literary narrative *alone* can suffice to produce a kind of insight, indeed that the narrative a literary work weaves *is* the object of understanding, when such there is. If this sounds entirely obvious, be assured that contemporary philosophers of literature have produced many arguments to the contrary. And they have done so by arguing that we need something *in addition* to a fictional narrative if literature is to lead the mind to genuine insight. The most common way of explaining what this additional thing might be is to invoke the image of something declarative and sentence-like, say a proposition, a claim, an assertion, or a kind of conclusion. The idea is that it is only once we have an entity such as a proposition that a work of fiction can be said to produce a proper object of cognitive attention: an item that embodies, or otherwise acts as the vehicle of, insight. We see such an approach, for example, when we attempt to model literature's cognitive value on *thought experiments* (hypothetical employments of thought that lead readers to embrace or dismiss a claim) or *enthymemes* (incomplete arguments the missing links of which readers are obliged to fill in).[7] I will not argue against the idea that literature can do such things, but something always feels bad-mannered about such a philosophicalization of our sense of how literature traffics in ideas. When literature offers gifts cognitive and epistemic in nature, we should expect it to deliver them in distinctly literary packaging, and my interest in

---

7. See Jukka Mikkonen, *The Cognitive Value of Philosophical Fiction* (New York: Bloomsbury, 2013) for an exhaustive survey of these and other such strategies, as well as for a sophisticated defense of the idea that literary narratives can function as enthymemes.

defending a notion of narrative understanding is motivated in part by a desire to take this seriously. It may be the case that narrative understanding is expressible in propositional form, or, more generally, that literary narratives can assert truth-valued claims about extrafictional reality, construct sound arguments, establish theses, perhaps even traffic in justified true belief itself. My claim is simply that a viable account of literary knowledge does not require any of this, and I trust that my discussion of *Hamlet* will make this clear.

Note that what we *explicitly* find presented in a literary narrative is a (linguistically mediated) picture of human comportment and relationship: of actions, events, happenings, sufferings, and sayings. These things are organized such that certain patterns of significance are made visible and hence critically salient. We find much more than this, needless to say; but the point I wish to make is that in the first instance we should attempt to find in this "weave of life," to use Wittgenstein's phrase, the raw material of literary knowledge and the primary form in which it is declared to the mind. When Wittgenstein speaks of the importance of coming to grasp "special patterns in the weave of our lives," part of his point is that *cultural practices*, socially organized forms of human activity, are themselves often the proper object of philosophical understanding (rather than, say, abstract propositions or extracultural matters of fact). Understanding typically requires more than that we possess the relevant concepts and representational capacities and that we can deploy them competently. It demands more than, as it were, definitional understanding. It requires a grasp of the role words and concepts play in constituting a "form of life."[8] Without this, in many cases understanding is merely conceptual and thus impoverished, incomplete. As such, it is a step short of that crucial grasp of the link

8. Ludwig Wittgenstein, *Philosophical Investigations*, ed. P. M. S. Hacker and Joachim Schulte, 4th ed. (Malden, MA: Wiley-Blackwell, 2009), 240. The German is *Muster auf dem Band des Lebens*.

between words, concepts, and the various forms of experience and circumstance in which we can fully see their significance, indeed what they "mean" for creatures such as ourselves. In respect to a certain range of concepts, understanding is fully articulated only once it is contextualized, enlivened, and tethered to the rhythms and ticks of cultural life.[9] None of this is to imply that a literary work is bound to existence and the way the world currently is, which would obviously be an insult to its imaginative powers, powers that permit it a very healthy degree of transcendence. But if literary works have the power to speak beyond our culture and material conditions such as they currently are, the claim is that this power also often functions to realign the heart and mind with the actual world.[10]

Works of narrative art should strike us as having an obvious role to play in this *acculturation* of understanding. It is, after all, in narrative form that we often represent actions and events, articulate the significance of experiences, and in general fashion a sense of how we hang together as persons, communities, and cultures. Add to this the claim that literary narratives provide us with many of our most complex and finely textured narratives, and the rudiments of an approach to the notion of literary knowledge becomes visible. I present these ideas in plainer philosophical terms below, but for the moment this will suffice to give a sense of my general orientation to the matter of how literary fictions can relate the mind to life.

A word to the skeptic. One might claim that everything I have said applies to the significance of *actual* weaves of life and not to the fictional ones works of imaginative literature place before us. Literature, as the young Nietzsche thought, necessarily falsifies life, precisely because it adds so much "art" to it.[11] For Nietzsche it does

9. I attempt to spell this out in proper philosophical terms in Gibson, *Fiction*.
10. I thank Tzachi Zamir for bringing this issue to my attention.
11. This is the Nietzsche of *The Birth of Tragedy*, trans. Douglas Smith (Oxford: Oxford University Press, 2000).

so in a way that makes life bearable, now presented as meaningful, beautiful, and significant, whereas in reality it is none of these things. Yet for just these reasons fictions cannot quite be said to show us the unadorned truth. The general worry this raises is obvious: the ordering of life one finds in a fictional narrative, and literature's manner of investing life with great expressiveness and meaning, can seem to raise a powerful question as to whether literature is suitable for representing *actual* life at all. I will return to this idea.

HAMLET'S PROBLEM

Hamlet, we know, is "sicklied o'er with the pale cast of thought" (3.1.84); he is "thought-sick" (3.4.49). This is Hamlet's problem: his predicament of thought and (in)action about which so much critical and philosophical hay has been made. Putting the problem this way makes it clear that I am concerned with the traditional question of why Hamlet hesitates; and while reducing his problem to one of "hesitation" is perhaps crude, we know perfectly well what is being highlighted. It is, especially, the force of Hamlet's self-questioning in his soliloquies as well as the text's various references to the oppressiveness of the "sun," "ears" as sites of penetration and potential contamination (by words, existence, other minds?), the expressions of disappointment with reason, language, and conscience, and, of course, sundry talk of skulls and suicide. "Hesitation" is a loose but serviceable way of referring to a series of problems and sites of potential significance in *Hamlet* that function as centers of interpretative gravity. I here elaborate one way of working through this familiar material so as to produce an example of how one might explain Hamlet's problem. The hope is that my reading will illustrate how we can draw from a literary work something that seems a candidate for the sort of thing literary knowledge might be knowledge *of*.

Sarah Beckwith argues that Shakespeare's later "post-tragic" plays develop a "grammar of forgiveness," and her claim provides an apt point of departure for my discussion. Plays such as *Cymbeline* and *A Winter's Take* conclude with, in her words, "a public spectacle, event, or ceremony in which private fantasy, isolation, grief, self-immolation, or despair is overcome, and the protagonists return to what is common and shared as the ground of their relations and as a place where their expression of themselves can have a local habitation and a name."[12] In other words, the terrible event that crushes the protagonist at the end of a tragedy is, in Shakespeare's post-tragic plays, presented as a premise rather than a conclusion, and dramatic tension is generated by exploring the link that extends from this event to, if not redemption, then a revitalization of the self and its community (the two things tragedy always threatens to destroy). A helpful way of thinking about *Hamlet* is that it is a sustained study of life at the other end of the process, in the days before the terrible act, as the self attempts to comprehend its significance and to give order to the various desires, anxieties, and doubts it has in respect to committing it. What is dramatized is the challenge of self-organization in the face of such an event: of our ability to arrange the moving parts of our psychological interior into a coherent self when called on to establish who we are through our actions. If forgiveness is what might be required in the aftermath of the act, prior to it the implicit plea is for something more akin to *resolution*, whose "native hue" (3.1.83) Shakespeare depicts not as the simple matter of committing oneself to a course of action but as a deeper, moral-psychological issue of achieving determinacy as a thinking and feeling self.

It is this resolution that defies Hamlet. There is something about the way Hamlet *thinks* that makes it so, and it is the particular manner

---

12. Sarah Beckwith, *Shakespeare and the Grammar of Forgiveness* (Ithaca, NY: Cornell University Press, 2011), 1.

in which his thinking appears to annihilate the possibility of both self-organization and action that presents the essential problem of understanding Hamlet. There are of course many literary characters whose motivational problems appear to raise, as Hamlet's do, great existential and moral questions. It is hard not to think of Melville's *Bartleby the Scrivener* in this context. Like Hamlet, Bartleby refuses to act, though clearly on much different grounds. While Melville gives us virtually no access to the inner workings of his character's mind, we at least know that Bartleby is possessed of a settled, and wholly negative, opinion on the value of action. We may not know *why* he thinks the world unworthy of his involvement; but his inaction reveals *that* he thinks this, since it is declared every time he says, "I'd prefer not to." Thus Bartleby achieves the requisite resolution as an actor on the stage of life; it is just that he is convinced that the most suitable way of performing his role is by doing nothing. Hamlet, however, is among the most psychologically transparent characters literature has given us. He stands as a puzzle not because he fails to share his mind with the audience. Unlike Bartleby, Hamlet opens his mind to us entirely, and the problem is one of sorting through the mess inside. In this way *Hamlet* implies a rebuke to the old idea that what limits our knowledge of others is lack of access to their psychological interiors, as though if we could just look inside a person, our questions about who they *really* are and why they behave as they do would be fully answered. The play suggests that even if we could look in on Hamlet's mind, what we would find there would be as vague and ambiguous as the self-image he offers the public world. This is because there is something essentially inchoate about Hamlet's inner life, some crucial aspect that we expect to be defined yet that he insists on leaving unformed. Let me explain.

For Hamlet thought propels one in precisely the wrong direction: back into the self rather than forward into the world. Hamlet does many things in the play, needless to say. But he does not do them as a coherent agent who is capable of self-legislated action: as one who wills himself to be thus and then steps out into the world according to plan. It is obviously a mistake to think that Hamlet retreats inward simply because he dislikes the options for action the world gives him, though he does dislike them: avenge his father and become a murderer, refuse the sin of murder and be a coward, or make himself a suicide, which God, he half-heartedly tells us, forbids (1.2.131). The murder of his father and remarriage of his mother to Claudius—all within the space of a month—surely brought on his intense "melancholy" (2.2.536; 3.1.164), but we cannot imagine him to have been a Laertes prior to all the bad news.[13] As Hamlet thinks through his possibilities, we see the gradual emergence of a *generalized* dissatisfaction, felt to reach out to much more than Hamlet's immediate predicament. Stating just what this generalized dissatisfaction is *with* is where the game becomes difficult. One has, in the broadest terms possible, two choices: (1) an externalist interpretation that sees Hamlet as articulating dissatisfaction with the world itself and the possibilities of experience it places before him; or (2) an internalist interpretation that makes features of the self—of what it means to be minded—the essential object of dissatisfaction. Strictly speaking, these two interpretations are not incompatible (logically, that is; they may well be dramatically incompatible—a specific performance may have to choose between the two—but that is another story). Nonetheless, each offers a very different way of articulating what *Hamlet* is, in a philosophical sense, *about*.

13. For discussion of the nature of social organization in Hamlet's world and its relevance for understanding his afflictions, see Paul A. Kottman, *Tragic Conditions in Shakespeare: Disinheriting the Globe* (Baltimore: Johns Hopkins University Press, 2009), chapter 2. In Kottman's reading, *Hamlet* is as much about our moral obligations to the dead and the confounding demands they place on us as it is about Hamlet's "self."

I favor an internalist approach, certainly as a starting point, and it is in good part because of how I think a critic ought to unravel Hamlet's claim that "there is nothing good or bad but thinking makes it so."[14] In the hands of ill-informed readers this can be taken in a resolutely externalist sense, as, say, suggesting constructivism or relativism about the moral realm. But this fails to do justice to our best hypothesis about Shakespeare's intellectual inheritance and the way *Hamlet* amends a central aspect of it. As A. D. Nuttall observes, the line looks not forward to edgy postmodernists but back to detached Stoics, whose ideas would have dotted the material of an Elizabethan classical education (Nuttall 2007, 193). In this case the lines take on a new meaning. It is not a sage invocation of antirealism but an attempt to make a despairing claim about the inescapability of the mind in experience.

Note that for the Stoics, as for many Greek and Roman philosophers, *passion* is the part of the self that causes the gravest problems in the economy of the mind ("soul"/ψυχή), though for the Stoics emotion cannot be neatly separated off from thought. Theirs was an essentially cognitive theory of emotion, according to which a passion is a complex psychological state with a *judgment* as its core. Passion, in effect, involves "thinking that makes it so," thereby presenting items in the world as disgusting, beloved, pitiable, and so on. But these are Stoics, and so emotions, certainly when intense, are seen as typically embodying *false* judgments about the value and significance of what befalls us (death as "mattering" or "horrible," though it is not in the grand scheme of things). This is what the Stoics offer as a route to addressing a more basic, and familiar, problem, that of *akrasia* ("weakness of the will" or "moral incontinence"): the phenomenon of acting against our best judgment. [15] In Plato's foundational

---

14. This line appears in the F but not in Q2 or in Q1. It appears in the Arden II edition (Harold Jenkins), which prefers but does not always privilege Q2, at 2.2.250.

15. The Stoics, unlike Plato and Aristotle before them, clearly cannot explain *akrasia* as simply conflict between thought and passion, since the latter so essentially enlists the former.

image, reason, a charioteer, holds the reins of the unruly horses of passion and appetite, and in *akrasia* one of the beasts pulls free, usually commandeering reason and so directing thought in the process. The upshot of all this is that on the classical model of mind a coherent self is one in which the passions we act on and the desires we satisfy are those that logos consecrates, in effect, as *mine*: as expressive of *my* values, *my* beliefs, *my* goals. In akratic behavior a mere (e.g.) desire gets expressed (for that cigarette, for another hour at the bar) and not quite a person. The failure of self-organization in akratic action implies a failure of self-expression: my behavior does not speak for who I take myself to be. When suffering *akrasia*, how I believe I hang together as a person is defied by, rather than declared through, my actions.

What makes *Hamlet* so fascinating to a reader concerned with the self and moral psychology is that in his figure reason alone, not passion or desire, comes to seem the culprit in the fits and paroxysms of the akratic mind.[16] In Hamlet *logos* just produces logorrhea, expelling an endless stream of "words, words, words." If reason is not right with the world, it is not due to an epistemic failure or the deceptions of passion but to the endless addition of another word when trying to render judgment. Yet the intimacy of reason, thinking, and the self

---

Nonetheless, they can distinguish between different ways in which different judgments can conflict, one, for example, that is rationally sanctioned and the other, embodied in a powerful emotion, that is not (my unshakable thought that another drink would make the evening better, even though I know, and rationally identify, with the judgment that it is best to be sober around colleagues). For a study of (early) Stoic moral psychology, see Brad Inwood, *Ethics and Human Action in Early Stoicism* (Oxford: Oxford University Press, 1985). For an excellent survey of the concept of *akrasia* in Greek philosophy, see A. W. Price, *Mental Conflict* (London: Routledge, 1995) and Martha Nussbaum, *The Therapy of Desire: Theory and Practice in Hellenistic Ethics* (Princeton, NJ: Princeton University Press, 1994). For discussion of the Platonic roots of *akrasia* and the "tripartite soul," see the essays collected in Christopher Bobonich and Pierre Destrée, eds., *Akrasia in Greek Philosophy: From Socrates to Plotinus* (Leiden: Brill, 2007).

16. This is also what makes *Hamlet* seem so prescient in respect to various modern critiques of rationalist views of the human.

yields a larger problem. As a phenomenologist might put it, the self is always in the "dative" position of experience, endowing it with an inescapable "for-me-ness."[17] It is omnipresent in conscious thought, and this is what Hamlet cannot tolerate: consciousness takes the form of "a prison."[18] He suffers the inevitable presence of the self as the rest of us experience white noise, a kind of buzzing of me-ness that makes him yearn for "quietus" (3.1.74). This quietus, death, strikes Hamlet as a viable avenue of self-escape, until thought, of course, keeps on going and asks, "what dreams may come / When we have shuffled off this mortal coil" (3.1.66). Thought effectively poisons Hamlet's hope that there is at least one place where he can escape the chatter of "conscience." If this is so, then when Hamlet says, "thus conscience does make cowards" (3.1.82), he laments not quite his failure of agency but the limitlessness of thought and its endless generation of—to borrow Gertrude's line—"noise so rude" (3.4.39). The problem of Hamlet is not inaction but hyperactivity, just reinterpreted in psychological rather than behavioral terms.

The text's various references to the ears now take on a distinct significance. As Tzachi Zamir notes, "for Shakespeare's contemporaries . . . [w]hatever enters the ear is conceived as a powerful, and at times violent, entity, capable of transforming the hearer."[19] In *Hamlet* this violence is given a very particular spin. The sense modality through which the thought of others is most commonly received is of course auditory, by way of spoken language (perhaps the Internet has rendered this false; it was certainly true in Hamlet's world). This is what *logos* traffics in, semantically packaged "accounts": descriptions, explanations, and theories. For Hamlet this openness to other minds compounds the problem

17. Zahavi 2011, 326–27.
18. This is the continuation of 2.2.250 in F, and while it refers to Denmark, the passage treats it as a synecdoche for a much wider landscape.
19. Zamir 2007, 168–69.

exponentially. The ears add to the noise inside the noise of others, turning what would be the solitary mumbling of one mind into a grating choir. Each of these voices adds one more statement of how the world and its affairs "seem" to it. In *Hamlet* there are some 166 mentions of "seems" and 182 of "appears." The repetition reinforces the sense of the ears as assaulted from within and from without by thought and the relentlessness of its manner of making things "appear" and "seem." Or so Hamlet feels.

"Seeming" is also a mark of determinacy, of something achieving sufficient form to appear as *this* or *that*. Hamlet, as nearly every critic notes, is marked by a refusal of self-definition. He feels "too much in the sun" (1.2.67), and his wish is to "resolve into a kind a dew" (1.2.130), that is, a liquescent, unformed state.[20] When he tells Gertrude, "I know not seems" (1.2.76), we initially hear his refusal to put on appearances as a claim to authenticity, though as the play progresses we gradually come to realize that his use of "seems" has a subtler meaning. In the semantic and symbolic play of the language of *Hamlet*, "being" is associated with "the sun" and "seeming," that is, with the illuminated world in which things appear as the things they presumably are. Hamlet is not, we know, quite at home in this world. He copes with it in part by dissociating his sense of self from those aspects of a person in which we habitually think self-identity resides. One way of stating this difficult idea is in terms of a fairly precise refusal of self-constitution. A central way in which we articulate a sense of self—an image of being a particular kind of person—is through an act of psychological identification. We all have perhaps an anarchy of different desires, emotions, beliefs, interests, and concerns that pass through us, if not in a single moment then certainly

20. In the Hegelian tradition of interpretation, this craving for indeterminacy is linked both to a kind of angst (with existence and the pressures it places on us), and to a desire for the freedom of pure potentiality. On this, see Kristin Gjesdal's "Reading Shakespeare—Reading Modernity," *Angelaki: Journal of the Theoretical Humanities* 9.3 (2004): 17–31.

over a span of time. As we saw hinted in the discussion of *akrasia*, the road to self-constitution is paved in part by *identifying* with certain of these desires (etc.), bestowing upon them the right to *stand* for us, that is, to be expressive of who we take ourselves to be.[21] Now I might be guilty of self-flattery or self-deception when I identify with my desire for a modest life or my love of animals, but in so identifying I begin to craft a self-image. I can now "appear" as a kind of person, to myself and, if I wish, to others. In fact, it now becomes possible to ask questions of *self-knowledge*: am I really as I take myself to be, and are those features of my mental life I tap as essentially expressive of *me* those which actually inform my agency? This is what Hamlet understands, and it is in effect this kind of self-identification against which he rebels. His problems of agency bear witness to an unwillingness to let various of our desires, wishes, beliefs to *speak* for us, indeed to give domicile to our identity. Of course throughout the play Hamlet desires various things, expresses values, endorses thoughts, and states preference for actions. The point, however, is that Hamlet lets none of them declare his identity. None of them function to constitute a self.

To distill these reflections on Hamlet's problem into a philosophical point, I conclude with two related claims. The first, clearly, is that *Hamlet* inherits and amends in a novel manner the traditional picture of *akrasia*. Hamlet is perhaps the first *cognitive* akratic, that is, the text renders

---

21. This way of thinking about the self comes into the philosophical literature by way of Harry Frankfurt's still highly influential theory of identification, according to which selves have (second-order) volitions regarding which (first-order) desires constitute our self-concept as agents (our "will"). See Harry G. Frankfurt, *The Importance of What We Care About: Philosophical Essays* (Cambridge: Cambridge University Press, 1988). This line of thought can also be developed in terms of so-called narrative conceptions of the self, in which case the important act of identification will not, or not just, be with desires but, crucially, with the events and experiences that provide the content of the stories we tell of ourselves and the lives we lead. See Marya Schechtman, *Staying Alive: Personal Identity, Practical Concerns, and the Unity of a Life* (Oxford: Oxford University Press, 2014) for an excellent defense of this.

intelligible an image of human moral psychology in which a cognitive state—*thought*, bluntly put—alone can make self-organization impossible in the face of action. In *Hamlet* logos does not hold the reins but itself is one of the beasts, and this raises a fascinating question about just what, and where, the self is for Hamlet and in *Hamlet*. Hamlet effectively dislodges his sense of self from any of the features of the mind traditionally imagined to be capable of housing it: not just desire and passion but even thought itself.[22] There would seem nowhere to go from here, no further feature of the psyche to make expressive of his self through a grand act of identification. But the play indicates a striking possibility.

To bring this possibility to view, we must first note that it is a mistake to think, as critics sometimes do, that *Hamlet* pushes the self deeper into the psychological interior, hiding it more thoroughly from the public world than classical models of mind could countenance. Hamlet's self is marked by radical *abstraction* and not *interiority* or *innerness*.[23] It is the image of a self, dim and merely implied, as what remains when I say, *I am not this*. As Hamlet wishes, it is formless, "dew-like," removed from "the sun," and thus a self largely without defining qualities. But herein lies the accomplishment: showing that one can generate, and identify with, a voice that functions

---

22. For elegance of argument, if it can be called that, I ignore a possibility. I have approached moral psychology with the classical picture of the tripartite self and claimed that *Hamlet* breaks its mold. But the tripartite picture of the self was effectively expanded by Augustine and later medieval moral psychology, and the amendment would have been very familiar to any Elizabethan who entered a church. It is the addition of a fourth element, the will (*voluntas*). There is perhaps an element of this in *Hamlet*, namely, that Hamlet effectively houses his identify in something will-like. In a sense, the will is just the voice of *agency*, the part of the person that makes pronouncements of identification with various desires, beliefs, and values. Nonetheless, *Hamlet* still can be said to revise the traditional view of even this picture, since the will is now conceived as generating an entirely negative voice, not as constituting agency through acts of psychological identification but in the refusal to do so.

23. On the idea of inwardness, interiority, innerness, and the like, see Anne Ferry, *The "Inward" Language: Sonnets of Wyatt, Sidney, Shakespeare, Donne* (Chicago: University of Chicago Press, 1983); Katharine Eisaman Maus, *Inwardness and Theater in the English Renaissance* (Chicago: University of Chicago Press, 1995); Stephen Greenblatt, *Hamlet*

only to express alienation from all that would otherwise make self-constitution possible: desires, thoughts, actions—the whole lot of it. This is of course a profoundly estranged self-image, and that is the point. Nietzsche calls it the "pathos of distance," which is achieved through "out-looking and down-looking" on those we deem beneath us.[24] For Hamlet it just happens that the objects of this pathos are internalized, not other people but all those features of ourselves upon which we can hang a determinate self-concept. Whatever we may think of the desirability of this self, the text pulls off an impressive philosophical trick: it reveals that self-constitution can consist in acts of self-alienation and refusals of self-expression (in the sense given here), and it shows that, despite appearances, there is nothing really contradictory about the idea. Hamlet is of course happy to accept the consequence of this: that it makes of the self an "airy nothing,"[25] a fiction not unlike the characters on the stage in his try at theater in act 3. But this fiction, this air of a self that is brought to view only obliquely, is, for all that, *an image of a self*: of one whose particular way of being consists in not being one way or another. There is nothing to know about this self; it has virtually no determinacy, except, of course, the determinacy of a refusal. Yet it has a voice—a

in Purgatory (Princeton, NJ: Princeton University Press, 2001); Christopher Tilmouth, *Passion's Triumph over Reason: A History of the Moral Imagination from Spenser to Rochester* (New York: Oxford University Press, 2007); and Tzachi Zamir, *Double Vision: Moral Philosophy and Shakespearean Drama* (Princeton, NJ: Princeton University Press, 2007).

24. Nietzsche, *Beyond Good and Evil*, trans. Helen Zimmern (New York: Boni and Liveright, 1917), 197. Parts of the passage in which this phrase appears would seem to offer much more for making sense of Hamlet: "Without the *pathos of distance*, such as grows out of the incarnated difference of classes, out of the constant out-looking and down-looking of the ruling caste on subordinates and instruments, and out of their equally constant practice of obeying and commanding, of keeping down and keeping at a distance—that other more mysterious pathos could never have arisen, the longing for an ever new widening of distance within the soul itself, the formation of ever higher, rarer, further, more extended, more comprehensive states, in short, just the elevation of the type 'man,' the continued 'self-surmounting of man,' to use a moral formula in a supermoral sense."

25. *A Midsummer Night's Dream* (4.1.16).

decisively negative one—and it can be heard, indeed even enacted on the stage, and it is thus a proper object of dramatic and philosophical appreciation.

THE MATTER OF MEANING

We can now return to the question with which we began. We have a candidate insight, into selfhood, as my interpretation has it. And so we have something that seems a potential object of understanding, perhaps even an example of the sort of thing literary knowledge might be knowledge *of*. To make a first pass at this, assume for a moment the aptness of my interpretation, just to see what follows from it.

Note that what my interpretation has yielded is the very thing that a common line of thought tells us will not do if we wish to assert literature's philosophical and cognitive value. What I have drawn from *Hamlet* is just an image: a *vision*, fictional at that, of a person burdened with a peculiar sense of self. And a certain kind of philosopher will complain that images, pictures, visions, and the like merely represent a state of affairs; they do not establish its truth.[26] Something must be *done* with an image if it is to lead the mind to truth and knowledge, some surrounding apparatus of argumentation must be provided, some reason must be proffered for *believing* that it gets things right; hence the desire for propositions and proofs mentioned in section "A Kind of Life". The worry, with us since Plato, is

---

26. What I canvass here are often described as arguments for aesthetic anticognitivism, that is, the idea that art, literature included, derives none of its value from its contributions to human understanding and the growth of knowledge. See Stolnitz, Jerome. "On the Cognitive Triviality of Art." *British Journal of Aesthetics* 32.3 (1992): 191–200 and Terrence Diffey, Terrence. "What Can We Learn From Art?" *Australasian Journal of Philosophy* 73.2 (1995): 204–11 for classic anticognitivist arguments.

that literature's manner of "showing" is *mimetic* and not *epistemic*. Art presents a picture but *demonstrates* nothing about it; that is, it does not show the picture to be reasonable, right, accurate, revelatory of reality: *anything* that could give the image a claim to properly *cognitive* significance. And my interpretation of *Hamlet* appears to walk us directly into this thicket of worry. It is worth adding that the picture of the self *Hamlet* inherits and amends is, it turns out, likely false: modern sciences of the mind do not countenance the existence of tripartite psyches or a thing called "logos." So how could *Hamlet* lead the mind to something called insight, to something one might *know*?

The above line of reasoning is too quick and too manifestly philosophical in respect to the terms it offers us for addressing the issue. First things first, *Hamlet* in fact does demonstrate something. It even shows something to be the case; it *establishes* something. It may not be the truth of a proposition about what selves—all or most of them—in fact are. Nor is it quite a conclusion about the nature of self-experience. But for all that, something is still made very clear. *Hamlet* demonstrates the *intelligibility* rather than the truth of a certain view of the self. The play makes *comprehensible* a way of thinking about mindedness and the inescapable presence of the self as a problem, as a "prison." It turns into an object of *understanding* how anxieties, fears, and material circumstances may conspire to make such an abstracted self desirable, even appear a sanctuary. Truth is important, but so is what *Hamlet* gives us: a refinement of thought, and an enlargement of our sense of the possibilities and complexities of experience. When I assert this, it is important to see that I am not reporting on something that I simply *feel* has happened to me when reading *Hamlet*, describing, as it were, the private glow of personal illumination. There may be some of that, but what bears primary witness to this refinement of understanding is the refinement of terms, concepts, distinctions, and habits of thinking about selves displayed *in the work of criticism*: in the struggle, public in nature, to state what one finds of significance in *Hamlet*. If one does not think that this is in evidence in my interpretation, it will be if one begins to work through the history of *Hamlet* criticism and its brighter achievements.

This form of demonstration is narratological and perhaps not in any interesting sense epistemic. A narrative demonstration aims not at establishing the truth of some matter but rather at showing that a coherent story can be told of it. It demonstrates, for instance, that a view of the self as formless, estranged, and abstracted can be given sense in the context of a kind of life. The story makes this view of the self meaningful, not, of course, by tracing the boundaries of a concept and defining it in propositional terms, but by showing us what it amounts to as a kind of human experience, as a way, that is, one might be in the world. Thus while it is fair to say that *Hamlet* demonstrates the intelligibility of a certain conception of the self, it is not a merely conceptual mode of presentation. It presents the "idea" of this self as *embodied*, placed on the concrete stage of human action and relationship. The concept is given flesh, indeed Hamlet's "too sallied flesh" (1.2.129), and so it becomes intelligible to us as a precisely shaped human situation. Literary works, because of their way with fictional narratives, can infuse understanding with a sense of what a certain slice of life looks like when configured in the light of the concepts and "ideas" upon which we habitually rely: despair, joy, alienation, or weakness of the will as *these* "patterns in the weave of our lives." It is essentially our understanding of this that I am claiming literature refines, expands, and enlivens. Fictions, for reasons entirely too obvious to be worth mentioning, give us infinitely more opportunities than the actual world does for providing these slices of life.

Noël Carroll argues that literary narratives are primarily concerned not with the discovery of new items of knowledge but with the clarification of our existing (moral) concepts and the demands they place on us.[27] My claim is kindred, at least to the extent that it takes the achievement of a kind of clarity to be paramount. It is literature's ability, as exemplified by *Hamlet*, to link thought to context, concepts to visions of lived experience, "ideas" to cultural conditions, that explains its particular gift to the mind: its "cognitive significance." This acculturation of understanding is what I am claiming to be literature chief's contribution to understanding: its ability, on occasion at least, to bring the contents of our minds more perfectly in line with the "form of life," to misuse Wittgenstein's phrase just slightly. This is, I submit, a fair answer to the question of what literature knows and so of what literary knowledge might be knowledge of. It is in effect a form of know-how: knowledge of how to use fictions, and the narratives that deliver them to us, to bring thought more firmly in line with the material of life: with practices, experiences, relationships, desires, and everything else that bears the mark of the world we are inclined to call ours. True, Hamlet is not real, but only a terribly misguided metaphysical view would lead us to conclude that his world is therefore not the human one. Fictional characters and real people are not of a piece, but the practices in which they engage, the relationships they cultivate, and the anxieties that animate them provide the needed undercurrent of shared life, a common stage upon which our ontological differences become visible yet appear to be much less of a big deal. Not every literary work, of course, establishes this shared stage, and some get us wholly wrong. But the terms in which I explicated *Hamlet* provide an example of how we speak when we wish to affirm success.

It is in this way that we can see how to handle the skeptic when she protests, "Hamlet does not exist, and thus the play only

27. See Noël Carroll, "Art, Narrative, and Moral Understanding," *Aesthetics and Ethics: Essays at the Intersection*, ed. Jerrold Levinson (Cambridge: Cambridge University Press, 1998), 126–60. His position is aptly labeled "clarificationism." I resist the temptation to refer to my position as "acculturationism," on obvious aesthetic grounds.

demonstrates that a certain view of the self applies to a fiction, not to us." If *Hamlet* does not establish the truth of a certain view, it by extension does not establish that it is true of any one of us. In other words, it does not attempt to say that this is how we, or even how some of us, *are*. To this extent, Nietzsche is vindicated. But the achievement of *Hamlet* is more fundamental than can be captured in these terms, and it enjoys a certain priority to matters of truth. The point is simple. Before we can query the truth of various ways of taking ourselves and our world to be, we must first have the vision itself. That is, what renders talk of truth and falsity meaningful is a more basic cultural accomplishment: the production of these visions of life and the fleshing out of a sense of the world and the possibilities of experience it contains. What *Hamlet* gives us in respect to the self is more akin to a moment of genesis than the discovery of a fact: the establishment of an image, in the form of Hamlet himself, that holds in place a cluster of concerns about self-organization, thought, and action. This is one way of explaining why *Hamlet* provides the framework for so many philosophical, psychoanalytic, theological, and existential analyses of the person. *Hamlet* creates the terms for the debate and so a ground on which it can be carried out. By rendering intelligible such a view of the self, *Hamlet* offers a refinement of our capacity to think about what it means to be minded and the burden of self-experience this can place on us, at least on those of us whose "melancholy" makes such a self seem desirable. The compliment to be paid to this is not to call it "true" but "foundational": it is the *establishment* of grounds for a manner of thinking about persons and their plights. That these grounds have proven productive and valuable is brought to relief not by, or just by, looking inside the work; we see it most asserted clearly in all the theories, arguments, and artworks built upon it in the four hundred years since its first performance. The general point one should take from this is it is often best to see literary narratives as intervening in the real by, as it were, *making* sense: by creating a distinct sense of the nature of some feature of human action and predicament. This does not flag the dull point that fictional narratives are intelligible; it highlights the more interesting fact that they can, as *Hamlet* has, play a role in creating the conditions of intelligibility.

Before concluding I have to address a final item of business. What happens if we no longer assume the aptness of my interpretation? What happens, that is, if we look out across the vast expanse of skeptical, theological, psychoanalytic (and so on) interpretations? Does everything I have just argued for suddenly become provisional, at least until I can refute all competing interpretations? Does the assertion of my interpretation commit me to the painfully conservative view that all other interpretations are illegitimate just to the extent they conflict with mine? I trust it does not, and while these questions open up all those great debates on the nature of interpretation— debates I clearly do not have the space to address here—I want to say why I think it would be an error to think that they vitiate the points I am putting on offer here.

The mistake, I think, is to think that conflicting interpretations necessarily assign conflicting *content* to a literary work. We can be inclined to think this when held captive by a bad picture of what content is in a literary context. The picture can be put a number of ways, though one way is to cast it in terms of a mistaken view of the relationship between text and meaning. It is to model our thinking of how literary works bear meaning on our model of how sentences do. As a sentence is a vehicle of a proposition, a text, on this picture, is a vehicle of a meaning. And as a proposition just *is* the content of a sentence, a meaning just *is* the content of a text. Thus my reading falsifies the very content of *Hamlet* if it turns out that the play is not really about selfhood—that it does not contain this meaning—or at any rate not about it in the manner I have claimed. But a literary work is very unlike a sentence. There are many reasons for this, but I trust a few simple examples will suffice. Consider the difference, radical indeed, between the meaning of "meaning" in these cases:

1. What is the meaning of the Gullah sentence, "A ain shame eben one leetle bit ob de Good Nyews"?[28]
2. What do the recent attacks on Paris mean?

And, more colloquially,

3. Exactly what were you reporting when you confessed that you threatened a man with a severed limb?
4. What does the Trump presidency say about us?

In cases 1 and 3 we are asking about the semantic meaning of a linguistic vehicle, and our knowledge of communicative intentions gives us very good reason to assume that they each attempt to generate one and only one content (if not, then the sentences are ill-formed or not a genuine attempt to convey a content). In cases 2 and 4, however, we are talking about *culture* and not *assertions*, events and not linguistic vehicles. We might find conflicting Marxist, libertarian, or Seventh-day Adventist interpretations of 2 and 4, but clearly here the conflict is between the values, concerns, and philosophical commitments different interpreters endorse. The "content" of these examples, like the content of a narrative, is a constellation of events, sayings, doings, and happenings, delivered to us through language but not themselves linguistic in nature (an attack on a city is *not* a sentence). In disagreeing in our interpretations, we call into question the terms we each deem appropriate for capturing the significance of these events, their "meaning" in a broadly "existential" sense. Still, each interpretation

---

28. It is a line from the Gullah New Testament and can be translated as, "For I am not ashamed of the Gospel of Christ."

takes itself to be attempting to specify the nature of these events: of what they are *about* and so of what they mean. If I call a certain act or practice violent, I take myself be saying something about its nature, about it the way that *it is*. Only a profound act of dissociation, or self-doubt, would permit me to experience the violence I see in a blow as a mere projection, a reflection of my attitudes but not also of the quality of the event.

It is at this juncture that we do well to think of *Hamlet* in its natural state, as a play, and to recall that literary works in general, though offering us a texture of words, function to bring before us the texture of a world: an image of a weave of life. When we ask what bears meaning, it is in the primary instance the configuration of life we might find on the stage or page. The "content" of this just is the actions, sayings, sufferings, and predicaments enacted before us. My interpretation, and most others that are philosophical in nature, are attempts to put to words the significance of life so configured. It is the attempt to find terms appropriate for revealing why this weave of fictional life suggests to us something of consequence about, if not exactly ourselves, then certainly selves and their complexity. It is the intricacy of the "form of life" we find in it that underwrites the variety and openness of manners in which we can, with apparent legitimately, specify what it means. An externalist interpretation that casts Hamlet as suffering from a disappointment in the world surely is in disagreement with an internalist one that casts him as disappointed with the self. Assuming neither of us has simply misperceived or misheard what is happening on the stage, then the conflict is ultimately between how we are inclined to make sense of life, not merely the "content" of *Hamlet*. We may of course disagree about the (semantic) meaning of various utterances in *Hamlet*, form varying hypothesis about the intentions of its author, discover that we mistook a historical reference, and much else besides. And this may lead us to a different sense of something rightly called the content of the play. These problems are perhaps inescapable in the interpretation of art, and I have no wish to deny this. My point, however, is that when the articulation of meaning is performed in the register outlined here, we are engaged in an activity different in nature than when we argue about whether Hamlet's flesh is "sullied," "sallied," or "solid" (1.2.29) and its broader implications for the meanings we find *in* the play.

In this respect, understanding *Hamlet*'s particular way with meaning obliges us to begin the good work of liberating the notion of "literary meaning" from the concept of linguistic meaning, to which the linguistic turn—in both philosophy and literary theory—of the last century yoked it much too tightly. *Hamlet* seems to bear meanings in excess of even our best interpretations not quite because its signification is such a challenge to pin down but rather because its significance strikes us as so potentially vast, perhaps even "unlimited." It is a work that seems to implicate us, in our very attempts to make sense of it, in the act of working through, and so making meaningful, basic and often elusive features of our ethical, familial, existential, and psychological condition. All these features of the basic stuff of "life" are, of course, constitutionally open to interpretation and reinterpretation, not because we do not know what they "mean" but rather because the sort of meaningfulness they bear is not the sort of thing that gets a final statement. We chip away at it, as philosophy and literature themselves do in respect to the issues and questions that animate them.

CONCLUSION

All this leads us round to a simple point. It is hardly surprising, even a truism, though certain trends in philosophy and literary theory have done their part to make such a mundane observation worthy of statement. It is this: what *Hamlet* offers as an object of understanding is

Hamlet. This, and not some further thing, is what it makes available to the mind as an object of cognitive attention. It is what it possesses that is worth knowing, at least if we wish to acquire knowledge of the complexity of our culture's concerns with the self and the varieties of ways it imagines it.

WORKS CITED

Beckwith, Sarah. 2011. *Shakespeare and the Grammar of Forgiveness.* Ithaca, NY: Cornell University Press.

Bobonich, Christopher, and Pierre Destrée, eds. 2007. *Akrasia in Greek Philosophy: From Socrates to Plotinus.* Leiden: Brill.

Bruns, Gerald L. 2006. *On the Anarchy of Poetry and Philosophy: A Guide for the Unruly.* New York: Fordham University Press.

Carroll, Noël. 1998. "Art, Narrative, and Moral Understanding." *Aesthetics and Ethics: Essays at the Intersection.* Ed. Jerrold Levinson. Cambridge: Cambridge University Press. 126–60.

Cavell, Stanley. 1987. *Disowning Knowledge in Six Plays of Shakespeare.* Cambridge: Cambridge University Press.

Critchley, Simon, and Jamieson Webster. 2013. *Stay, Illusion: The Hamlet Doctrine.* New York: Pantheon Books.

Cutrofello, Andrew. 2014. *All for Nothing: Hamlet's Negativity.* Cambridge, MA: MIT Press.

Diffey, Terrence. 1995. "What Can We Learn From Art?" *Australasian Journal of Philosophy* 73.2: 204–11.

Eldridge, Richard. 2008. *Literature, Life, and Modernity.* New York: Columbia University Press.

Felski, Rita. 2008. *Uses of Literature.* Malden, MA: Blackwell.

Ferry, Anne. 1983. *The "Inward" Language: Sonnets of Wyatt, Sidney, Shakespeare, Donne.* Chicago: University of Chicago Press.

Frankfurt, Harry G. 1988. *The Importance of What We Care About: Philosophical Essays.* Cambridge: Cambridge University Press.

Gaskin, Richard. 2013. *Language, Truth, and Literature: A Defence of Literary Humanism.* Oxford: Oxford University Press.

Gaut, Berys. 2007. *Art, Emotion and Ethics.* Oxford: Oxford University Press.

Gibson, John. 2007. *Fiction and the Weave of Life.* Oxford: Oxford University Press.

———. 2008. "Cognitivism and the Arts." *Philosophy Compass* 3.4: 573–89.

Gjesdal, Kristin. 2004. "Reading Shakespeare—Reading Modernity." *Angelaki: Journal of the Theoretical Humanities* 9.3: 17–31.

Greenblatt, Stephen. 2001. *Hamlet in Purgatory*. Princeton, NJ: Princeton University Press.

Harrison, Bernard. 2015. *What Is Fiction for? Literary Humanism Restored*. Bloomington: Indiana University Press.

Inwood, Brad. 1985. *Ethics and Human Action in Early Stoicism*. Oxford: Oxford University Press.

Kottman, Paul A. 2009. *Tragic Conditions in Shakespeare: Disinheriting the Globe*. Baltimore: Johns Hopkins University Press.

Lamarque, Peter. 2014. *The Opacity of Narrative*. London: Rowman & Littlefield.

Massey, Joseph. 2015. *Illocality*. Seattle: Wave Books.

Maus, Katharine Eisaman. 1995. *Inwardness and Theater in the English Renaissance*. Chicago: University of Chicago Press.

Mikkonen, Jukka. 2013. *The Cognitive Value of Philosophical Fiction*. New York: Bloomsbury.

Mousley, Andy. 2013. *Literature and the Human: Criticism, Theory, Practice*. New York: Routledge.

Nietzsche, Friedrich Wilhelm. 1917. *Beyond Good and Evil*. Trans. Helen Zimmern. New York: Boni and Liveright.

———. 2000. *The Birth of Tragedy*. Trans. Douglas Smith. Oxford: Oxford University Press.

Nussbaum, Martha C. 1994. *The Therapy of Desire: Theory and Practice in Hellenistic Ethics*. Princeton, NJ: Princeton University Press.

Nuttall, A. D. 2007. *Shakespeare the Thinker*. New Haven: Yale University Press.

Price, A. W. 1995. *Mental Conflict*. London: Routledge.

Schechtman, Marya. 2014. *Staying Alive: Personal Identity, Practical Concerns, and the Unity of a Life*. Oxford: Oxford University Press.

Stolnitz, Jerome. 1992. "On the Cognitive Triviality of Art." *British Journal of Aesthetics* 32.3: 191–200.

Tilmouth, Christopher. 2007. *Passion's Triumph over Reason: A History of the Moral Imagination from Spenser to Rochester*. New York: Oxford University Press.

Wittgenstein, Ludwig. 2009. *Philosophical Investigations*. Ed. P. M. S. Hacker and Joachim Schulte. 4th ed. Malden, MA: Wiley-Blackwell.

Zamir, Tzachi. 2007. *Double Vision: Moral Philosophy and Shakespearean Drama*. Princeton, NJ: Princeton University Press.

Chapter 2

Staging Wisdom through *Hamlet*

PAUL WOODRUFF

INTRODUCTION

Shakespeare's *Hamlet* stages wisdom to its audiences. By this I mean two things: the play is the product of its author's wisdom, and audience members stand to gain in wisdom if they watch a wisely staged performance of the play, and do so wisely. But this is against expectations. Shakespeare wrote to please an audience so as to realize a profit, and we would not expect that he could do that by staging wisdom. Plato long ago argued that a poet who aims at pleasure cannot stage wisdom—at best such a poet fakes wisdom.[1]

If a play were to stage wisdom, where would we find it? There is no wisdom in the obvious places in *Hamlet*—nothing we might find to call the moral of Hamlet's story, and nothing reliably wise in any of

---

1. We may have no doubt that Plato's criticism of tragedy is sincere, as we find it voiced by both Socrates, in the *Republic* (10.605a–607b), and by the Athenian in the *Laws* (2.658d–659c). See also: "We ourselves (the lawgivers) are poets of the finest and best tragedy possible; our entire *politeia* is a mimesis of the finest and best life" (*Laws* 817b2–5), and consider the importance of the Third Chorus in the *Laws*, which is to take the place of tragic performances in the city under construction (2.665d–671a). The essence of the criticism in both dialogues is that Athenian tragic poetry is governed by its aim of pleasing a general audience.

the messages delivered by the characters in their lines. But if there's no wisdom in a moral or in the messages of *Hamlet,* where could it be?

Morals and messages are what I call *doubles* of wisdom—things that merely look like nuggets of wisdom. The virtues have many doubles. A clear example of a double is fearlessness, as a double for courage. Fearlessness looks like courage, and people are often taken in by the resemblance. Fearlessness seems to be a good thing in some cases. But it causes foolish devastation in others. In truth (I have argued elsewhere), courage is a kind of wisdom, and so is justice. Wisdom has many names and many doubles.[2]

Wisdom (so long as it is wisdom) does not fail to be wise, but messages and morals may be wise in some ways and foolish in others. The platitudes of Polonius may be wise to follow in some circumstances, but foolish in others. For example, Polonius's advice to "Give thy thoughts no tongue" is sometimes good advice, but often it is not (1.3.58). Such pithy messages look like wisdom, but Shakespeare's staging—which is theatrically captivating—shows clearly that they are not. Polonius is a joke.

In this essay I will be working from a Platonic-Socratic conception of wisdom, as I am using *Hamlet* to answer a question that has been active in philosophy since Plato asked it.[3] At the center of this conception of wisdom is the realization that—while divine wisdom would teach us how to live—human wisdom is not worth much. Human wisdom is what Socrates says he is learning and relearning every day—it is not a lesson he could learn at one time for always.[4] He learns it by reflecting on his judgments as he makes them and on his life as it unfolds.

---

2. On the doubles of virtues, see Paul Woodruff, "Good Things and Their Doubles," *The Ajax Dilemma: Justice, Fairness and Rewards* (New York: Oxford University Press, 2011), 131–39.

3. A valuable exercise in the history of ideas would be to study *Hamlet* in the light of conceptions of wisdom contemporary with Shakespeare, but that is not my project here.

4. *Apology* 23ab, cf. *Phaedrus* 229e–230a.

Strange as it may seem, we may learn and relearn human wisdom of this kind from our experience of *Hamlet* on stage. Somehow we must find it possible to watch what Hamlet does and reflect on our own lives at the same time in a way that enhances our own wisdom. Shakespeare learned how to stage wisdom from his practice in the theater—not from reading Plato. For human wisdom, theater is a brilliant teacher. Shakespeare made his plays wise by his way of making them theatrical, that is, by his way of making plays worth watching. This he does preeminently in *Hamlet*. The wisdom of the play grows from its theatricality.

I have set myself two hard questions: How can we grow wiser through an experience of theater—how, in particular, from an experience of *Hamlet*? And, second, how could a playwright learn from the practice of theater itself what to do in order to make this possible—how, in particular, could Shakespeare have learned to write, wisely, a play such as *Hamlet*?

About Theater

The art of theater is the art of making a play in performance worth watching for a given audience. Such success depends on the success of three subordinate practices: the playwright and dramaturge must provide a watchable text, the production staff and performers must provide watchable action, and the audience must know how to watch such things and be willing to do so. The text, the performers, and the watchers need to be right for each other.[5]

A play that is worth watching usually engages its watchers emotionally. Then the watchers care about the people in the play and

5. Here I am summarizing the main points of my book *The Necessity of Theater: The Art of Watching and Being Watched* (New York: Oxford University Press, 2008). I have nothing to say there or in this chapter about readers of scripts for plays. A few readers trained in theater know how to read a script and imagine it in performance, but they are rare. Shakespeare

want to know what happens to them. The thing is not worth watching if it bores its watchers, puts them to sleep, or drives them out of the theater. Such a failure results from a bad text, a good text badly performed, a good text well performed for a bad audience—or from all three being good but not in alignment.

About Growing Wiser

First a general point about the virtues, including wisdom: For any good quality of character, no one can start from scratch. Only the wise can grow wiser. If you are not already wise, you will not know how to gain wisdom from any experience. Similarly, only the brave can grow braver. A fool will never become wise. But please do not be insulted. None of my readers are fools, none of them totally devoid of wisdom—though it may take some effort to scratch their way down to the wisdom they have, beneath the partial knowledge, the confusions arising from past certainties, and the conceit that grows on success.[6]

Second, a point specific to human wisdom: Socratic wisdom grows through self-examination and is nourished by reflection. Theater draws our attention to other people (as we shall see) and charms us with humor or engages us through our emotions. Are we free to reflect on ourselves while watching a play? Are we free to deploy our reasoning powers in the theater? Plato thought not. Theater of the pleasure-giving sort, he feared, teaches its audiences to set reason aside. How then could wisdom survive?

---

wrote for performance. He may also have given his edited scripts for publication, but that cannot be proved. His income came from performance.

6. Theories of virtue such as the one I use assume that normal humans are born with at least the tender beginnings of virtues, which Mencius likens to the shoots of rice plants. See my "How Can I Become Reverent?," *Reverence: Renewing a Forgotten Virtue*, 2nd ed. (New York: Oxford University Press, 2014), 68–69.

PLATO'S CHALLENGE

What could wisdom be doing on the stage? Perhaps it should have no place there, if I am right that theater is the art of watching and being watched. Wisdom can't be watched at all. The wise are silent about their wisdom. When speakers try to show off their wisdom, they fail, because showing off is a clear sign that they lack wisdom (at least on the Platonic conception of wisdom I am using here). At the same time, those who seem wise but don't show off are not worth watching; they are boring. On the other side, people who spout wisdom are worth watching only when they are funny, and they are funny because their self-proclaimed wisdom shows them to be fools. That's how Shakespeare uses Polonius. He uses characters differently when, like Macbeth, they make no pretense to wisdom but suffer into an understanding of their lives anyway.[7]

Plato concludes that the playwrights of his time could put nothing but fake wisdom on stage. Because they aim to please, they must put before an audience only what it wants to watch, and no audience wants to watch the silence of the sage, even if, like Socrates, the sage gives shape to silence through asking unanswerable questions.

The most pedantic modern playwright has been Bertolt Brecht. His *Lehrstücke* were directly and unabashedly instructive. If Brecht makes them worth watching, we will want to know how he accomplishes this. And if he succeeds, we should then ask whether we should count what his plays teach as wisdom. Perhaps, like Polonius's wise sayings, Brecht's messages lose whatever wisdom they had, once

---

7. Macbeth reflects on the meaningless he has found in his own life, and generalizes the point in his famous "tomorrow and tomorrow and tomorrow" speech (5.5). He has reached a personal moment of recognition, but it is partial at best; he does not recognize his own faults or the absurdity of projecting his failures on others. See the chapter on the nihilism of this speech in Tzachi Zamir, *Double Vision: Moral Philosophy and Shakespearean Drama* (Princeton, NJ: Princeton University Press, 2007).

they are put on stage—or, equally likely, they lose stageability. Brecht was too theatrical a playwright to keep up his experiment with the most pedantic plays.

In ancient times, poets staged facsimiles of wisdom which were so credible that Plato concluded they must be banned from the stage of his ideal city. They were too much like the real thing—but without being wise. Indeed, the plays of Plato's time presented on stage an alternative to the wisdom which he thought should guide civic life. They did this mainly by presenting characters who, in Plato's view, were modeling behavior that Plato thought should not be countenanced in a healthy community. They also larded speeches and choruses with wise-sounding aphorisms—but these, for reasons I have already given, cannot be reliably wise. All of this they did in order to please a popular audience.

Plato's objections are not to the aphorisms, but to plot and character, and to the effect of these on an audience. Tragic plots, as Aristotle later pointed out, turn around characters who, like Oedipus, are *spoudaios*, zealous of being good, but are subject to overreaching and other errors. As a result, characters on the tragic stage are not role models for the youth of Athens. There is no one shown on stage whom they should try to be like. These characters are models of what to avoid, as the choruses often point out. Plato is not impressed with this sort of plot and he is right: there is no great wisdom in showing how proud men stumble, and no wisdom is gained by laughing at their stumbles or mourning for their fate. We already knew that proud men stumble, before we entered the theater. Besides, watching them stumble gives us a sense of superiority. In fact, the tragic chorus often emphasizes the moral superiority of the common man (understand: the audience) to the tragic heroes.[8] Feelings of superiority are fatal to human wisdom. The point is obvious: a sense of superiority

8. See for example, the choruses in Euripides's *Bacchae*: 386–401, 430–33, 910–11.

is just another sort of pride that leads to a fall, as so often illustrated on the tragic stage.

The effect of tragic performance on an audience, Plato believes, is entirely bad. Such performance arouses unhealthy emotions, as a way to give pleasure. Reading between the lines, we can see what was so upsetting to Plato. The wise, he believes, express grief moderately if at all. Because the wise do not believe that death is a bad thing, they neither fear it on their own behalf nor grieve for others who die. Pity and fear are not for the wise. But the chorus in a tragic play set an example for the audience of how to feel; they are like cheerleaders in our time, except that they lead the audience not in cheering but in grief and compassion—emotional responses that Plato believes are entirely unhealthy.

Plato argues, rightly I think, that if theater aims to give pleasure to its audience, it cannot put truly wise people on stage; they would be unexciting and therefore boring. He considers his own writing to be an alternative to tragic poetry. In the *Laws* he will replace spectator theater with a participatory art form derived from theater: In Athens, everyone watched choral performances of song and dance; in Magnesia, everyone, young and old, will take part in singing and dancing to celebrate the virtues. Again, Plato appears to be right. Performing is more fun than watching, and is more likely to affect our behavior in ordinary life.

GREEK TRAGEDY

Ancient Greek tragic plays often put wise-sounding comments in the songs of a chorus, which represented common opinions of the audience. A famous case is the Second Stasimon from the *Oedipus Tyrannus*, where the first antistrophe begins (873): "Hubris grows from tyranny." Or perhaps "Hubris begets tyranny." Scholars are divided. The manuscripts have "Hubris begets tyranny," but that does not apply to the plot of this play; hubris had no part in Oedipus's rise to power. So it seems more likely that his hubris grew from his power. Either way, this appears to be a nugget of tragic wisdom—but, either way, the chorus gives us no hint as to how to apply such wisdom to the action of the play.

Wise-seeming messages from the chorus are often mysterious in this way. For example, in the *Antigone*, the famous Ode to the Human (the First Stasimon) simultaneously celebrates and deplores the wonders and terrors that have come to the human species through innovation:

> Many wonders, many terrors
> But none more wonderful than the human race
> Or more dangerous.
>
> (332–34)[9]

But whose inventiveness brings this on? Antigone's appeal to unwritten law, unparalleled at the time the play was produced? Or Creon's decree that a rebel be unburied, which, though unusual, had tradition behind it? Sophocles gives no hint.

Characters also use wise-seeming generalizations, often when they present an argument within a debate. In these cases, the application is clear. In *Antigone*, when Creon and his son Haemon debate, they both use wise-sounding generalizations:

> CREON: The public knows that a man is just
> Only if he is straight with his relatives.
>
> (661–62)

---

9. Translations of Greek plays are my own, from Peter Meineck and Paul Woodruff, trans., *Sophocles: The Theban Plays* (Indianapolis: Hackett, 2003).

HAEMON: If a man believes that he alone has a sound mind,
And no one else can speak or think as well as he does,
Then, when people study him, they'll find an empty book.
But a wise man can learn a lot and never be ashamed.

(707–10)

This last line appears not only to be a nugget of wisdom; it is a piece of wisdom *about* wisdom.

We often find wise seeming utterances at the end of messenger speeches. For example, also in *Antigone* the messenger tells how Haemon kills himself after finding the corpse of his beloved Antigone, and then makes a general comment about wisdom:

He took his blade
And leaned on it, drove it into his lungs.
Then, still conscious, he pulled the girl into the curve
Of his sagging embrace. He gasped and panted,
Spattered blood on her white cheek, a spurt of scarlet.
Then he was dead. His body lay with hers;
They'd brought their marriage off at last in the house of Death—
Which proves the point: In a human life,
It's deadly for bad judgment to embrace a man.

(1235–44)

This comes as an anticlimax: Why say something so obvious after describing such a grisly scene? The triteness lowers the tone and perhaps gives the audience a moment to relax before they receive the next blows, the howls of Creon and the suicide of Haemon's mother. But the aphorism is also a puzzler: Whose bad judgment? Haemon's, for loving Antigone? Or his fathers, for refusing to take the boy's advice? Who is to blame for this tragic scene? Again, no hint. If we are to learn from this, we must bring our wisdom to the theater.

Sometimes a messenger's message is not merely inappropriate (as this case was) but is downright comic. The watchman who reports the burial that set off this tragic sequence ends with a bromide: "No one loves the man who brings bad news" (277). He has already been set up as a comic character, one who shares attitudes with the audience. So this line should bring a sympathetic laugh from the audience. But it often seems true, for all that.

Often the plot of Greek tragedy seems to drive home the vulnerability of human beings, the danger of hubris, and the consequent need for reverence. Sometimes the poet will have the chorus state this in a message to the audience. There is a kind of wisdom in this, but Plato would not count it as true wisdom. On his view we are immortal, vulnerable only to temporary setbacks due to ignorance. While the tragic poets warn us against competing with the gods, Plato urges us to emulate them.

Ideally wise human beings, if there were any, would be like the gods (according to Plato); they would eschew reverence and compassion, since gods (as the Greeks understood them) are neither reverent nor compassionate. But we are not gods. What is wisdom for a human being?

WHAT IS THE WISDOM PLATO SEEKS?

Wisdom may be ideal or human. Ideal wisdom would be an unfailing guide to living well—the sort of thing Socrates knows he does not have. Human wisdom is self-understanding or self-knowledge. At Apollo's command, the Greeks inscribed at their most sacred place the two words "Know Thyself." That is no easy thing to do. Plato's Socrates said that it was a life-consuming task to know himself; to stop examining his life would be to abandon the quest. Knowing yourself is not like knowing a theorem in geometry, which you learn and then have for life. To know yourself thoroughly you need to keep on under-standing yourself at the point of each action or refusal to act. You can never say, "Now I know what I am: I am brave and smart and wise, so I can expect to act that way the rest of my life." If you say such things, expect disaster. Socratic human wisdom grows partly from reflection on our own individual experiences, and partly from reflection on the cumulative experience of our species. Human wisdom sees patterns of behavior in ourselves and others; often these patterns set ambition against a spotty record of success and failure. Always human wisdom sees that human joy and hope and sorrow end in death.

Plato's Socrates found himself confined to human wisdom, but he seems to have wanted his ideal state to be guided by the ideal wisdom that ideal philosophers would bring brought back from outside the cave, infused with the joy of knowing that a human soul never dies, that humans can come to share with gods the very highest knowledge. It is a paradox that the Socrates who tells the parable of the Cave has, in other dialogues, declared his limitations with respect to wisdom.[10]

Such limitations are at the heart of tragic poetry. Tragic poets offer us a wisdom that is all too human, that reminds us of our limitations, our potential for error, our destiny for death—and, above all, para-doxically, of the folly of believing that one has found wisdom. That's the wisdom of the ancient Greek stage: Oedipus's conceit of wisdom, for example, contributes to his downfall. But there is a danger here for an unwary audience: "Aren't we wise," we might say, "compared to Oedipus, now that we have learned how dangerous it is to be proud of one's wisdom?" No. The effect has been to make us more foolish than we were before. Watching other people stumble, learning to feel superior, is no way to become wise.

We have come to a more serious challenge than Plato's. A theatri-cal experience separates you from your living for a measured time;

10. See note 4.

you are safe from living your own life while watching a play (unless, like Claudius, you wind up watching a play aimed directly at you). Human wisdom grows on reflection about one's own life. Theater asks you to set yourself aside and reflect, if at all, on the lives of others. If you reflect on your own life, then, like Claudius, you stop watching the play and theater has failed. So the obvious tragic way of staging human wisdom backfires. Theater is watching, but wisdom is not to be learned by watching others; it grows from reflection on how one lives. But such reflection, if it is serious, blocks the experience of theater.

Human wisdom is least evident in the mockery of others—which is common in theater—and most evident in self-mockery. Some comic scenes represent the audience on stage and give the real audience a chance to laugh at representations of themselves. Wisdom would grow from that, if the experience did not distance the audience from its representations, as it so often does. "We, at least, are not as bad as Strepsiades," an Athenian audience might think while watching the *Clouds* of Aristophanes, or an Elizabethan audience might feel superior to the audience in *A Midsummer's Night Dream*, which mocks the actor playing Moonshine offstage (5.1.239–56).

Nevertheless, in the face of all these difficulties, I would argue that ancient tragedies did succeed in staging human wisdom; how they did that is material for another paper. Plato was wrong about the tragic poets, who earned their place in the wisdom literature of their time. He would have been even more wrong about Shakespeare.

WHERE IN *HAMLET* MIGHT WISDOM BE FOUND?

Shakespeare succeeded in staging wisdom, most notably in *Hamlet*. How did he get away with that? Does he go about this differently from his ancient forebears? And how did he learn this from the practice of theater?

Hamlet integrates wisdom into language, character, and plot more smoothly than did any of the ancient Greek plays. Shakespeare wrote to please his audience, but in writing *Hamlet*, especially, he pleased his audience by staging wisdom. He does not, however, succeed in staging wisdom in the ways we might expect from our survey of Greek tragedy.

Plot

A distinctly theatrical way to stage wisdom might be to stage the effects of folly or wickedness. Plot can be wisely drawn and characters wisely developed—or so it would seem. True, tragic plots show foolish (but universal) patterns of overconfidence and vulnerability: power leads to confidence, confidence to blindness, and blindness to a fall. Look at this tale: this is the shape of a human life. In such a plot, well-drawn characters illustrate what it is to be human, with the blend of strength and weakness, wisdom and folly that is so characteristic of our species. I remarked earlier on the moral danger of reflecting on the folly of others.

Remember how Hamlet invites the court to watch a play about fratricide and incest. "You shall see anon 'tis a knavish piece of work," Hamlet admits to Claudius, "but what of that? Your Majesty, and we that have free souls—it touches us not" (3.2.233–35). Indeed the play will touch no one but Claudius, and that effect will be an anomaly. Successful theater depends on keeping the audience in their seats until the end of the play. The company fails with Claudius. No normal actor or director wants an audience to respond as Claudius does, calling for lights and conspicuously storming out. (The play was performed in full lighting; Claudius needs lights to help him find his way down through the corridors of the castle.)

The art of theater asks us to stay and watch till the end of a play. In order to stay, we must enjoy the play, and not feel so threatened by it that we will leave. We must forget ourselves. At the end, then, we will turn our minds back to ourselves and leave with our confidence reinforced. "Yes, we have free souls. Hamlet was right. This touched us not; it might have touched others, but not us." That leads us to this question: If *Hamlet* were to touch us in a way that leads to wisdom, how would it do that, when the play within the play does not—indeed cannot—touch others the way it touches Claudius?

The answer lies in the unique plotting of this play. In a standard revenge tragedy, the audience would see ambition or some other wickedness leading to crime and crime to revenge carried out by the victims or their friends. But such a plot is routine and boring. Even Shakespeare's lesser contemporaries had to distort the genre in order to make plays worth watching. *The Duchess of Malfi*, for example, has the basic shape of a revenge tragedy, with this notable difference—that the agent of revenge is also the agent of the crime that cries out to be revenged. The actual killer—Bosola—becomes the most interesting and sympathetic figure, the one an actor would most want to play and the audience to watch. The evil cardinal is scarcely human, but Bosola, who has been under great pressure to act as he does, is all too human and all too like us. He is no fool and no villain, but a complex person beset by complex situations.

The plot of *Hamlet* distorts the genre in a similar direction, making us more sympathetic to the agent of the crimes than to their avenger. The agent is Hamlet, for all the crimes that take place during the play's action. The murder of Polonius, the betrayal of Ophelia, and the execution of Rosencrantz and Guildenstern—for all of these our hero is responsible. They are the things Hamlet does while *not* avenging his father. A revenge tragedy there will be, but it will be the revenge of Laertes against Hamlet for killing Polonius; we do not want this, and it will not satisfy us when justice is done. Yet this is the only act of revenge that is planned and carried out in the play. Yes, the king and queen will die, but the queen's death will be an accident, and the king's will not come as the climax of any plan Hamlet could concoct.

Here we do not witness the familiar pattern of wickedness, crime, and punishment. Instead, we see a man we suppose to be intelligent and good-hearted on the whole, who does terrible things while trying to do what the occasion demands. No room for complacency here on the part of the audience. Nothing in the play suggests that we might have done better ourselves. In many tragedies we are in danger of the folly of thinking ourselves superior to the hero. Not in this one. We are in awe of Hamlet's brilliance; he is too clever, and too complicated, for us to second-guess him, as we might second-guess, say, Creon, in *Antigone*. We don't know what he will say next, and neither does he. He dazzles us. We in the audience may well feel that we are wiser than Creon. We would not make his mistakes; we would pay attention, as he does not, to young people who know what is being said in the streets. But on what score could we think ourselves wiser than Hamlet? Thus are we saved from the folly of superiority.

Shakespeare learned to write *Hamlet* in the school of theater for profit; theater taught him to vary the plot, to create surprising new characters, and to leave an audience unsatisfied, reflecting on a problem ending. Few of his plays conform strictly to their official genres, and many have problem endings. None is more perplexing than the ending of *Measure for Measure*, which leaves us deeply unsettled over issues of justice, compassion, and power. At the end of *Hamlet*, we see a brilliant prince's plans failing, a royal family strewn dead upon the stage, and a kingdom up for grabs. Watchers who are wise are drawn to wonder and reflect and to consider the futility of human effort without any feelings of superiority. *Hamlet* is uniquely constructed in such a way that we cannot reflect on the lead character without reflecting on ourselves.[11]

Hamlet lifts our hopes for wisdom and then dashes them again and again. Displays of wisdom are undercut by irony, aphorisms show their foolish sides, self-explorations end in failure, and choices turn back upon themselves. Out of such dashed hopes arises the most human wisdom.

Character

No character in Shakespeare reveals more of himself than Hamlet, with his six soliloquies. But what he reveals is a puzzle as to what sort of character he is. A character, Aristotle wrote, should be plausible; an audience will not be moved to pity or fear on behalf of a character who is not believable. Believable characters, he thought, would be consistent in that they would act in ways that were either necessary or probable in view of who they are and what they have done so far.[12] A good Aristotelian character has an identifiable ethos.

Hamlet does not have such a character. We know he is brilliant with words and given to self-examination. We see that he is resourceful in stratagems—the play within a play that will catch the king's conscience, for example, or the exchange of letters that will kill his old school-friends. But his actions and his words do not conform to each other, or allow us to form an assessment of his character. Nothing explains him, as Tolstoy noted:

> One moment he is awestruck by his father's ghost, another moment he begins to chaff it, calling it "old mole"; one moment

---

11. Contrast our reactions to Othello, whom we find too credulous of Iago, or to Romeo, whom we see as immature and impulsive. We would not make such mistakes. Hamlet is unique.
12. See my "Aristotle on Character, or, Who Is Creon?," *Journal of Aesthetics and Arts Criticism* 67.3 (2009): 301–9. "Probable" is the usual translation for *eikós*, which means what is

he loves Ophelia, another moment he teases her, and so forth. There is no possibility of finding any explanation whatever of Hamlet's actions or words, and therefore no possibility of attributing any character to him.[13]

We find a similar uncertainty in Sophocles's *Philoctetes*, in which the young hero, son of Achilles, vacillates between compassionate honesty on one hand, and ruthless dishonesty on the other. This is because the young man's character is not yet formed, and we will not be able to assess it properly until his life is over. This, I think, shows the wisdom of the poet. In life, if not on the stage, character remains mysterious, for any human being.

It is unwise for any of us to believe that we are characters of certain sorts. John Doris has argued convincingly that we should not rely on having the virtues we think we have. Social science shows that human beings are not reliably brave or generous or resistant to temptation.[14] Only the wisest of us know ourselves as well as we think we do, and that is because the wisest of us know, by means of constant self-investigation, that we always have more to learn about ourselves.

Tolstoy is partly right about Hamlet. We cannot know who Hamlet is, because he himself cannot know who he is. He does not play any of the parts listed in "all the world's a stage." At thirty, he is neither young nor old. As a sidelined prince he is neither royal nor ordinary. He is an expert swordsman, but not a soldier, a scholar but not at school, a passionate lover but not so passionate he cannot hide his love. He puzzles himself. The relentless self-examinations of the

reasonable to expect. Aristotle recognizes that it is probable for improbable things to happen; he does not wish to rule out surprises in drama.

13. *Shakespeare and the Drama* quoted from the Norton Critical Edition, ed. Robert S. Miola (New York: Norton, 2011), 254.
14. John Doris, *Lack of Character: Personality and Moral Behavior* (Cambridge: Cambridge University Press, 2002).

soliloquies lead only to this self-baffling result—that here is a self that cannot find itself, no matter how hard it tries. Wise watchers of the play, seeing this, may recognize themselves—or, rather, the mystery that we all are to ourselves.

Tolstoy approaches the play in the wrong way, as an analytical reader rather than as a watcher or potential watcher reading a script. The script of a play is not for reading but for performing and watching. *Hamlet* is not written to satisfy the questions of a reader like Tolstoy, but to enthrall an audience by keeping it guessing. The same could be said of the *Philoctetes*, which baffles readers but keeps watchers on the edge of their seats with suspense. (Of course, readers with a trained theatrical imagination can see a performance in their minds' eyes as they read a play, but this ability is rare.)

In the hands of a less able playwright, a character as mysterious as Hamlet might ruin a play. But not here. Shakespeare has probed the art of theater deeply in search of what captivates an audience. What he has discovered is a prince who surprises us at every turn, who keeps us wondering and watching, who remains breathtakingly believable. Hamlet is far more human than any of the stereotypical characters that Tolstoy or Aristotle would prefer in a play. We see ourselves in him and are reminded of the never-ending task of self-study.[15]

Irony

Human wisdom cannot have much confidence in itself, or it slides into human foolishness. Irony befits a sage, and irony plays well on stage. Socrates, of course, is the father of wisdom's ironies, in the European tradition, but irony was already familiar from the comic

---

15. "Hamlet is spectatorproof. He fascinates every member of the audience, who recognizes—always—something of himself or herself in the dramatic ebb and flow of Hamlet's moods, his inhibiting self-realizations and doubts, his pitiful failure to control events." Laurence Olivier, ["On Hamlet's Character,"] from his *Confessions of an Actor: An Autobiography*, cited in the Norton Critical Edition of *Hamlet*, ed. Miola, 169.

stage when Plato wrote, and it was present on the tragic stage as well—sometimes comic even there, sometimes excruciatingly painful. Usually, in ancient Greek theater, wise proverbs are given to the most ordinary people to pronounce—the chorus and the messengers—rather than to people with authority. But in *Hamlet*, they are given to the stars.

Hamlet is packed with nuggets of wisdom, gnomic utterances, proverbs, or aphorisms. Many of these catch in our memories, and we quote them without knowing their source. I count thirty-seven, give or take a few. Of those, nine are delivered by Polonius in a scene laced with irony. Polonius, the old courtier, is pompous and silly. His son, the gallant Laertes, has just delivered his own set of bromides, advising his sister to guard her virtue, concluding "best safety lies in fear" (1.3.35–43). Now, later in the same scene, we can see him and his sister stifling their laughter as their father pops off nine bromides as if from an automatic wisdom machine (1.3.58–80).

Here, if the scene is well directed, the irony will be palpable. We see Ophelia stifling her own reaction to Laertes's pomposities.[16] Like any teenager, she has heard it all already, and she knows better. (She is right, too: Hamlet does truly love her.) Like comic actors everywhere she can share the moment and the feeling with the audience, with a look that says, "My big brother is at it again." Then, when Laertes makes the same faces during his father's pomposities, we cannot miss the irony. Displays of wisdom are comical, because they always reveal a failure of self-understanding. The truly wise are silent.[17] Shakespeare has put this fact of comedy to exquisite use in this play.

Polonius may be laughable, but he is not a fool through and through. We laugh because he does not see how silly he seems to his

---

16. Here we see the difference between watching a play and reading its script. In reading, we are aware only of Polonius's words; in watching, we cannot forget that Laertes and his sister are also watching and reacting.

17. See my "The Silent Teacher," in *Reverence*, 213–28.

adult children, who have no doubt heard him unload his wisdom machine many times. At the same time, however, we let his maxims stick in our memories, and we take them to heart while observing their limitations. Polonius's advice is not good for all seasons, and it will not save the life of his son. But it is good advice nonetheless, worth remembering. So are his four nuggets delivered in other scenes (1.3.114–19; 2.1.61–63; 2.2.90–91; 3.1.46–48). One of these, too, comes with irony: he speaks "Brevity is the soul of wit" in the center of a speech marked by prolixity. That's right, most of the time. The wise say little. Most of the time.

Hamlet, with fifteen nuggets of wisdom, is only slightly behind Polonius, and if we count the six soliloquies, he is way ahead. His wisdom too is hedged in irony. When the ghost makes him suspect his uncle of murder, he realizes that "One may smile, and smile, and be a villain!" (1.5.108), but before blurting it out he reaches for his little notebook ("my tables! Meet it is I set it down") and right after saying it he partly withdraws it: "At least I am sure it may be so in Denmark." "It may be so?" Certainly it is so, anywhere, as everyone knows. This is one of the very few aphorisms that are reliably true. Hamlet is self-consciously academic in undercutting this well-known point as he does. Yet, overall, he is the wisest of Shakespeare's characters, painfully wise through successive crippling doses of self-knowledge and self-doubt. Of the latter, this is our first glimpse.

Nuggets of Wisdom?

Wise-seeming aphorisms pepper ancient tragedy, and they are even more frequent in *Hamlet*. Why do these not put wisdom on the stage? A well-composed aphorism makes its message memorable. If it is well worded, metrical, even rhyming, it will stick in the minds of the audience. The more quotable the better. Once it is in your mind it is ready for you to call on when you need it. But when is that?

Polonius says, "Neither a borrower nor a lender be": good advice, some of the time. Borrowing and lending can destroy a friendship, drive family members apart, and sink fortunes forever—but it can also save lives. The trick, with any aphorism, is to be wise enough to know when to apply it and when not. No aphorism can carry that kind of wisdom. Indeed, the reaction of the wise to an aphorism is to be wary of it.

Greek tragedies leave aphorisms unexamined, unquestioned. Their aphorisms are popped into speeches and choruses, not integrated into the action of the plays. Shakespeare folds aphorisms neatly into his scenes and shows us how to question them—through irony (as we have seen in the case of Polonius), through the structure of the scenes, and through revealing the characters behind them.

Hamlet has penned this line for the Player Queen: "None wed the second but who killed the first" (3.2.174)—a nice jingle but plainly false—except, perhaps in the case of Gertrude. Claudius, on the opposite tack, speaks to reassure Gertrude of their safety. But he too uses a slogan that is plainly false: "There's such divinity doth hedge a king / That treason can but peep to what it would" (4.5.123–24). Of course he knows this is not true (though it sounds good). After all, Claudius has done quite well at treason, and so have many others. His very need to utter this nugget betrays it.

Hamlet, on seeing Fortinbras lead his army across Denmark to claim a useless patch of land, remarks on the futility of war (4.4.24–28). He sees nothing to admire in what Fortinbras is doing, and yet he does admire him for taking some sort of action. He will find, in the end, that revenge is no less futile than war, but still he hates himself for not yet having taken it. Into his mind comes an argument from Aristotle by way of Thomas Aquinas:

> What is a man
> If his chief good and market of his time

Be but to sleep and feed? A beast—no more.
Sure he that made us with such large discourse,
Looking before and after, gave us not
That capability and god-like reason
To fust in us unused.

(4.4.32–38)

But he sees that his reason has been holding him back from action. Perhaps he would be better off if he did let his reason fust unused for a while. Shakespeare has given this nugget of wisdom a context—a theatrical reason for its being said—and at the same time cut the ground from under it. We human beings are designed for both thinking and acting, but how to balance the two? Hamlet does not know, and neither do we.

Hamlet has not agreed with himself about human nature from the beginning. He has been depressed, and finds no one pleasing to him, even though he admires the human species, delivering yet another Aristotelian sentiment: "What a piece of work is a man! . . . The beauty of the world, the paragon of animals!" (2.2.269–73). Yet soon after, in the same scene, he takes a Christian tack. When Polonius says he will treat the players as they deserve, Hamlet objects: "Use every man after his desert and who shall scape whipping? Use them after your own honor and dignity; the less they deserve the more merit is in your bounty" (2.2.467–70). Good advice, in keeping with the sort of wisdom that Polonius himself dispenses, very close to the wisdom of Christian mercy: "All the souls that were were forfeit once," as Isabella says in *Measure for Measure*, pleading for mercy (2.2.73). But Hamlet himself is loath to follow the advice he gives. He wants to treat Claudius as he deserves—wants this so fervently that he wants to deprive him of God's mercy by sending him to heaven unshriven—as he will do, and as he will do also for Rosencrantz and Guildenstern, for whom he orders execution without time for absolution.

One after another, the nuggets of wisdom fall in this play, well motivated by the immediate theatrical context, but almost always undercut by the larger context of the plot. This is a kind of wisdom, to watch a character like Hamlet steeped in learning, ready to cite wisdom of the ancients as needed, and equally ready to show that he cannot apply it in his life.

But there is one sort of wisdom that survives the action of the play: mortals will die. That is a tautology we never forget but one that rarely comes home to us. It will come home to Hamlet at last when he sees Ophelia in the grave.

GRAVE WISDOM

Delivering a challenge from Claudius, the foppish Osric says, indirectly, that Hamlet must know the excellence of Laertes. Hamlet says he doesn't dare confess that he does, for that would be to compare himself to Laertes, and continues: "But to know a man well were to know himself" (5.2.124).[18] This cuts both ways: To know Laertes, he must first know himself, and vice versa. In context, this may mean only that he could gauge Laertes's skill as a swordsman only by measuring himself against the other in a duel. But Hamlet often means something deeper than the context allows.

There is someone Hamlet knew, and freely confesses that he knew, and that is Yorick (5.1.171). To know the mortality of Yorick is to know his own. Greek tragedy harps on the theme of mortality, but no scene from the Greek stage is as memorable as the gravedigger scene in *Hamlet*. We have been prepared for this by Hamlet's pun, "Your worm is your only emperor for diet" (4.3.21). He is acutely aware of

---

18. This exchange, found in the Second Quarto, was not printed in the First Folio. So we may entertain some doubt as to its importance for Shakespeare.

the fate that awaits us all, to pass through the guts of a worm. Then comes the black humor of the gravedigger and sexton, their banter and songs, their light tossing of skulls—a prelude to the horror of Ophelia's funeral, when, for once, Hamlet finds an emotion that is his own—his grief for Ophelia, which he does not want to share with her brother.

Hamlet's first line in the gravedigger scene is about emotion: "Has this fellow no feeling of his business?" He has heard the digger singing of love and considers such behavior inappropriate. But, ironically, his own behavior in what follows lacks gravity. His remarks on the finality of death and the vanity of life's efforts are delivered lightly and laced with puns. He imagines Yorick's skull in "my lady's chamber," trying to fetch a laugh at the truth that not even heavy makeup will save her beauty from death, and he pictures the dust that was a conqueror stopping a bung hole. Then the joking ends: a body is brought to the grave, and Hamlet now goes beyond grasping the finality of death intellectually. He now feels the pain of losing to death the one he truly loves:

> I loved Ophelia—forty thousand brothers
> Could not with all their quantity of love
> Make up my sum.
>
> (5.1.258–60)

For the investor, when he is dead, his parchment deeds to land mean nothing, and they will mean no more to his heir when he too has gone to earth (5.1.98–105). But to the living Hamlet, the death of Ophelia means everything.

The scene is intensely visual, from the bouncing skulls to the leap into the grave and the confrontation with Laertes. It must be seen to be appreciated. I would ask my students to perform it in class before discussing it; they will understand it far more deeply than they would by reading it in silence. The standard wise-seeming irony and cant about death give way here to a climax of grief.

Elsewhere in Shakespeare, characters are made to speak about death, as Claudio does in *Measure for Measure* ("Death is a fearful thing," 3.1.116). Claudio's speech is as moving to us when we read it on the page as when we hear him deliver it on stage. But that scene does not have a fraction of the sheer theatrical power of the gravedigger scene in *Hamlet*, when we see our hero jolted out of his schoolboy wit about death, into its terrible reality for those who survive.

Recognizing mortality is at the root of human wisdom. Easy enough to say we are mortal (and not especially wise) but hard to take this truth to heart, as Hamlet has done, and as the audience is invited to do in this unforgettable scene. To make this common wisdom theatrical, entertaining, even pleasurable, and still make it strike home—that calls for Shakespeare's extraordinary capacity to stage wisdom.

ACKNOWLEDGMENTS

A version of this chapter was presented at the conference "Occasioning Philosophy: Celebrating Philosophy and Theater on the 400th Anniversary of Shakespeare's Death," University of Mississippi, April 22, 2016.

WORKS CITED

Doris, J. 2002. *Lack of Character: Personality and Moral Behavior*. Cambridge: Cambridge University Press.
Meineck, Peter, and Paul Woodruff, trans. 2003. *Sophocles: The Theban Plays*. Indianapolis: Hackett.
Miola, Robert S., ed. 2011. *Hamlet*. Norton Critical Edition. New York: Norton.

Woodruff, Paul. 2008. *The Necessity of Theater: The Art of Watching and Being Watched.* New York: Oxford University Press.

———. 2009. "Aristotle on Character, or, Who Is Creon?" *Journal of Aesthetics and Arts Criticism* 67.3: 301–9.

———. 2011. *The Ajax Dilemma: Justice, Fairness and Rewards.* New York: Oxford University Press.

———. 2014. *Reverence: Renewing a Forgotten Virtue.* 2nd ed. New York: Oxford University Press.

Zamir, Tzachi. 2007. *Double Vision: Moral Philosophy and Shakespearean Drama.* Princeton, NJ: Princeton University Press.

Chapter 3

Philosophical Sex

DAVID HILLMAN

The degree and kind of a person's sexuality reach up into the ultimate pinnacle of his spirit.

—Friedrich Nietzsche[1]

PHILOSOPHY AND SEX

Imagine Hamlet having sex.

Why not? The preoccupations of Hamlet's own imagination seem to invite the thought. Hamlet watches in his mind's eye pretty much everyone around him in the act—Claudius ("honeying and making love / Over the nasty sty," 3.4.91–92); Gertrude (living "in the rank sweat of an enseaméd bed," the "heyday in [her] blood" undiminished by age, 3.4.90 & 67); himself and Ophelia ("Lady, shall I lie in your lap?" 3.2.108); the entire natural world ("if the sun breed maggots in a dead dog, being a good kissing carrion . . . ," 2.2.178–79). For much of the play it is the "couch for luxury and damned incest" (1.5.83), far

---

1. Friedrich Nietzsche, *Beyond Good and Evil: Prelude to a Philosophy of the Future*, trans. Walter Kaufmann (London: Vintage Books, 1973), 75.

more than the murder of his father, that transforms Hamlet's imagination into a place "as foul / As Vulcan's stithy" (3.2.79–80). He rails
against bestial oblivion, his own whorishness, his father's cuckoldry,
his mother's adultery, his uncle's incest, is disgusted at the sexual act
and its "contagious blastments" (1.3.41). Sex is the central target of
Hamlet's skepticism; in his mind, in Vulcan's stithy, sex is a base element forged of adultery, incest, and defilement. But who could stop
themselves from wishing to look in? From his opening soliloquy in
1.2 through the play-within-the-play and his visit to his mother's
closet, Hamlet can hardly staunch the intrusion of thoughts of sex;
the Ghost's instruction—"taint not thy mind" (1.5.85)—is in vain.
And he seems to feel his inner self to be sullied by these imaginings
("Let me not think on't!" 1.2.146). Yet he—like many of us, one
feels inclined to add—is unable to avoid such ideas of what he terms
"compulsive ardour" (3.4.84). Both the ardour and the thoughts are
compulsive.

"Kissing carrion" encapsulates the way Hamlet's disgust at sexuality and breeding is intimately linked to his preoccupation with death
and decomposition (his puns on "matter" and "mater" bring together
this charged relation to both the material into which we dissolve and
the matter from which we are formed).[2] More generally, Hamlet is
preoccupied with the gross materiality of the body: "O that this too
too solid [or: sallied] flesh should melt . . ." (1.2.129); "the thousand
natural shocks / That flesh is heir to . . ." (3.1.61–62); "how a king
may go a progress through the guts of a beggar" (4.3.29–30); "I'll
lug the guts into the neighbour room" (3.4.210); "How long will a

2. On Hamlet's "sexual disgust," see especially Janet Adelman, *Suffocating Mothers: Fantasies of Maternal Origin in Shakespeare's Plays, "Hamlet" to "The Tempest"* (New York: Routledge, 1992), chapter on *Hamlet* plus 250 n. 14—though many critics, as Adelman points out, have written about Hamlet's recoil from Gertrude's sexuality. On "matter" in *Hamlet*, see Adelman, 255 n. 36, and Margaret Ferguson, "*Hamlet*: Letters and Spirits," in *Shakespeare and the Question of Theory*, ed. Patricia Parker and Geoffrey Hartman (New York: Methuen, 1985), 295.

man lie i'th'earth ere he rot?" (5.1.154); "my gorge rises at it" (l.177). Critics have often enough observed *Hamlet's* concern with the body, from Samuel Taylor Coleridge's comment upon the play's "compelled attention to bodily feelings" to Stephen Greenblatt's description of the play's "obsession with corporeality."[3] At the same time, it has long been felt that Hamlet is the most philosophical of Shakespeare's characters—from Coleridge's own "I believe the character of Hamlet may be traced to Shakespeare's deep and accurate science in mental philosophy" to Franz Rosenzweig's "the hero is to all intents and purposes a philosopher."[4] The protagonist of the play is introspective, pensive, speculative regarding some of the fundamental questions about human life. Yet his philosophical bent is rarely brought into relation with his crude materialism, let alone his sexualizing imagination. The Romantic idea of the prince's delicacy of spirit can sit ill beside the discomfiting texture of so much of what the play's protagonist says; this is especially true of his sexual jibes at Ophelia and of his repugnance at Gertrude's sexuality.

In discussions of *Hamlet* and elsewhere, philosophy and sex have seemed to be uncomfortable bedmates, the *philo* (at least in its erotic aspect) apparently radically at odds with the *sophia*. The intimacy of philosophy and sex, though, is Platonic. Plato found desire (not excluding sexual desire) at the root of higher philosophy. As David Halperin has argued, "Plato refuses to separate—he actually identifies and fuses—the erotics of sexuality, the erotics of conversation,

3. Samuel Taylor Coleridge, *Coleridge's Writings on Shakespeare*, ed. Terence Hawkes (New York: Capricorn Books, 1959), 140; Stephen Greenblatt, *Hamlet in Purgatory* (Princeton, NJ: Princeton University Press, 2001), 243. See also, among others, John Hunt, "A Thing of Nothing: The Catastrophic Body in *Hamlet,*" *Shakespeare Quarterly* 39 (1988): 27–44; and David Hillman, *Shakespeare's Entrails: Belief, Scepticism and the Interior of the Body* (Basingstoke: Palgrave Macmillan, 2007), 80–116.
4. *Coleridge's Writings on Shakespeare*, 164; Franz Rosenzweig, *The Star of Redemption*, trans. William W. Hallo (Notre Dame, IN: University of Notre Dame Press, 1985), 210, cited in Paul Kottman, ed., *Philosophers on Shakespeare* (Stanford, CA: Stanford University Press, 2009), 9.

and the erotics of philosophical enquiry."[5] In *The Symposium*—one of the founding discussions of sexual and other forms of love in the Western philosophical tradition—Socrates's friend Alcibiades proposes that sleeping with Socrates might give him more profound insight into the philosopher's true self than anything Socrates says or does.[6] So it is worth asking, with Alcibiades: what would give one more insight into the internal life of a person, or a character—say into their unconscious: overhearing them speak, even soliloquize (the epitome, as we imagine it, of privileged access to the inward realms of the other, and the form of speech most closely associated with the character of Hamlet)—or experiencing them having sex? And what would such an experiencing entail exactly? Intuiting? Watching? Listening? Having sex with them? (And what, indeed, would constitute "having sex"?) What might we learn about someone from the latter that we couldn't learn about them from the former (and vice versa)? What are the different kinds of knowledge you might gain (and lose) via these different avenues? If the core of one's subjectivity is—as Nietzsche would have it in my epigraph, and as Freud would emphasize throughout his writing[7]—hardly properly to be separated from one's sexuality, an interest in the philosophical prince's sexual being (and not merely his genderedness or his misogyny) is not misplaced. Perhaps if one abstains from sex, as Hamlet apparently does,

---

5. David M. Halperin, "Plato and Erotic Reciprocity," *Classical Antiquity* 5 (1986): 60–80, 79; see also Shadi Bartsch, "Eros and the Roman Philosopher," in *Erotikon: Essays on Eros, Ancient and Modern*, ed. Shadi Bartsch and Thomas Bartscherer (Chicago: University of Chicago Press, 2005), 59–83; writing of the well-known image of the philosopher's wings in Plato's *Phaedrus*, Bartsch writes: "The abstract force of the beautiful . . . is well grounded in the physiology of arousal and of erotic desire, however far the growth of the soul's wings will eventually carry us from this corporeal response" (61).

6. See *Symposium*, §215–22, in *Plato: The Collected Dialogues*, ed. Edith Hamilton and Huntington Cairns (Princeton: Princeton University Press, 1961), 566–73, and Simon Goldhill, "On Knowingness," *Critical Inquiry* 32.4 (Summer 2006): 708–23, esp. 712–13.

7. Though of course it is worth bearing in mind Foucault's historicization of this understanding as a distinctly modern phenomenon.

"that within" inevitably "passes show" (1.2.85); quite possibly this is a major motivation for abstaining from sex.

"Sex" is close to undefinable; in what follows, however, I refer to an ideal—but not, I think, idealized—form of sex as relational and mutually open (rather than a concept of sex as either forced or coming from a position of insulated monadicity). Sex in this sense is exemplary in its involvement of the whole self, body and mind: does anything else one does intertwine the two, *make* them quite as inseparable, as sex does? Hence, sex offers a—perhaps *the*—royal road to exposure and expression of the self. [8]

G. Wilson Knight reads Hamlet's "To be" as "not merely to live, to act, to exist, but really *to be*; to be, as an integrated and whole person . . . in the Nietzschean sense."[9] "To be," on such a reading, would include—perhaps even privilege—being a sexual being, taking upon oneself not only (as Stanley Cavell has argued in relation to *Hamlet*)[10] the fact of one's origins in one's parents' sexual congress but also one's own sexual existence. It may not be irrelevant that the verb "to be" was known in this period as the "copula," which the *OED* defines as "the present tense of the verb *to be* (with or without a negative)."[11] To be (or not to be): that is the copula.

8. Recent work on gender/sexuality/identity which moves away from "essential" categories and focuses on *desire* as a more holistic way of thinking about sexual being includes Deborah Cameron and Don Kulick, eds., *The Language and Sexuality Reader* (London: Routledge, 2006) and Keith Harvey and Celia Shalom, eds., *Language and Desire* (London: Routledge, 1997).
9. G. Wilson Knight, *The Wheel of Fire: Interpretations of Shakespearean Tragedy* (London: Methuen, 1930), 308. Compare Emmanuel Levinas's emphasis on "being in the verbal sense of the word, in which being is suggested and understood, in a sense, as a process of being, an event of being, an adventure in being." Levinas, *Entre Nous*, trans. Michael B. Smith and Barbara Harshav (London: Continuum, 2006), vi.
10. See Stanley Cavell, "Hamlet's Burden of Proof," in *Disowning Knowledge in Seven Plays of Shakespeare* (Cambridge: Cambridge University Press, 2003 [updated edition]), 179–91.
11. *OED*, s.v. "copula," n., 1. Though the *OED* gives as its first example 1650, texts from much earlier in this period reiterate this definition: "*Copula* is the verbe Substantive, that in construction standeth betwixt them [i.e. *Subiectum* and *Predicatum*]" (Robert Crowley, *A setting*

Such an understanding of "being" would imply that "not to be" can denote a turning away from or a suppression of one's sexuality, perhaps in response to the forms of policing—our parental, educational, penal, and legal institutions, our social milieu—which administer desire. Polonius's and Laertes's emphatic instructions to Ophelia (do not "your chaste treasure open," 1.3.30), an instruction repeated by Hamlet to both Ophelia ("Get thee to a nunnery!" 3.1.120)[12] and Gertrude ("go not to my uncle's bed," 3.4.157) are the precepts of a moralizing "conscience," the part of the self that, in Adam Phillips's words, "prevents us from finding, by experiment, what may be the limits of our being."[13] The internalized representative of our milieu, the judgmental superego, with "its all too impoverished vocabulary" (*UP*, 106), Phillips suggests, overly impresses or burdens conscience, inhibiting "imaginative redescriptions" (*UP*, 107) of what is permissible, and indeed pleasurable. But at the same time, in linking this conscience to cowardice ("conscience does make cowards . . ."), "Hamlet's great soliloquy perhaps suggests . . . a morality, a conscience, that had a different relation to the unknown," a morality "inspired by desire" (*UP*, 104)—something akin to what Plato famously called (in describing *erōs* as *mania*) "the divine release of

---

open of the subtyle sophistrie of Thomas Watson [London: Henry Denham, 1569], 6); "The *Copula*, whereby the Attribute is knit with the Subject, is the Verbe Substantive *IS*" (Lucas Trelcatius, *A briefe institution of the common places of sacred divinitie* (London: Francis Burton, 1610), 369). On "copulate" as a common Elizabethan sexual term, see Gordon Williams, *A Dictionary of Sexual Language and Imagery in Shakespearean and Stuart Literature*, 3 vols. (London: Athlone Press, 1994), 1:305–6 (s.v. "copulation"; cf. *As You Like It*, 5.4.56). *Hamlet* is, moreover, a play extraordinarily full of hendiadyses (as was first recognized by George T. Wright, "Hendiadys and *Hamlet*," *PMLA* 96:2 (1981): 168–93)—and the conjunction deployed in this rhetorical figure is known as a "copulative conjunction." Wright in fact suggests at one point that in some of its uses in the play, hendiadys can have an "erotic suggestiveness" (177).

12. This, recall, immediately after his "To be or not to be" soliloquy.

13. Adam Phillips, *Unforbidden Pleasures* (London: Hamish Hamilton, 2015), 103; further references appear as "*UP*" in parentheses in the text.

the soul from the yoke of custom and convention."[14] Such a morality, beyond good and evil, would thoroughly embrace one's own (and the other's) sexual being, in all its unknown, unknowable fullness (and emptiness). It would, to quote Hamlet himself, "as a stranger give it welcome" (1.5.164).

CARNAL KNOWLEDGE

If conscience—in a sense hovering between introspection and morality—can make us cowardly, conscience in its original sense, of "knowing with" (con-scientia), can lead us in other directions too. Alcibiades's section of The Symposium plays with the notion that knowing can have different meanings; and that carnal knowledge— knowing in one's body—might be no less valuable than epistemological, intellectually understood forms of knowledge. After all, we used to use the word "know" to mean "have sex with," to know in the carnal sense: "Adam knew Eve" (and it is upon eating of the tree of knowledge that fallen sexuality enters the world).[15] In early modernity, sexual congress was sometimes referred to, along these biblical lines, as "the Act of Knowledge."[16] But this must refer to knowledge of a different order from epistemology—an act-ive form of knowledge,

---

14. Plato, Phaedrus, 265a. On this passage, see especially Douglas Cairns, "The Imagery of Erôs in Plato's Phaedrus," in Erôs in Ancient Greece, ed. Ed Sanders et al. (Oxford: Oxford University Press, 2013), 233–50. Compare Mark Johnson's description of "a conception of morality as a means of exploring possibilities for human flourishing—a conception that is primarily expansive and constructive" (rather than constructive): Mark Johnson, Moral Imagination: Implications of Cognitive Science for Ethics (Chicago: University of Chicago Press, 1994), 31.

15. Shakespearean examples include All's Well that Ends Well, 5.3.281; Measure for Measure, 5.1.187; Macbeth, 4.3.125. For more examples, see the entry for "know" in Williams, A Dictionary of Sexual Language, vol. 2, 770–71.

16. See, e.g., Middleton's A Game at Chesse, 4.1.150 (in Thomas Middleton: The Collected Works, ed. Gary Taylor and John Lavagnino (Oxford: Clarendon Press, 2007), 1809.

akin to savoir faire. As Maurice Merleau-Ponty puts it: "there is an erotic 'comprehension' not of the order of understanding, since understanding subsumes an experience, once perceived, under some idea, while desire comprehends blindly by linking body to body."[17] This implies that the "com-prehension" or con-science[18] offered by sex is of a different order from or irreducible to that of rational hermeneutics. It is, rather, a relational knowing that cannot be subsumed under the category of empirical knowledge or understanding.

"In Plato's version of Platonic love," writes Glenn Most, "sexuality, so far from being extirpated, is incited, enhanced, and sublimated in order first to create and then to liberate large quantities of psychic energy that can be put to the service of philosophical knowledge."[19] Plato, unsurprisingly, wanted to bring sexuality under the domain of knowledge; but this may be precisely because sex is so inherently resistant to conceptual control. Recent writing on the topic has emphasized the hermeneutic complexity as well as the radically unstable outlines of the very term "sex."[20] (And, as Valerie Traub argues brilliantly in *Thinking Sex with the Early Moderns*, the intrinsic inscrutability of sex is redoubled when the impasses of historical difference and distance are brought to bear on the issue.)[21] Sex is in fact the thing par excellence *not* subject to what Cavell calls

17. Maurice Merleau-Ponty, "The Body in Its Sexual Being," in *Phenomenology of Perception*, trans. Colin Smith (London: Routledge, 1962), 158.
18. It has been suggested by some critics (Stephen Booth, *Shakespeare's Sonnets* (New Haven: Yale University Press, 1977), 526; Janet Adelman, *Suffocating Mothers*, 255 n. 37) that Hamlet's "conscience" "puns on the female genitals" (i.e., "con" = cunt; hence "conscience" = knowing the female genitals).
19. Glenn W. Most, "Six Remarks on Platonic Eros," in Bartsch and Bartscherer, *Erotikon*, 33–47, 41.
20. See, e.g., James M. Bromley and Will Stockton, eds., *Sex before Sex: Figuring the Act in Early Modern England* (Minneapolis: University of Minnesota Press, 2013). See also James M. Bromley, *Intimacy and Sexuality in the Age of Shakespeare* (Cambridge: Cambridge University Press, 2013).
21. Valerie Traub, *Thinking Sex with the Early Moderns* (Philadelphia: University of Pennsylvania Press, 2015). We might here add that, at least according to Foucault, sex *becomes* an object

"knowledge under the aegis of dominion, of the concept of a concept as a matter, say, of grasping a thing":[22] we can measure aspects of it, be knowing (all-too-knowing) about it, but "it" is never an entity observable in any scientific or epistemological way. Indeed, "it" is not, properly speaking, an "it" at all: sex is, to use Hamlet's terminology, "nothing," no *thing*: yet "This nothing's more than matter" (4.5.168).[23] "Nothing," says Hamlet, is "a fair thought to lie between maids' legs" (3.2.112). "Nothing" here is both a gerund (early modern "nothing" = "noting" = copulating = lying between a maid's legs) and a noun ("nothing" = "no thing" = vagina = what lies between a maid's legs). Is sex an action, a thing, or nothing? Or, like the king, "a thing . . . Of nothing" (4.2.26–28)? It can no more be caught than a conscience.

The sexual is in-com-prehensible; it cannot be grasped like a thing; but neither is it abstract (this is why sexual desire cannot be satisfied, any more than knowledge of the sexual can ever be full). "Sex," writes Richard Poirier, is "a subject in which every reader is a kind of expert";[24] by the same token, no one can sensibly claim expertise in this area. To vary Lacan's famous dictum (*Il n'y a pas de rapport sexuelle*): *il n'y a pas de savoir sexuelle* (there is only ever savoir faire).[25] Nothing is more likely than sex to remind us that epistemology and ontology are radically at odds; that the facts of life are not really

of discursive knowledge at a particular historical moment—one not all that distant from the turn of the seventeenth century: see esp. *The History of Sexuality* vol. 1.

22. Cavell, *Disowning Knowledge*, 9.

23. As Traub writes of the word "nought," "Forging analogical but also incommensurate notions of nothingness, negativity, lack, worthlessness, and immorality, on the one hand, and pleasure, interpersonal contact, bodily integrity, and affective connection, on the other, 'naught' accretes, compounds, and expands into a resounding obliquity" (*Thinking Sex*, 222).

24. Richard Poirier, "The Powerful Secret," *New York Times*, January 14, 1979. (https://www.nytimes.com/books/00/12/17/specials/foucault-sexuality.html, accessed March 10, 2016).

25. See Jacques Lacan, *Le Séminaire. Livre XVII. L'envers de la psychanalyse*, ed. Jacques-Alain Miller (Paris: Seuil, 1991), 134.

matters of fact (but of tact and tactility). Montaigne—an undisputed influence on *Hamlet*—is perhaps our best philosophical observer of the (comic and tragic) madnesses of the sexual body, writing candidly and probingly, with his curious blend of serenity, curiosity, and openness about the strangeness of its potent (and impotent) demands. Montaigne is also, not coincidentally, our least abstract philosopher—one who writes not with the aim of achieving propositional knowledge but with the aim of sharing the intimate self.

Sexual desire is maddening, as writers from Plato to Montaigne and from Freud to Lacan have pointed out, because it is shot through with irony: it always points both to and beyond its object (as David Halperin succinctly puts it, "I want you, but you are not what I want").[26] Indeed, paradox is "the exactest center of eros"—"linked to both death *and* life, pleasure *and* pain, the child of lack *and* plenty"[27] Sex is irreducibly both culture-bound and natural, both linguistically constituted and essentially corporeal, a "thoroughly constructed yet totally fundamental and pervasive structure through which the rest of existence is experienced: neither outside or prior to language and culture, nor merely a contingent ideological effect of language and culture, but a coeval element of the human."[28]

Sex is paradoxical: it both is and isn't a thing, and therefore both is and isn't knowable as things are. There is virtually nothing objective about sex—its unstable definition, its myriad forms of enactment, our limited understanding of it; and while this may be true of many

---

26. David M. Halperin, "Love's Irony: Six Remarks on Platonic Eros," in Bartsch and Bartscherer, *Erotikon*, 48–58, 55.
27. As Shadi Bartsch and Thomas Bartscherer argue: Bartsch and Bartscherer, *Erotikon*, 8.
28. Christine Varnado, "'Invisible Sex!': What Looks Like the Act in Early Modern Drama?," in *Sex before Sex: Figuring the Act in Early Modern England*, ed. James M. Bromley and Will Stockton (Minneapolis: University of Minnesota Press, 2013), 29–30; cf. Nancy on "the linguistic redundancy of sex, or indeed a sexual redundancy of language, which moves these two major modes of relation towards one another." *Corpus II: Writings on Sexuality*, trans. Anne O'Byrne (New York: Fordham University Press, 2013), 103.

things—grief, or pain, for example—sex isn't as internally-oriented as grief or pain; it is relational in its essence (and if knowledge of the sexual is never anything but partial, it is never more partial than when *not* relational). Sex only exists in the between—between self and other, between mind and body, between thing and nothing. In *Corpus II: Writings on Sexuality*, Jean-Luc Nancy suggests that the sexual entails "a mingling that is not just a mingling of these bodies but at the same time the blurring of all distinctions, roles, or operations"; its enactment entails "the shattering of the identical and the one-in-itself."[29] Hence "knowledge of jouissance, . . . knowledge of [sexual] relation, is a matter of knowing exactly what is not an object of knowledge."[30] An "object of knowledge" may be interpreted as that which is amenable to our post-Enlightenment mode of rationality: an experience become a concept, dominated by our intellectual capacities. In contradistinction to this "object of knowledge" Nancy emphasizes the non-objectivity of sex, imagining it as an invitation to unknow, to let go of the distinctions and roles we habitually impose upon things, experiences, bodies. "Lovemaking is a way of living, in the flesh, the aporias of figure," writes J. Hillis Miller.[31] Sex "puzzles the will" (3.1.79; elsewhere in the play, "will" in several places has an unambiguous sexual meaning).[32] Nancy suggests that sex produces

29. Nancy, *Corpus II*, 93, 10.

30. Nancy, *Corpus II*, 13.

31. J. Hillis Miller, "The Critic as Host," in *Deconstruction and Criticism*, by Harold Bloom et al. (London: Routledge and Kegan Paul, 1979), 246–47.

32. E.g., "won to his shameful lust / The will of my most seeming-virtuous Queen" (1.5.45–46); most editions gloss "will" here as "sexual desire." Cf. 1.3.15–17 ("no soil nor cautel doth besmirch / The virtue of his will"); 2.1.99–101 ("the very ecstasy of love . . . leads the will to desperate undertakings"); 3.3.39 ("Though inclination be as sharp as will"); 3.4.86 ("reason pardons [or panders] will"). (Given the strong sexual undertones of Ophelia's final speeches and songs and the sexual elements in Gertrude's description of her death ["long purples / That liberal shepherds give a grosser name," 4.7.167–68], it may be that the choice of a *willow* as the tree from which Ophelia falls to her death owes something to the sexual connotation of "will" that have accrued through the course of the play. The same may be said of Desdemona's willow.)

a form of understanding that is nonepistemological, beyond what is objective, observable or provable; that the sexual is *con-fusing*, both defeating epistemology and (not coincidentally) opening possibilities for the undoing of the boundaries of the self. But the invitation to unknow, as we know, isn't always accepted. Human sexuality straddles the tension between an impulse to control (and know) and a welcoming of the unknown.

For Lee Edelman, sex "has something to do with experiencing corporeally, and in the orbit of the libidinal, the shock of discontinuity and the encounter with nonknowledge."[33] But this begs a question: what is my attitude to this shock, my relation to this encounter? Is it something I welcome (as a stranger)—or something I reject or fear (as a stranger)? Perhaps a good part of our moralizing vis-à-vis sex is an expression of discomfort with the discontinuity and nonknowledge—the negative capability—which Edelman wishes to celebrate. Sexuality is always pulled between these impulses—to know and to unknow, to control and to lose control, to open the other and to be open to the other. As Cavell writes (vis-à-vis *Othello*):

> Human sexuality is the field in which the fantasy of finitude, of its acceptance and its repetitious overcoming, is worked out; the way human separateness is turned equally toward splendor and toward horror, mixing beauty and ugliness; turned toward before and after; toward flesh and blood.[34]

This is why sex can, on the one hand, be the ur-topic of repulsion, as when it becomes the obsessive material of tragic skepticism, or, on

---

33. Lauren Berlant and Lee Edelman, *Sex, or The Unbearable* (Durham, NC: Duke University Press, 2014), 4. In Lauren Berlant's view, however, "the affective experience of sexual or any non-knowledge is not usually a blockage or limit but is actually the experience of the multiplication of knowledges that have an awkward relation to each other, crowd each other out, and create intensities" (6).

34. Cavell, *Disowning Knowledge*, 137.

the other, offer the redemptive possibility of engagement, as in much of Shakespeare's comedy, where the generative potential of human sexuality offers release.

SKEPTICISM AND SEX

While the desire for knowledge is, according to Freud, a constituent element of sexual desire,[35] sexuality's epistemological recalcitrance may be precisely one of the things we want from sex. But this recalcitrance also means that sex can become the primary site for the expression of our skepticism. Insofar as sex is conceived of as subject to knowledge, it is by the same token subject to doubt: do I satisfy the other? Is the other faithful? Chaste? It is unsurprising therefore that the main target of the Shakespearean protagonist's skepticism tends to be the sexuality of the other (think of Othello, Leontes, Claudio, Troilus, Posthumous; the gendered asymmetry is striking). Hamlet too expresses a large part of his skepticism by targeting his mother's and Ophelia's sexuality. We can posit that his sexual loathing is closely connected to his epistemophilic bent. It is, for example, notable that the very scene in which he is meant to be establishing his uncle's guilt—the play-within-the-play—is also the scene in which he is at his most sexually provocative, aggressively "interpret[ing]" the scene under the sign of Eros:

> HAMLET: I could interpret between you and your love, if I could
> see the puppets dallying.
> OPHELIA: You are keen, my lord, you are keen.

35. See Sigmund Freud, *Introductory Lectures on Psycho-Analysis*, S.E. 15: 327–28; and Melanie Klein, "A Contribution to the Theory of Intellectual Development," in *The Writings of Melanie Klein*, vol. 1, 236–47. For Freud, the sexual impulse is primarily appetitive and possessive, rather than fluid and itinerant.

HAMLET: It would cost you a groaning to take off mine edge.

OPHELIA: Still better and worse.

(3.2.239–44)

And again:

HAMLET: Lady, shall I lie in your lap?

OPHELIA: No, my lord.

HAMLET: I mean, my head upon your lap?

OPHELIA: Ay, my lord.

HAMLET: Do you think I meant country matters?

OPHELIA: I think nothing, my lord.

HAMLET: That's a fair thought to lie between maids' legs.

OPHELIA: What is, my lord?

HAMLET: Nothing.

(3.2.108–14)

Much has of course been said about these exchanges. Here I wish simply to direct attention to the fact that Hamlet's "keen" (i.e., sharp, incisive) "edge"—his penetrativeness—appears more immediately aimed at Ophelia's sexuality than at Claudius's "occulted guilt." He may be trying to "tent" his uncle "to the quick" (2.2.532), but his probing is at least equally directed toward Ophelia's "nothing." There are many ways to understand this observation: perhaps Hamlet's excitement at the imminent revelation of the truth of his father's murder spills over into sexual arousal; perhaps (Cavell's thesis) he is staging the murder of Gonzago as "a fantasy that deciphers into the memory of a primal scene," and hence as always already sexual;[36] perhaps he is merely fooling (about), distracting everyone from the Mousetrap that is about to be sprung. In any case, there appears to be an overlap here between the epistemological (trap for Claudius)

---

36. Cavell, *Disowning Knowledge*, 183.

and the sexualizing (provocation of Ophelia)[37]—though Hamlet appears bent on establishing the factual truth, the veracity of the Ghost's story and the guiltiness of Claudius and Gertrude as a prelude to taking action ("I'll have grounds / More relative than this," 2.2.538–39). Action and knowledge and the relation between them are of course central concerns of *Hamlet*. But it is as if the idea of "*the act*" (as the sexual act was often known in early modern England)[38] stymies his ability to take action (or at least the action he has been urged to take by the Ghost), or as if all action is tainted by the idea of the (sexual) act.

We might draw a distinction here between the sexual (as I have defined it here) and the sexualizing: Hamlet's crude wit in this scene is certainly the latter, but should we think of it as sexual? In his railing against his mother, in 3.4, the "closet" scene (though often, in the wake of Freud's interpretation of Hamlet's Oedipal desires, misnamed "the bedroom scene"), Hamlet repeatedly urges his mother to refrain from having sex—while lingering upon the details of what he is insisting she not do:

> Not this, by no means, that I bid you do—
> Let the bloat king tempt you again to bed,
> Pinch wanton on your cheek, call you his mouse
> And let him for a pair of reechy kisses,

37. It is almost as if Hamlet sees Ophelia as the guilty party here, and is goading *her* to find *her* occulted guilt—the guilt he seems to feel is native to all women ("Frailty, thy name is woman"; "You lisp, you gambol . . ."). On the transferal of disgust and apparent guilt from Claudius to the female characters in the play, see Adelman, *Suffocating Mothers*, and the very full notes on pp. 247–50.

38. "The act" was a common euphemism for sexual congress in early modern England (and beyond)—as in Iago's "the blood is made dull with the act of sport" (*Othello*, 2.1.225), or Troilus's "the desire is boundless, and the act a slave to limit" (*Troilus and Cressida*, 3.2.79), or Shylock's "when the work of generation was . . . in the act" (*Merchant of Venice*, 1.3.77). See Williams, *A Dictionary of Sexual Language and Imagery*, s.v. "act."

Or paddling in your neck with his damned fingers,
Make you to ravel all this matter out.

(3.4.179–84)

The king's foreplay is imagined as unraveling the queen, and Hamlet's disgust is, it seems, aimed at both his uncle's sexuality and his mother's openness to it. Hamlet's vivid sexualized imagining, here and elsewhere in the play, has been taken, in a Freudian vein, to indicate Hamlet's desire for his mother. But the language seems directed more to *separating* his mother from her sexual desires than to expressing his own veiled impulses. Hamlet does express his wish for his mother to be more open, but this seems far from an erotic opening. When he speaks of her heart, at the beginning of this scene, as being potentially "proof and bulwark against sense" (l. 36), he implicitly contrasts his desire for her to be open to sense (reason) with her propensity to be open to Claudius' sensuality. A little later in the same scene, Hamlet returns to the word "sense":

Sense, sure, you have—
Else could you not have motion. But sure, that sense
Is apoplexed, for madness would not err
Nor sense to ecstasy was ne'er so thralled
But it reserved some quantity of choice
To serve in such a difference. What devil was't
That thus hath cozened you at hoodman-blind?
Eyes without feeling, feeling without sight,
Ears without hands or eyes, smelling sans all,
Or but a sickly part of one true sense
Could not so mope. O shame, where is thy blush?
Rebellious hell,
If thou canst mutine in a matron's bones,
To flaming youth let virtue be as wax

And melt in her own fire; proclaim no shame
When the compulsive ardor gives the charge,
Since frost itself as actively doth burn
As reason panders will.

(3.4.69–86)[39]

It is precisely the senses' propensity to deceive that forms the centerpiece of most skeptical recitals. Like a Classical skeptic (though without a trace of the requisite equanimity), Hamlet insists that his mother's senses (sight, hearing, smell, touch) have betrayed her—they have "cozened" or cheated her, "pander[ing]" her "reason" and placing it in "thrall" to her "will," her sexual desire. Her shift of sexual choice, from Old Hamlet to Claudius, is, for Hamlet, the ultimate insensitivity. The "moping" or aimlessness of this libidinal transferal threatens to reduce his mother's (and, by extension, all human) sexuality to a purely sensual drive—one in which the corporeal senses have become divorced both from each other ("feeling without sight, / Ears without hands or eyes") and from the guiding light of sensibility or judgment—from sense-as-reason.

Sex is thus paradigmatic both of our sensory relation to the world and of the ways in which we can be led astray by the senses, both in terms of morality and in terms of knowledge. More than most things, sex ineluctably "reveals us humans to be in the same boat of sensuous endowment, fated to the five senses"—to use Cavell's words—and this is "the position from which alone the skeptic's doubt demands to be answered."[40] Early modern natural philosophers, though, struggled to define the relation between the sexual and the sensory. On the one hand, as Francis Bacon suggested, sex offered "the greatest of

---

39. Most of this passage was omitted from the Folio; the final line in Q2 is "And reason pardons will"—that is, reason forgives or makes excuses for passion. F's "panders" is stronger and fits better with Hamlet's all-out attack on Gertrude's sexuality.
40. Cavell, *Disowning Knowledge*, 7.

the *Pleasures* of the *Senses*."[41] On the other hand, though, so singular a phenomenon—so heightened and so unlocalizable—was this pleasure that sex seemed to transcend the modality of touch, or indeed any single sensory modality, to stand apart from the senses and to constitute a separate (sixth) sense in its own right, the *sensus veneris*, or sexual sense. In terms of our sensory immersion in the world, sex appears as both paradigmatic *and* anomalous. Calling it the *sensus veneris*, however, is akin to a throwing-up of hands, an admission that the relation of the senses to sexuality is so unique, so unassimilable to anything else, that it needs its own separate category. In the *New Organon*, as Joe Moshenska has shown, Bacon declares the *sensus veneris* to be irreducible, "a mystery, made all the more compelling by the fact that it is so common and incidental, so necessary to life."[42] Here again, the attempt to pin down or categorize sexuality fails.

The sexual, as Nancy puts it, "is an order of *sense*—and the *senses* of *sense*—where signs are in play but do not make significations; they make pleasure-desire instead."[43] In the sexual sphere, suggests Nancy, signs do not signify something *other*, say some normally hidden interior; the body here is not (as Hamlet sees it) a signifier of an ulterior inwardness—which can be either revealing ("If 'a do blench, / I know my course," 2.2.532–53) or concealing ("O shame, where is thy blush?" 3.4.79). Hamlet's struggle for epistemological assurance is embodied in his perception of the ever-present potential gap between the inner and the outer, and his concomitant isolation and corporeal boundedness—his sense of being in a solitary confinement of the body ("I could be bounded in a nutshell and count

41. Francis Bacon, *Sylva Sylvarum: or, a Naturall Historie* (London, 1631), 171; cited in Joe Moshenska, *Feeling Pleasures: The Sense of Touch in Renaissance England* (Oxford University Press, 2014), 186.
42. Moshenska, *Feeling Pleasures*, 187; see pp. 186–87 for his fine discussion of Bacon and the *sensus veneris*.
43. Nancy, *Corpus II*, 19.

myself a king of infinite space").[44] It is as if the body is an obstacle to knowledge. Such skepticism expresses itself as a rejection of physical openness, a denial of the accessibility or exposure of the interior (of self or other), a sense of selves as solitary, impenetrable entities. At the core of Hamlet's skepticism is an imagining of the embodied world in this claustrophobic way, and a concomitant disdain for that which is "common" ("Ay madam, it is common," 1.2.74; Common here = just part of nature; shared; open to the other; not royal/ sovereign), as well as a distrust of all conjoining or "union" ("Is thy union here? Follow my mother," 5.2.310–11).[45]

From such a position, sexuality inevitably appears dangerous. For Hamlet, as Janet Adelman has written, "all sexuality—licit or illicit—is imagined as an adulterating mixture."[46] Sex is in its essence a being-in-relation to the other—"an encounter with the estrangement and intimacy of being in relation."[47] It entails an opening of and to the other, or—better—a putting-into-relation of the self's and the other's preexisting (originary) openness, involving "something like a self-exposing, or a self-ex-porting outside oneself before even being constituted as 'self,' and therefore a being ex-posed and a being in relation that precedes and opens in advance all possible 'being.'"[48]

44. For a fuller discussion of Hamlet's sense of confinement, see Hillman, *Shakespeare's Entrails*, 80–116.
45. On "common," "union," and "Hamlet's [habitual] mocking echoes of courtly language which turn the meanings of 'common' or ordinary words back towards the body and sexuality," see Phillipa Berry, "Hamlet's Ear," in *Shakespeare and Language*, ed. Catherine M. S. Alexander (Cambridge: Cambridge University Press, 2004), 201–12, 206. "Union" here interestingly combines a sense of separateness—from the Latin *unio*, unique ("as a man would say, Singular, and by themselves alone" [Holland's Pliny, 255])—and a sense of conjoining (the union of man and wife). ("Vnion" or "union" are the Folio [and Q1] readings—here and at line 249; Q2 has [at 249] "Vnice" [in the Q's uncorrected state] and "Onixe" [in Q2's corrected state], and [at 310] "Onixe.")
46. Adelman, *Suffocating Mothers*, 28.
47. Berlant and Edelman, *Sex, or The Unbearable*, viii. As Nancy writes, sex is "nothing but relation": *Corpus II*, 10.
48. Nancy, *Corpus II*, 101–2.

Hamlet, by contrast, *demands* such an opening ("You go not till I set you up a glass / Where you may see the inmost part of you," 3.4.18–19) as a consequence of (and revenge for) the perception of closure. It is the conception of the world and its denizens as sealed that finds its corollary in Hamlet's urge to penetrate others ("I'll tent him to the quick," 2.2.532; "It would cost you a groaning to take off mine edge," 3.2.243; "I will speak daggers to her, but use none," 3.2.429; "let me wring your heart; for so I shall / If it be made of penetrable stuff," 3.4.33–34).

Hamlet's view of sexuality bears comparison to that of Lucretius's famous description of the futility of Eros: "All is vanity, for they [human lovers] cannot penetrate and be absorbed body in body [*nec penetrare et abire in corpus corpore totus*]."[49] On the face of it, these are opposed positions: for Lucretius, sexual desire involves a (vain) urge to interpenetrate corporeally; for Hamlet, interpenetration is not the desideratum but the danger. Yet this may bring us close to one of the central paradoxes of sex: even as—and just *because*—sexual relations come as close as humanly possible to fusion with the other, they can by the same token exacerbate the frustration (the inability to achieve fusion) and the doubt about the other. If the aim is to close the gap between self and other, the impossibility may end up emphasizing the sense of an abyss. So the skeptic's apparent rejection of openness may be preemptive. The impossible yearning to transcend the boundaries of selfhood and of the body *becomes* the insistence on the truth as somehow inner, beyond a bourn, in need of aperture (rather than always already open).

But this may be precisely a *dis*owning of knowledge, to use Cavell's formulation. In Cavell's view, the skeptic's epistemological doubt is a cover story; "the essential object or event of the skeptical

---

49. Lucretius, *De Rerum Natura*, trans W. H. D. Rouse, rev. Martin Ferguson Smith (Cambridge, MA: Harvard University Press, 1975), 4.1109–10.

question" is the uncertainty regarding "the existence or occurrence of the woman's satisfaction," centrally the woman's sexual satisfaction. The only assurance available in this realm is one that "must be conferred, given, not one that I can cause or determine on the basis of my senses"—"the reception of sensuous intuitions":[50] "My senses go out; satisfaction happens in my absence, only in it, by it."[51] "The working out of skepticism in *Hamlet*," writes Cavell, is a manifestation of the protagonist's "struggle not to know what he knows"—an embodiment of this struggle.[52] Hamlet cannot achieve what Cavell calls "the transformation of incestuous knowledge into erotic exchange"—the move (as I understand the phrase) from the disowned knowledge of incestuous desire to Eros as a different modality of knowledge, one more closely aligned with acknowledgment and "exchange."[53] Sex is more apt or appropriate, as Cavell might put it, to acknowledgment than to knowledge (and doubt).

SEX AND ACKNOWLEDGMENT

Sex might be thought of, in short, as less a matter of sensory evaluation than of consent; less of assurance than of openness; less an active grasping (of an object) than a receptivity (to a relation). Acknowledgment in the sexual sphere entails several dimensions of

50. Cavell, *Disowning Knowledge*, 9.
51. Cavell, *Disowning Knowledge*, 34–35.
52. Cavell, *Philosophy the Day after Tomorrow* (Cambridge, MA: Harvard University Press, 2006), 26. As Simon Critchley puts it, this is being in "a relation with that which cannot be comprehended or subsumed under the categories of the understanding. In Stanley Cavell's terms, it is the very unknowability of the other, the irrefutability of scepticism, that initiates a relation to the other based on acknowledgement and respect." Simon Critchley, *Ethics-Politics-Subjectivity: Essays on Derrida, Levinas, & Contemporary French Thought* (London: Verso Books, 1999), 97.
53. Cavell, *Contesting Tears* (Chicago: University of Chicago Press, 1997), 82.

acceptance, and all of these are relevant to *Hamlet*: the acceptance that one's origins lie in a sexual congress—and one, moreover, to which one has no access; an embrace of our natural (part-bestial, part-aggressive) creatureliness—even as we retain a belief in what is distinctly human in human sexuality; and—perhaps most difficult of all—an acknowledgment that the human organism is always already open (and thus not fully separable from the other)—even as one acknowledges "one's individuality or individuation or difference, say one's separateness"[54] and one's unknowability.

Sex thus always returns us to origins—to both phylogenetic and ontogenetic origins. "In the 'primal scene,'" write Jean Laplanche and J.-B. Pontalis, "it is the origin of the subject that is represented."[55] The scene of sexual relation between the parents, whether observed in reality or fantasized, points beyond itself to the (inevitably inaccessible) moment of one's conception—to what Cavell calls Hamlet's fantasy of "the origin of the individual (of the subject *as* individual)."[56] In redescribing Hamlet's staging of the Mousetrap as the staging of a primal scene, Cavell suggests that Hamlet is wrestling with the (unanswerable) question, "Why of all the ones I might have been am I just this one and no other, given this world and no other, possessed of exactly this mother and this father?" Hamlet's "To be or not to be" soliloquy, on this reading, is "first of all [a question about] how he or anyone lets himself be born as the one he is"[57]—a question derived from what Cavell calls Hamlet's "presiding wish to deny his existence (that ever he was born)"—as if trying to undo the sexual liaison between his parents that led to his existence.[58]

54. Cavell, *Disowning Knowledge*, 188–89.
55. J. Laplanche and J.-B. Pontalis, *The Language of Psychoanalysis*, trans. Donald Nicholson-Smith (New York: Norton, 1973), 332.
56. Cavell, *Disowning Knowledge*, 187; my emphasis.
57. Cavell, *Disowning Knowledge*, 187.
58. Cavell, *Philosophy the Day after Tomorrow*, 26.

Of this problem of whether it would have been better not to have been born, Adam Phillips has pointed out that

> it tends to be in adolescence that versions of this question begin
> to occur. That is to say, with the emergence of sexuality. It seems
> worth saying that if it would have been better not to have been
> born it is also true that everyone has been born only because two
> people have had sex. It is, in other words, at least from a psycho-
> analytic point of view, a question about, and a questioning of,
> both the parents and sexuality. Is sex worth it? Are the conse-
> quences of sex worth having, or living with? (UP, 184)

Hamlet's answer to these questions, at least at the start of the play, appears to be no: "O cursed spite / That ever I was born to set it right!" (1.5.186–87). From the beginning, Hamlet's orientation to the world could be described as antisexual. What we see in his open-ing soliloquy is a character out of love with the world and disgusted with his mother's sexuality.[59] "How weary, stale, flat and unprofit-able / Seem to me all the uses of this world!" (1.2.133–34) evinces a disposition—evocative, perhaps, of a sort of postcoital tristesse—that was to become the model of Freud's melancholic, whose libido has been withdrawn from the world.[60] He has ceased to be "erotically bound to the world"; Freud calls this process "desexualization."[61] We could surmise that this, and the indistinct featurelessness of this (stale, flat) world, are related to a perception that his mother's sexual lack of selectivity has rendered sex "bestial" (4.4.39), bringing out its potential as mere unindividuated reproduction.

59. As Philip Edwards (the editor of the New Cambridge Shakespeare edition of the play) puts
it, "All he says is backed by a loathing of the world, a loathing of himself, and a loathing of
sex": Introduction to Hamlet (Cambridge: Cambridge University Press, 1985), 50.
60. See Freud, "Mourning and Melancholia," S.E. 14: 249.
61. Jonathan Lear, Love and Its Place in Nature: A Philosophical Interpretation of Freudian
Psychoanalysis (New York: Farrar, Strauss and Giroux, 1990), 153; Freud, The Ego and

Careful distinction is one of the prized features of human sexual behavior: "it is through sex that human technology activates nature by practicing selective reproduction," writes Nancy.[62] Or, as Eric Santner has put it, explicating the work of Nietzsche: "Eros is not simply an unfolding of natural capacities": "this is at least in part what Nietzsche means when he says that love must be learned."[63] We impart values to sex (whether these are moral, religious, legal, or matters of individual taste). For humans, the sexual life is a life that is always already within the space of meaning, never simply a biological drive: "'Sblood, there is something in this more than natural, if philosophy could find it out" (2.2.303–5).[64]

Human sex humanizes sex. If sex impels a fusion of self and other, its myriad forms of expression nonetheless offer myriad paths to individuation. It is on the basis of this assumption that we are able to bring love into sex, both moderating and complicating the aggressive and individuating qualities of desire. What Hamlet sees in his mother's transferal of love and desire from his father to his uncle is an insufficient will to distinguish between individuals. Her failure, in Hamlet's eyes, to properly differentiate between Hyperion and a satyr (that hypersexual half-human figure) renders sex mere rutting. She has not "reserved some quantity of choice / To serve in such a difference" (3.4.73–74). Hamlet challenges his mother to sustain the difference between the natural and human realms in

the Id, S.E. 19, 30. Lacan links this libidinal loss to the inherent problem of desire: "only insofar as the object of Hamlet's desire has become an impossible object [viz., the dead Ophelia] can it become once more the object of his desire." "Desire and the Interpretation of Desire in Hamlet," in Shoshana Felman, ed., Literature and Psychoanalysis: The Question of Reading: Otherwise (Baltimore: Johns Hopkins University Press, 1977), 36.

62. Nancy, Corpus II, 10.

63. Eric L. Santner, "Was Will der Philosoph?," in Bartsch and Bartscherer, Erotikon, 192–95, 194 (to be precise, Santner is summarizing the previous essay in this volume—by Robert B. Pippin, "The Erotic Nietzsche: Philosophers without Philosophy," 172–91).

64. "'Sblood" is omitted (expurgated?) in the Folio, but it can serve to remind us of the connection between philosophy and the body in Hamlet.

this sphere. After all, it is Gertrude's "falling-off" (not his father's murder, about which Hamlet knows nothing at the opening of the play) that has made him feel that "things rank and gross in nature / Possess it [this world] merely" (1.2.136–37). It is her remarriage that has put in doubt the meaningfulness of sex as such, its special place in human organization (codified in the institution of marriage) as an upholder of profound distinctions—in contrast to the mere (pleasure-seeking, meaningless) natural transmission of life, the idea of sex as nothing more than the passage between life and death and another life—the sun breeding maggots in a dead dog, something that "a beast that wants discourse of reason" (1.2.150) might indulge in.

> What is a man
> If his chief good and market of his time
> Be but to sleep and feed? A beast—no more.
>
> (4.4.32–34)

To sleeping and feeding Hamlet might have added copulating. Paul Kottman has suggested that "the dramatic horizon of tragic conditions in Shakespeare can be understood as a struggle over how particular human beings aim to properly suture the claims of nature and the demands of culture."[65] For Kottman, the threat to the "transmissability . . . of human sociality" is manifested in *Hamlet*'s investment in the care of the dead: "Hamlet's challenge with respect to his dead father . . . is to make the limits of culture belong to culture, as it were, rather than to nature."[66] This may be the case vis-à-vis his father; but with respect to his mother, it is not so much the proper

65. Paul Kottman, *Tragic Conditions in Shakespeare: Disinheriting the Globe* (Baltimore: Johns Hopkins University Press, 2009), 21.
66. Kottman, *Tragic Conditions*, 4; 50.

care of the dead that is at issue as the proper uses of sex, a wish to bring sex into line with "the demands of culture," to make it part of a distinctly *human* transmissibility. Here again, sex has a divided status for humans—as both linking us to and dividing us from the natural world. The challenge is to humanize sex without idealizing it, to build into desire a higher dimension while embracing its inescapable aggressivity and materiality.

A TOUCH, A TOUCH

Sex is undoing; it is, in Edelman's words, "the encounter with what exceeds and undoes the subject's fantasmatic sovereignty."[67] Through sex we explore the frontiers of self at its meeting points with another. As Lauren Berlant defines it, the subject is "that which is structurally non-sovereign in a way that's intensified by sex."[68] Sex, as I have been arguing, entails an exposure to the otherness or heterogeneity that underlies all individuality, propriety, self-identity, and claims to empirical knowledge.

Hamlet the *Prince* of Denmark is precisely *not* the King. Fortinbras's strange final assertion, that "he was likely, had he been put on, / To have proved most royal" (5.2.381–82) seems wildly inaccurate, and in any case highlights Hamlet's permanently non-sovereign status. Indeed, by this final act, Hamlet seems not only to have moved away from any ambitions of becoming king, but also, and more profoundly, to have abandoned any illusion of self-sovereignty,

---

67. Berlant and Edelman, *Sex, or The Unbearable*, 2. This is cognate with the sense, in George Bataille's seminal writings on eroticism, of sex as jarring the stability of the self: "The whole business of eroticism is . . . to destroy the self-contained character of the participators," he writes in *Death and Sensuality: A Study of Eroticism and the Taboo* (New York: Walker, 1962), 17.
68. Berlant and Edelman, *Sex, or The Unbearable*, 5.

discarding the idea that one can control one's fate or the fate of one's body. In act 4, Hamlet acknowledges that even a king cannot achieve self-identity ("The body is with the King, but the King is not with the body," 4.2.25–26) or immunity ("a King may go a progress through the guts of a beggar," 4.3.29–30), or indeed one-in-itselfness ("Man and wife is one flesh," 4.3.50). The shift we witness in act 5 is akin to the one James Kuzner has recently described (vis-à-vis the final act of *The Winter's Tale*) as a move from "a closed . . . form of sovereignty to a radically exposed and open one."[69] The shift involves both a different conception of self-sovereignty and a relinquishing of an attachment to corporeal impermeability. In the graveyard scene, Hamlet tries to come to terms with matter, with the inevitable dissolution of the fabric of the human body and the pointlessness of trying to keep inner and outer separate:[70]

> Imperious Caesar, dead and turned to clay,
> Might stop a hole to keep the wind away.
> O, that that earth which kept the world in awe
> Should patch a wall t'expel the water's flaw.
>
> (5.1.202–5)[71]

The decomposition of the body works to dissolve Hamlet's prior sense of solitary confinement and the concomitant disgust at conjoining,

---

69. James Kuzner, *Shakespeare as a Way of Life: Skeptical Practice and the Politics of Weakness* (New York: Fordham University Press, 2016), 95. Kuzner's later elucidation of Bataille's account of a different kind of sovereignty is succinct and apropos to my sense of the final movement of *Hamlet*: "Unlike the self-possessed sovereignty that Shakespeare often entertains, in Bataille's model of sovereignty we no longer cling to ourselves as possessive subjects with protected interiors . . . . This requires just the opposite of bounded selfhood: an embrace of useless expenditure, existence in a pure present that excludes the wish for life and the fear of death alike" (150).

70. For more on Hamlet's sense of the indistinguishability of inside and outside in this scene, see my *Shakespeare's Entrails*, 109–14.

71. Folio has "winter's" for Q2 "water's."

including the revulsion from sex. This begins to be replaced by a
sense that the precise contours of one's individual self may not, in the
end, be that important; that "to be" and "not to be" may after all not
be so far apart. In act 5, we get a Hamlet unbound, a Hamlet who, as
Walter Benjamin wrote, "wants to breathe in the suffocating air of fate
in one deep breath."[72]

The move from "To be or not to be" to "Let be" (5.2.201–2) is
among other things an implicit repudiation of the earlier self that
had wished not to have been born: Hamlet no longer seems to wish
to undo the sexual liaison between his parents that led to his existence. It is indeed telling that he is no longer, in act 5, kicking against
the pricks of sexuality at all. We hear nothing of the sexual loathing, previously so florid. No longer is the "ardour" "compulsive."
We could say that Hamlet is only *ready* for a sexual relation in act
5; when his potential sexual partner, Ophelia, is dead and buried.[73]
The bouts with Laertes—the grappling in the grave and at the
duel—are perhaps the closest Hamlet comes to having the kind of
relation, of setting the body into relation with another body, entailed
by sex: a risking of one's body's tremulous, uncertain boundaries, an
opening of one's corporeal self to the potential for dissolution, what
Levinas refers to as "a savagery excluding deliberation and calcula-
tion, violence in the guise of beings who affirm themselves 'without
regard' for one another in their concern to be."[74] If in Shakespeare's

72. Walter Benjamin, *The Origin of German Tragic Drama*, trans. John Osborne (London: Verso, 1977), 137.
73. Cavell suggests that Hamlet's overcoming of his skepticism "is undertaken by Hamlet as some preparation, or explanation, for his leap into Ophelia's grave, as if facing the death of love is the condition of announcing one's separate existence": *Philosophy the Day after Tomorrow*, 26. That Hamlet's self-recognition takes place over the corpse of Ophelia and in the context of masculine, homosocial self-assertion and competitive declarations of love is significant in terms of the gender dynamic at stake here—the woman again the object, not the subject, of the triangular relation on display (I thank Valerie Traub for helping me see this clearly).
74. Levinas, *Entre Nous*, viii.

tragedies—and especially at their endings—sex and death are often fused, might there not be something of this sense at the end of *Hamlet*? In sex, as in death, one is faced with the limits of graspable knowledge, the limits of the definable, sovereign self. In act 5, and especially in the bout with Laertes, Hamlet exposes himself to the touch of the other:[75] "A hit, a very palpable hit" (5.2.262); "you do but dally" (280); "I am sure you make a wanton of me" (282): the terminology is unmistakably sexual.[76] "A touch, a touch" (F 268):[77] perhaps the best summation of sex, after all, is the one provided by Jean-Luc Nancy: "The sexual relation is the epiphany of touch."[78]

As he nears his, and his play's, end, Hamlet seems to approach the kind of nonanxious sense of self-dissolution regularly made possible by sex. What we are offered at the end of *Hamlet* is, I believe, an intimation of a paradoxical form of nonsovereign self-possession—a sense that letting go of the delusions of sovereignty and boundedness *is* precisely what allows Hamlet to claim, with apparently self-possessed assurance: "This is I, / Hamlet the Dane" (5.1.270–71).

75. On "touch" in *Hamlet*, see Carla Mazzio, "Acting with Tact: Touch and Theater in the Renaissance," in *Sensible Flesh: On Touch in Early Modern Culture*, ed. Elizabeth D. Harvey (Philadelphia: University of Pennsylvania Press, 2003), 159–86.

76. Cf. also "He's fat and scant of breath" (269) and "I pray you, pass with your best violence" (281). We have seen "dally" already: "I could interpret between you and your love, if I could see the puppets dallying" (3.2.241). On "dally" and "hit" as having the common meaning "have coitus with" or "indulge in sexual games" in this period (as well as on "fencing" as "having sex"), see Williams, *A Dictionary of Sexual Language and Imagery*, 1:362–63 and 2:667 (and on "fence," 1:476); on "hit," see esp. *Romeo and Juliet*, 2.4.55; *Titus Andronicus*, 2.1.96; *Love's Labour's Lost*, 4.1.118; and on "pass" and "dally" (alongside "wanton"): *Twelfth Night*, 3.1.14–41; see Keir Elam's notes in the Arden III edition of *Twelfth Night*, which bring out the clear sexual connotations of these words, especially in close proximity to one another (Elam refers to this passage in *Hamlet*).

77. "A touch, a touch" appears only in the F and Q1. On "touch" as "sexual contact" see *Antony and Cleopatra*, 3.12.30 and *Winter's Tale*, 1.2.416 as well as Williams, *A Dictionary of Sexual Language and Imagery*, 3: 1407.

78. Nancy, *Corpus II*, 99.

ACKNOWLEDGMENTS

I would like to offer my warm thanks to Joe Moshenska, Mike Schoenfeldt, Adam Phillips and Valerie Traub for their generous and helpful comments on early drafts of this essay. The essay could not have been written at all without many conversations with Adelais Mills. It is dedicated to her.

WORKS CITED

Adelman, Janet. 1992. *Suffocating Mothers: Fantasies of Maternal Origin in Shakespeare's Plays, "Hamlet" to "The Tempest"*. New York: Routledge.

Alexander, Catherine M. S., ed. 2004. *Shakespeare and Language*. Cambridge: Cambridge University Press.

Bacon, Francis. 1631. *Sylva Sylvarum: or, a Naturall Historie*. London.

Bartsch, Shadi. 2005. "Eros and the Roman Philosopher." *Erotikon: Essays on Eros, Ancient and Modern*. Ed. Shadi Bartsch and Thomas Bartscherer. Chicago: University of Chicago Press. 59–83.

Bartsch, Shadi, and Thomas Bartscherer. 2005. "What Silent Love Hath Writ: An Introduction to 'Erotikon.'" *Erotikon: Essays on Eros, Ancient and Modern*. Ed. Shadi Bartsch and Thomas Bartscherer. Chicago: University of Chicago Press. 1–15.

Bataille, George. 1962. *Death and Sensuality: A Study of Eroticism and the Taboo*. Trans. Mary Dalwood. New York: Walker.

Benjamin, Walter. 1977. *The Origin of German Tragic Drama*. Trans. John Osborne. London: Verso.

Berlant, Lauren, and Lee Edelman. 2014. *Sex, or The Unbearable*. Durham, NC: Duke University Press.

Berry, Phillipa. 2004. "Hamlet's Ear." *Shakespeare and Language*. Ed. Catherine M. S. Alexander. Cambridge: Cambridge University Press. 201–12.

Booth, Stephen. 1977. *Shakespeare's Sonnets*. New Haven: Yale University Press.

Bromley, James M. 2013. *Intimacy and Sexuality in the Age of Shakespeare*. Cambridge: Cambridge University Press.

Bromley, James M., and Will Stockton, eds. 2013. *Sex before Sex: Figuring the Act in Early Modern England*. Minneapolis: University of Minnesota Press.

Cairns, Douglas. 2013. "The Imagery of *Erôs* in Plato's *Phaedrus*." *Erôs in Ancient Greece*. Ed. Ed Sanders, Chiara Thumiger, Chris Carey, and Nick J. Lowe. Oxford: Oxford University Press. 233–50.

Cameron, Deborah, and Don Kulick, eds. 2006. *The Language and Sexuality Reader*. London: Routledge.

Cavell, Stanley. 1997. *Contesting Tears*. Chicago: University of Chicago Press.

———. 2003. *Disowning Knowledge in Seven Plays of Shakespeare*. Updated ed. Cambridge: Cambridge University Press.

———. 2006. *Philosophy the Day after Tomorrow*. Cambridge, MA: Harvard University Press.

Coleridge, Samuel Taylor. 1959. *Coleridge's Writings on Shakespeare*. Ed. Terence Hawkes. New York: Capricorn Books.

Crowley, Robert. 1569. *A setting open of the subtyle sophistrie of Thomas Watson*. London: Henry Denham.

Edwards, Philip. 1985. Introduction to *Hamlet*. Ed. Edwards. Cambridge: Cambridge University Press.

Elam, Keir, ed. 2008. *Twelfth Night*. Arden III ed. London: Methuen.

Felman, Shoshana, ed. 1977. *Literature and Psychoanalysis: The Question of Reading. Otherwise*. Baltimore: Johns Hopkins University Press.

Ferguson, Margaret. 1985. "*Hamlet*: Letters and Spirits." *Shakespeare and the Question of Theory*. Ed. Patricia Parker and Geoffrey Hartman. New York: Methuen. 291–308.

Foucault, Michel. 1984. *The History of Sexuality*. Vol. 1. Trans. Robert Hurley. London: Penguin.

Freud, Sigmund. 1962. *The Ego and the Id*. Trans. Joan Riviere, revised and ed. James Strachey. *The Standard Edition of the Complete Psychological Works of Sigmund Freud*, vol. 19. London: Hogarth Press.

———. 1963. *Introductory Lectures on Psycho-Analysis*. *The Standard Edition of the Complete Psychological Works of Sigmund Freud*, vol. 15. London: Hogarth Press.

———. 1964. "Mourning and Melancholia." *The Standard Edition of the Complete Psychological Works of Sigmund Freud*, vol. 14. London: Hogarth Press. 243–58.

Goldhill, Simon. 2006. "On Knowingness." *Critical Inquiry* 32.4: 708–23.

Greenblatt, Stephen. 2001. *Hamlet in Purgatory*. Princeton, NJ: Princeton University Press.

Halperin, David M. 1986. "Plato and Erotic Reciprocity." *Classical Antiquity* 5: 60–80.

———. 2005. "Love's Irony: Six Remarks on Platonic Eros." *Erotikon: Essays on Eros, Ancient and Modern*. Ed. Shadi Bartsch and Thomas Bartscherer. Chicago: University of Chicago Press. 48–58.

Harvey, Elizabeth D., ed. 2003. *Sensible Flesh: On Touch in Early Modern Culture*. Philadelphia: University of Pennsylvania Press.

Harvey, Keith, and Celia Shalom, eds. 1997. *Language and Desire*. London: Routledge.

Hillman, David. 2007. *Shakespeare's Entrails: Belief, Scepticism and the Interior of the Body*. Basingstoke: Palgrave Macmillan.

Hunt, John. 1988. "A Thing of Nothing: The Catastrophic Body in *Hamlet*." *Shakespeare Quarterly* 39: 27–44.

Johnson, Mark. 1994. *Moral Imagination: Implications of Cognitive Science for Ethics.* Chicago: University of Chicago Press.

Klein, Melanie. 1975. "A Contribution to the Theory of Intellectual Inhibition" (1931). *The Writings of Melanie Klein*, vol. 1, *Love, Guilt and Reparation and Other Works, 1921–45.* New York: Free Press. 236–47.

Knight, G. Wilson. 1930. *The Wheel of Fire: Interpretations of Shakespearean Tragedy.* London: Methuen, 1930.

Kottman, Paul, ed. 2009a. *Philosophers on Shakespeare.* Stanford, CA: Stanford University Press.

———. 2009b. *Tragic Conditions in Shakespeare: Disinheriting the Globe.* Baltimore: Johns Hopkins University Press.

Kuzner, James. 2016. *Shakespeare as a Way of Life: Skeptical Practice and the Politics of Weakness.* New York: Fordham University Press.

Lacan, Jacques. 1977. "Desire and the Interpretation of Desire in *Hamlet*." *Literature and Psychoanalysis: The Question of Reading. Otherwise.* Ed. Shoshana Felman. Baltimore: Johns Hopkins University Press. 11–52.

———. 1991. *Le Séminaire. Livre XVII. L'envers de la psychanalyse.* Ed. Jacques-Alain Miller. Paris: Seuil.

Laplanche, Jean, and Jean-Bertrand Pontalis. 1973. *The Language of Psychoanalysis.* Trans. Donald Nicholson-Smith. New York: Norton.

Lear, Jonathan. 1990. *Love and Its Place in Nature: A Philosophical Interpretation of Freudian Psychoanalysis.* New York: Farrar, Strauss and Giroux.

Levinas, Emmanuel. 2006. *Entre Nous.* Trans. Michael B. Smith and Barbara Harshav. London: Continuum.

Lucretius. 1975. *De Rerum Natura.* Trans W. H. D. Rouse, revised by Martin Ferguson Smith. Cambridge, MA: Harvard University Press.

Mazzio, Carla. 2003. "Acting with Tact: Touch and Theater in the Renaissance." *Sensible Flesh: On Touch in Early Modern Culture.* Ed. Elizabeth D. Harvey. Philadelphia: University of Pennsylvania Press. 159–86.

Merleau-Ponty, Maurice. 1962. *Phenomenology of Perception.* Trans. Colin Smith. London: Routledge.

Middleton, Thomas. 2007. *The Collected Works.* Ed. Gary Taylor and John Lavagnino. Oxford: Clarendon Press.

Miller, J. Hillis. 1979. "The Critic as Host." *Deconstruction and Criticism*, by Harold Bloom et al. London: Routledge and Kegan Paul.

Moshenska, Joe. 2014. *Feeling Pleasures: The Sense of Touch in Renaissance England.* Oxford: Oxford University Press.

Most, Glenn W. 2005. "Six Remarks on Platonic Eros." *Erotikon: Essays on Eros, Ancient and Modern.* Ed. Shadi Bartsch and Thomas Bartscherer. Chicago: University of Chicago Press. 33–47.

Nancy, Jean-Luc. 2013. *Corpus II: Writings on Sexuality*. Trans. Anne O'Byrne. New York: Fordham University Press.

Nietzsche, Friedrich. 1973. *Beyond Good and Evil: Prelude to a Philosophy of the Future*. Trans. Walter Kaufmann. London: Vintage Books.

Parker, Patricia, and Geoffrey Hartman, eds. 1985. *Shakespeare and the Question of Theory*. New York: Methuen.

Phillips, Adam. 2015. *Unforbidden Pleasures*. London: Hamish Hamilton.

Pippin, Robert B. 2005. "The Erotic Nietzsche: Philosophers without Philosophy." *Erotikon: Essays on Eros, Ancient and Modern*. Ed. Shadi Bartsch and Thomas Bartscherer. Chicago: University of Chicago Press. 172–91.

Plato. 1914. *Phaedrus. Euthyphro; Apology; Crito; Phaedo; Phaedrus*. Trans. Harold North Fowler. Loeb Classical Library. Cambridge, MA: Harvard University Press. 407–579.

Poirier, Richard. 1979. "The Powerful Secret." *New York Times*, January 14. https://www.nytimes.com/books/00/12/17/specials/foucault-sexuality.html, accessed October 3, 2016.

Rosenzweig, Franz. 1985. *The Star of Redemption*. Trans. William W. Hallo. Notre Dame, IN: University of Notre Dame Press.

Sanders, Ed, Chiara Thumiger, Chris Carey, and Nick J. Lowe, eds. 2013. *Erôs in Ancient Greece*. Oxford: Oxford University Press.

Santner, Eric L. 2005. "Was Will der Philosoph?" *Erotikon: Essays on Eros, Ancient and Modern*. Ed. Shadi Bartsch and Thomas Bartscherer. Chicago: University of Chicago Press. 192–95.

Traub, Valerie. 2015. *Thinking Sex with the Early Moderns*. Philadelphia: University of Pennsylvania Press.

Trelcatius, Lucas. 1610. *A briefe institution of the common places of sacred divinitie*. London: Francis Burton.

Varnado, Christine. 2013. "'Invisible Sex!': What Looks Like the Act in Early Modern Drama?" *Sex before Sex: Figuring the Act in Early Modern England*. Ed. James M. Bromley and Will Stockton. Minneapolis: University of Minnesota Press. 25–52.

Williams, Gordon. 1994. *A Dictionary of Sexual Language and Imagery in Shakespearean and Stuart Literature*. 3 vols. London: Athlone Press.

Wright, George T. 1981. "Hendiadys and *Hamlet*." *PMLA* 96.2: 168–93.

Chapter 4

Self-Uncertainty as Self-Realization

PAUL A. KOTTMAN

In the *Poetics*, as everyone knows, Aristotle stressed that plot-structure (*mythos*) is the "soul" of tragedy, and he connected this to an account of the impact of tragic dramas on audiences.[1] Tragic plots—thought Aristotle—present a shared understanding of the worldly conditions for the protagonists' actions and sufferings, a collective understanding of the things in view of which the drama's main events might occur. The events in a tragic plot must be plausible, after all, and they must unfold on account of one another in some intelligible way. If a tragic story moves us, Aristotle thought, it is because the events depicted seem to us "likely enough" and rational in this way, as if they *could* happen to any of us. What we watch happen in a tragedy is not likely enough to justify "real" fear, but the events are too close (and too significant) to ignore.[2] The way audiences are moved by

1. See Aristotle, *Poetics*, chapter 6. Although the influence of Aristotle's *Poetics* was less evident in Shakespeare's England than in, say, sixteenth-century Italy or France—Sir Philip Sidney's *Defense of Poetry* (1595) is probably the first appearance of Aristotelian ideas about poetry in English—"Aristotelian" attempts to develop generic definitions of tragedy were increasingly visible in Shakespeare's England, as witnessed in the use of Horace's *Ars Poetica* in education.
2. Any interpretation of the *Poetics* is open to contestation, especially in view of the long and complicated history of its influence and transmission. And there is of course far more to say about the issues broached here than I can say in this context. Here, I only wish to mention

what happens—indeed, *whether* audiences are moved—thus gauges this collective understanding of matters generally, and confirms the "universality" of a shared human condition.[3] Our affective response, Aristotle insists, is linked to the ultimate rationality of the events themselves, and the meaningfulness of the world in which they occur.

And so, for Aristotle, even when tragedies depict the breakdown of deep, abiding social bonds, this does not occur without leaving behind the possibility of our making sense of the crisis. Our affective response to tragedy, and the pleasure we take in the play, are colored by our relief at being able to achieve this kind of sense making, while risking nothing.[4] Histories or epics also portray sequences of events by which we can be moved; but tragedies go further—Aristotle proposes—by condensing those sequences (in a unification of time and place, for instance) so as to intensify and reveal the shared sense we make of what human beings might do or say. According to Aristotle, all of this is structured around a temporal interval between a significant deed and a subsequent "recognition" in tragic plots, where "events occur contrary to expectation yet on account of one another."[5] Through this retrospective view—this unexpected but intelligible consequentiality—we learn something about the actions, their conditions, and implications. And in this way, the basic rationality of the world in which the events occur is also affirmed.

some basic tenets as background for what I have to say about Shakespeare's *Hamlet*. For specific readings of Aristotle's *Poetics* with which I am agreement, at least with respect to the broad issues raised here, see Amélie Oksenberg Rorty, "The Psychology of Aristotelian Tragedy" and Jonathan Lear, "Katharsis," in A. O. Rorty, ed., *Essays on Aristotle's Poetics* (Princeton, NJ: Princeton University Press, 1992).

3. Aristotle's repeated emphasis on the "universality" of these elements in tragedy is connected to his remark that tragedy is "more philosophical" than history in the simple sense that, out of the morass of particular or contingent "happenings" in human affairs, an audience can discern the general sorts of things that "someone like us" might typically do or say.

4. Were the events "really happening," we would feel pain, not pleasure. Aristotle, *Poetics*, chapter 4.

5. Aristotle, *Poetics* 1452a3–4 (*The Poetics of Aristotle*, ed. Stephen Halliwell [Chapel Hill: University of North Carolina Press, 1987], 63).

In Shakespeare's *Hamlet,* the threats to the sense we make of the world proliferate considerably, when compared to Aristotle's view of *Oedipus Rex.*[6] If the *Oresteia* or the Oedipus myth could capture anxieties about the balance between matrilineal ties and the structure of the polis, for instance, the complexity of the social-historical world in which Shakespeare wrote (and *of* which he wrote) seems less suited to the tight plot-structure of these Attic tragedies. As Johann Gottfried Herder put it, in his critique of the appropriateness of Aristotle's *Poetics* for an understanding of Shakespeare's drama: "Shakespeare's age offered him anything but the simplicity of national customs, deeds, inclinations, and historical traditions which shaped Greek drama."[7] As every student of Shakespeare knows, not only do Shakespeare's plays resist easy "plot-summary" (the way that the story of Oedipus might be told in a few sentences); Shakespeare's drama also has to solve for itself, again and again, with each new play and performance, just what the main events in the play *mean,* exactly. For instance, Hamlet must work out for himself—and each performance of *Hamlet* must figure out anew—the meaning of Claudius's coronation, or his mother's remarriage, or his dead father's call for revenge, or what it means to be a "courtier" or "son" or "Prince."[8]

In contrast to Oedipus's predicament, Hamlet's knowledge of past events is in not in question; he is not blind to *what* he and others

6. Broad comparisons of Shakespeare and ancient tragedy are helpful only to a point, and I wish to make no large historical claims about the relation between ancient and modern tragedy in this context. By invoking Aristotle and Sophocles (hence, leaving aside Euripides, Seneca, and others), and with Herder's similar invocation of Aristotle in his "Shakespeare" essay in mind, I mean only to frame a few points of relevance to my discussion.

7. Johann Gottfried Herder, "Shakespeare" in *Philosophers on Shakespeare,* ed. Paul A. Kottman (Stanford, CA: Stanford University Press, 2009), 28. For a helpful discussion of Herder's essay on this point, see Kristin Gjesdal, "Literature, Prejudice, Historicity: The Philosophical Significance of Herder's Shakespeare Studies," in *The Insistence of Art: Aesthetic Philosophy after Early Modernity,* ed. Paul A. Kottman (Bronx, NY: Fordham University Press, 2017).

8. Just what is Hamlet supposed to *do* at Elsinore, exactly? Read books? Practice his swordsmanship? Learn the art of flattery? Avenge his dead father? Take up arms, like Fortinbras? It depends largely upon who asks the question, and when.

have done. But the *meaning* of what Hamlet knows is not clear; so, what is known—along with the practical response that knowledge requires—remains open to conjecture and interpretation. This not only characterizes Hamlet's predicament internal to Shakespeare's play—it also characterizes the way *Hamlet* looks to Herder, as well as to us today. And it helps explain the sheer variety and quantity of critical responses occasioned by Shakespeare's play in schools, playhouses, and popular culture.

This is largely because the social-historical world in which the events of the play occur ("Elsinore" or "Denmark" or "Shakespeare's England," or any other sociohistorical world in which they might plausibly occur) is complicated enough to render each of these events, and all these "types of people," problematic and unclear. There is, for a start, no universal perspective from which to secure a sense of *who* Shakespeare's characters are, exactly, that would be shared *by* all. Instead, Shakespeare shows us how different situations and individuals look from the standpoint of one individual (Hamlet)—as well as from other standpoints *on* that individual (Claudius, Gertrude, Polonius, Ophelia, each of whom has a worldview of their own)—without ever showing how or whether these multiple, individual viewpoints might coincide. Indeed, the events in *Hamlet* are motivated by the noncoincidence of these various subjective points of views—the lack of an objective, shared understanding of the situation. Think, for instance, of how different perspectives on Hamlet's behavior drive much of what actually occurs in the play. (By contrast, to compose an Aristotelian plot meant grasping *who* the protagonists are, essentially, in light of what they do. Sophocles saw—*had* to see—that Oedipus was both king of Thebes [hence, Jocasta's husband] and Jocasta's son [hence, Laius's murderer] in order to show how Oedipus himself was brought to "see" the whole picture. While Oedipus's viewpoint is at first partial and subjective—*he* thinks he is Jocasta's husband, even as he is ignorant of the fact that he is her son—the unfolding of events will bring him, too, to see the whole picture as the rest of us see it [within the play, and in the audience].) In Shakespeare, however, any understanding of "what happens in *Hamlet*," as John Dover Wilson once put it, is deeply provisional, historically bounded, and dependent on context. In *Hamlet* (and other Shakespeare plays), no one ever learns the "whole truth" of who he, or anyone else, fundamentally *is*. The plot offers no panoptic perspective on human affairs or particular actions and events that could eventually be shared by participants and spectators alike. Subjective-individual viewpoints and an objective grasp of the "way things really are for everyone" never fully coincide.

Because the conditions for human activity generally—social, political, economic, physical—have undergone radical transformations, and must therefore be seen as transformable still, any representation of human actions (*our* dramatic art) must also be seen as transformable in ways that no poetic "rules" can govern. If the world of Shakespeare's *Hamlet* is to be an intelligible one—and not just chaotic or meaningless—explanatory satisfaction and affective force must come from something other than a kind of Aristotelian plot-structure.

In what follows, I want to suggest some ways that Shakespeare's play addresses these challenges from two sides. First, my proposal will be that Shakespeare's *Hamlet* is framed by the historical breakdown of the social bonds—military life, family or kinship roles, economic activity, monarchical rule, feudal hierarchies—on which the protagonists depend for the meaning and worth of their lives together, for something like a coherent "practical identity."[9] The play shows these bonds to be dissolvable, in spite of that dependence. To be clear, I do not mean only that these *particular* forms of social life fall into crisis in Shakespeare's play—though that happens, too. (No

---

9. I have in mind Christine Korsgaard's definition of practical identity as "a description under which you value yourself, a description under which you find your life to be worth living and your actions to be worth undertaking." See *The Sources of Normativity* (Cambridge, MA: Harvard University Press, 1996), 100.

social world can outlive its ability to transmit its own values and commitments, and "something *is* rotten in the state of Denmark," 1.4.90). I mean that, as a result of this situation, the constitution of a practical identity via reflective commitments to broadly sharable norms itself starts to look uncertain. The incoherence of Hamlet's possible role as "obedient" son to Gertrude and "avenger" of his father, for instance, does not lie in any tragic, mutual exclusivity of these two "duties" or in a latent contradiction at the heart Elsinore's beautiful *Sittlichkeit*. (Hamlet *can* kill Claudius while leaving Gertrude out of it, as the Ghost in fact suggests.) It lies in the fact that the fulfillment of *any* duty (loving obedience to Gertrude or Claudius, vengeful murder) seems *to Hamlet* to fall short of offering him a chance to live his life. Hamlet is thus not only caught between competing "possible" practical identities—different ways in which he might "become Hamlet the Dane" in Denmark (each of which would come with its own problems and challenges). He also becomes uncertain whether any kind of coherent practical identity is possible for him at all, whether he can really *lead* a life—*become* Hamlet at all—just by reflectively endorsing the practical identities on offer (obedient son, avenger, Prince).

At the same time, I shall argue, Hamlet's predicament does not leave us with a desperate nihilism—with the sense that it does not matter what people do, or suffer, or that all we are left with is mere "vanity."[10] On the contrary, the play shows how the meaning of a life as individually lived is perhaps best gauged by the way it "bears up" under the collapse of traditional, inherited ways of life—as if the *way* in which individuals "bear up" completes, and perhaps even helps explain the significance of, the collapse of social conditions which sustain practical identities.

---

10. Compare A. C. Bradley's apt remark: "[Shakespearean tragedy] makes us realize so vividly the worth of [the life] which is wasted that we cannot possibly seek comfort in the reflection that all is vanity." *Philosophers on Shakespeare*, 98.

Hamlet himself, for instance, *does* undergo a kind of existential crisis, as just stated. But that crisis is—I think—different from the way in which it has often been portrayed. When Hamlet says things like, "O that this too too sallied flesh would melt" (1.2.129), he is not expressing the meaninglessness of his life so much as his experience of the meaningless of its possible worth, according to prevailing social norms. ("How weary, stale, flat and unprofitable / Seem to me all the uses of this world!" 1.2.134–35). Indeed, precisely because his life as Hamlet—as the person he might become—*matters to him* so keenly, he feels the meaningless of the social values according to which he feels called to live. Hamlet's crisis is thus not the expression of nihilism, but of the seriousness with which he tries to take up the task of "becoming himself." It is a kind of fidelity to the possibility of taking up a practical identity, without quite knowing what direction it will take in view of the social pretenses on offer.[11]

Consider, Hamlet can be identified with any number of deeds. He *does* all sorts of things. For instance, he openly disrespects Claudius, he berates Ophelia, speaks daggers to his mother, and kills Polonius. And yet no one in the play knows exactly what to make of Hamlet's deeds, or how to assess them in view of any collective "reasons" that adhere in any shared understanding of the world, or any social form of life. Indeed, Hamlet himself does not seem to know; though he seems to think that *something* in what he does *ought* to somehow

---

11. Which is not the same as saying that Hamlet *manages* the task. Although I do not recall that he mentions *Hamlet* in the course of his interpretation of Kierkegaard, I think that Jonathan Lear's recent discussion of Kierkegaardian "irony" (and his riposte to Christine Korsgaard) might be usefully brought into conversation with Hamlet's predicament. Lear himself seems to be alert to the possibility, when he speaks of irony as the possible cultivation of "an experience of oneself as uncanny, out of joint." And his overall discussion of irony as "a peculiar disruption of inherited way[s] of facing life's possibilities" is pertinent here. But perhaps Shakespeare's *Hamlet* helps us to see what it would be to—as Lear puts it—"get the hang of" living ironically, precisely insofar as Hamlet does *not* quite manage to "get the hang" of living his life. See Jonathan Lear, *A Case for Irony* (Cambridge, MA: Harvard University Press, 2011), 37, 31.

connect with his "task" of becoming a good son, or a worthy prince. Consider his behavior after his father's death (which Hamlet seems to think is appropriate to the occasion), or of his treatment of Ophelia, or his refusal to treat Polonius's corpse with appropriate care. Whenever Hamlet seeks the meaning of his actions in the clarity of others' responses, his social world seems incapable of answering him. (Gertrude: "O me, what hast thou done?" / Hamlet: "Nay, I know not," 3.4.23–24.) At most, others voice incomprehension; or, finally, they send him away to England. And yet, in each of the cases, Hamlet does not seem to be merely rejecting or repudiating the worth of these roles—lover, mourning son, avenger—rather, he seems to be looking for the right way of faithfully carrying out those roles.

Hamlet's challenge, under these conditions, is thus not just to figure out how best to carry out what is ostensibly being asked of him in terms of available social pretense—revenge, filial love, loyalty to the court—but to try to take up these "practical identities" under the realization that none of the available social pretenses are sufficient, even in combination. Moreover, it is not that Hamlet "steps back" with a "detached irony" and "critiques" his various roles—as "lover-to-Ophelia" or "avenger-to-his-father." Rather, by berating Ophelia ("get thee to a nunnery") or even by slaying Polonius, he is trying to find a way to *take up* those very commitments, while recognizing that the historically available, "known," ways of taking up those commitments according to available social pretense are insufficient and stand in need of disruption. Hamlet *is* committed to the life he is living, or trying to live; but the form that commitment takes, in practice, is the avowal that known ways of being a lover, son, or avenger can collapse. For Hamlet, to cite one instance to which I shall return, saying "I loved you not" (3.1.119) *can* be a way of trying to be a lover, beyond available social pretense.

My suggestion, then, is that a central issue in *Hamlet* is Hamlet's attempt to live his life as *his*—his efforts at discerning a course of action that might amount to provisionally "leading" a life, rather than just suffering it; or to at least to attaching himself meaningfully to what he has done, under the historical conditions just described.[12] At the same time, if *we* (in the audience) feel moved in response to Hamlet's fate, then it must be because we regard Hamlet's freedom, his *leading* a life, as important, as being of "universal" concern in Aristotle's sense—over and beyond what he actually does, accomplishes, or leaves undone. Our affective response to *Hamlet* thus brings to light our understanding of the importance of individual freedom, in a world where our deepest social bonds can turn out to be insubstantial.

I want to further flesh out these thoughts, in this short essay, by considering Hamlet's fate in light of three competing forms of social organization, upon which Hamlet depends, but each of which fail to afford Hamlet a livable, coherent normative framework in view of which to establish a practical identity. The first is Hamlet's natural blood-ties to Gertrude, or what might be called the principle of "matrilineal descent"; the second is revenge, or Hamlet's duty as his father's first son, connected to the right of primogeniture; the third stems from the election of Claudius, connected to "courtier" culture, and the assertion of state-sanctioned property rights irrespective of natural geniture.[13] (Again, my point is not just that *these* forms of social organization are in crisis—and that others need to emerge to take their place; rather, I mean that the crises in these forms of life leave Hamlet uncertain about the possibility of *any* practical identity he might hope to take up.)

---

12. I see this reflected, with different implications, in the respective fates of Ophelia or Laertes, as well. But I think Hamlet experiences a deeper ambivalence or uncertainty about what to *do* under these conditions than either Ophelia or Laertes; and it the significance of this uncertainty on which Shakespeare asks us to reflect by placing Hamlet at the drama's center.

13. This is a reconsideration and elaboration of an interpretation that I first sketched in my *Tragic Conditions in Shakespeare* (Baltimore: Johns Hopkins University Press, 2009), chapter 2.

Consider, first, that Hamlet is unable and unwilling to sever the filial ties that chain him to Elsinore, prevent his return to Wittenberg, and oblige him to his mother—and, consequently, to Claudius (who repeatedly calls him "son") and to the incestuous bed, or "nasty sty," whose image he cannot get out of his head.[14] This is not to suggest that the elective monarchy of Shakespeare's fictional Denmark conceives of itself in matrilineal terms. But we should remember that it is central to the play's dramatic force that Claudius's accession to the throne appear adjoined to his sexual conquest of Gertrude.[15] Proximity to Gertrude's womb, to the matrix of power imbued by the flow of her blood, remains an essential bond between one generation and the next.[16]

Hamlet's disgust at this "incestuous" union has received plenty of critical attention, but it is likely that the intensity of Hamlet's disgust is linked to the very real possibility of his disinheritance, were Claudius and Gertrude to have a child. (In an inversion of the Oedipus model, it is precisely because Hamlet did *not* have a child with his mother, and thereby insert himself between her and any further offspring, that he stands to lose everything.)[17] At any rate, it is clear that Hamlet

14. Gertrude also has Hamlet's bed on her mind, as at 5.1.232–34.
15. This is emphasized at many points in the play—for instance, in the dumb show, where the murderer woos the queen; in the ghost's lament that Claudius "won to his shameful lust / The will of his most seeming-virtuous queen" (1.5.45–46); at 4.3.48, where Hamlet calls Claudius "dear Mother." "Father and mother is man and wife / Man and wife is one flesh. So—my mother" (4.3.49–50); and at 5.2.309–10, "Here, thou incestuous damned Dane! / Drink of this potion. Is the union here? / Follow my mother."
16. Another way of looking at Gertrude's importance can be found in Janet Adelman's suggestive study, which develops work by Coppélia Kahn and others. Adelman argues that Gertrude marks "the origin of [Shakespeare's] great tragic period." Whereas the histories and comedies had unfolded "without any serious confrontation with the power of female sexuality," *Hamlet* subjects "to material presence the relationships previously exempted from that presence." Janet Adelman, *Suffocating Mothers: Fantasies of Maternal Origin in Shakespeare's Plays* (New York: Routledge, 1992), 11.
17. As Margreta de Grazia puts it, "That a son's feelings for his mother should be sexual may have seemed less transgressive than prudent at a time when endogamous unions

SELF-UNCERTAINTY AS SELF-REALIZATION

is allowed to live, breathe, eat, command servants, speak publically, stage plays, welcome guests, and wield a sword in large part because he is acknowledged to be of royal blood—meaning, he is unquestionably Gertrude's child, "too much in the 'son'" (1.2.67). In this sense at least, Hamlet's social place is to some extent determined by a natural fact, the conjugal blood of which he is both loving proof and vessel. Already in his first appearance, Hamlet seems to note this when he pledges allegiance to his mother—"I shall in all my best obey you, madam"—only to then, moments later, lament his situation. Such thoughts lead to further disgust.[18] For in their very adolescence they are also founding questions for human culture generally, as it seeks a nonnatural foothold within natural processes: *Am I anything more than natural offspring? Am I—am I at all—without my natural family? Is my life nothing more than a natural interlude, between womb and grave? What is a family for?*

In the *Phenomenology of Spirit*, G. W. F. Hegel posed these same questions, and offered a startling answer which foresees an entire field of subsequent anthropological inquiry: Care for the dead, for one's own dead. "Blood-relationship," writes Hegel, "supplements the natural process by . . . interrupting the work of Nature and rescuing the blood-relation from destruction; or better, because destruction is necessary, the passage of the blood-relation into mere being, it takes on itself the *act* of destruction."[19] (After someone dies, we "rescue" their body from decay through embalming or some other ritual, only to then "accomplish" the destruction for ourselves, in burial or cremation—turning

were used to keep dynastic power and property intact." See her *Hamlet without Hamlet* (Cambridge: Cambridge University Press, 2007), 106–7. Also, Lisa Jardine, *Reading Shakespeare Historically* (New York: Routledge, 2006), 46–47.

18. Including sexual disgust; for more, see my discussion in *Tragic Conditions in Shakespeare*, chapter 2.

19. G. W. F. Hegel, *The Phenomenology of Spirit*, trans. A.V. Miller (Oxford: Oxford University Press, 1977), 271, paragraph 452, my emphasis.

the natural "fact" of death into a human "deed.") Care for one's own dead is, of course, one of Hamlet's primary challenges. For, it is this very "nature"—"whose common theme / Is death of fathers" (1.2.103–4)— that Claudius invokes when berating Hamlet for "persever[ing] / In obstinate condolement" (1.2.92–93). Indeed, Claudius faults Hamlet precisely for failing to recognize his father's death as a *merely* natural event—as the *exemplary* natural event. He sees Hamlet's grief as "unmanly," "a fault against the dead, a fault to nature" (1.2.94, 102). But what Claudius misses are the questions to which both Hamlet and Hegel draw our attention: What happens to someone once they are dead? Do they retreat immediately *back* into natural life? ("To what base uses we may return, Horatio!" 5.1.192.) If being dead is a merely natural state, if individual deaths are a mere natural occurrence, then the death of Hamlet's father has no *human* meaning, no "particular" meaning. There would be no way to distinguish Hamlet's father from Caesar, Alexander the Great, from Hamlet himself, or any of the other crumbs of nature littering the earth.

This is why Gertrude's initial query to Hamlet is so galling. "All that lives must die," she chides, "passing through nature to eternity. "Why?" she asks, "seems it so particular with thee?" (1.2.73, 75) Hamlet's responses, as everyone knows, is to assert that it does not "seem" particular; it *is* particular with him (1.2.76). For, without holding to this particularity, there can be no difference between seeming and being—no way to determine what is essential within the ceaselessness of temporal change. But *how* to make Hamlet's father's death (and, hence, his lived life) *particular*? How to make the loss of his father worthy of particular note? More generally, how to prevent care for the dead from become a hollow, ritual response enacted in obsequious debt to mere natural facts?

Consider the sequence of failed, botched or perverted funerals in Shakespeare's play. "Hamlet," thunders Claudius upon learning what he has done with Polonius' murdered corpse, "for that which thou hast done—must send thee hence" (4.3.41–42). Tellingly, the deed to which Claudius here refers is not just the actual killing of Polonius but also the obscenity of his "secret" disposal of Polonius's body, the "guts" he "lug[s]" (3.4.210). Claudius is, I take it, genuinely horrified at Hamlet's actions here, and by Hamlet's subsequent extemporization on maggots, worms, and fish, which shows "how a king may go a / progress through the guts of a beggar" (4.3.29–30). But is this not Hamlet's direct riposte to Claudius's and Gertrude's earlier remarks about the "commonness" of death of fathers? Is he not mocking Gertrude's callous truism, "all that lives must die / Passing through nature" (1.2.72–73). "Ay, madam, it is common," sneers Hamlet— and his disposal of Polonius punctuates the sneer. *You say the passage from life to death is accomplished by nature? Fine, I'll leave your courtier's body under the stairs. No offense in the world.*

Hamlet's response to his mother, here and elsewhere, signals a breakdown in the ritual organization of social pretense around birth, and care for the dead. What we see emerge, between Hamlet and his parents, then, is a way of life in which such care is still routinely provided but no longer operates as an uncontested matrix for human self-understanding. "Do not for ever with thy veiled lids / Seek for thy noble father in the dust," Gertrude implores (1.2.70–71). The dead must be buried, and "yet"—Claudius adds—"so far hath discretion fought with nature / That we with wisest sorrow think on him / Together with remembrance of ourselves" (1.2.5–7).

With this in mind, let me now turn to the second principle of social organization that falls into crisis in the play: Revenge, or Hamlet's duty as his father's first son. In a general sense, revenge tragedies symptomize the failure of funerary rites and obsequious care for the dead to do the "cultural" work that is being asked of such rituals. Indeed, revenge is called for when those "rites" are not enough, when the bonds between the living and the dead remain sundered by an individual's death, by *this* death. Like care of the dead, successful vengeance seeks to *particularize* the avenged one, and recuperate the individuality of his connection to the community of the living.[20] So, too, Hamlet must avenge his father in order to properly bury him, as it were; to let him rest in peace.

This inadequacy of funerary rites is marked at several points in Shakespeare's play. In the first place, the burial was not sufficiently separated—in its ritual doing—from the marriage of Claudius and Gertrude ("Thrift, Horatio, thrift . . . ," 1.2.179–81). Indeed, what Hamlet finds vexing in the "most wicked speed" with which his "mother's wedding" followed his "father's funeral" (1.2.156, 176, 178) is not only the implicit substitutability of his father, but the confused substitution of burial for marriage, love of the dead and love of the living. In the second place, the Ghost calls upon Hamlet to, in effect, accomplish what the funeral itself did not manage— namely, the formation of a practical identity capable of binding son and father. He asks Hamlet to *act* like his son—"If ever didst thy dear father love . . ." (1.5.23).

Of course, it could be said that revenge *is* Hamlet's duty, the norm to which he ought to adhere in the face of whatever might lead him astray; certainly, it is recognizable as such. But, then, to put the question in its traditional form: Why the delay, if Hamlet's course of action is so clear? It is worth remembering that it also takes Hieronimo and Bel-Imperia an awfully long time to achieve revenge in Thomas Kyd's *Spanish Tragedy* (c. 1590). Indeed, delayed revenge is so pervasive in the "revenge" tragedies of the late sixteenth and early seventeenth centuries that it might be called a convention of the genre, like the happy marriage at the end of a typical comedy.[21] But in *Hamlet* this convention reaches a kind of apotheosis insofar as it is connected a

20. As Laertes later makes clear, it is the "natural" bond of blood that also motivates revenge. See 5.2.240–42.
21. My thanks to Thomas Pavel, to whom I owe this observation and comparison.

perceived shortcoming in the duty itself. As if the duty is not *enough* for Hamlet—necessary, but not sufficient, for a fully lived life: an indicator that his life (any life) might be lived *more* fully or *less* fully.[22]

By delaying, Hamlet himself experiences and also shows (us, in the audience) by sheer force of procrastination that his life is not reducible to the doing of this duty; that his life *might* be more fully lived as his. After all, Hamlet's delay also serves to show, if nothing else, his individuality or distinctness—his own "sense of self"—with respect to his "role" as avenger; the *possibility* that Hamlet might distance himself from his father's demand, at least temporally—by taking his time in the carrying out of his obligation, or by doing it "his way." And this is true, even if Hamlet's self-individuation (the "fuller" life he seeks) turns out to be little more than the achievement of this delay, or whatever we watch him do in the "interim." It is true, in other words, even if he fails to lead a life—or, better, even if the possibility of failure seems intrinsic to the possibility of Hamlet's succeeding.[23] "It will be short. The interim's mine, / And a man's life's no more than to say one" (5.2.73–75).

At the same time, the delay tests *our* patience by seeking to make a drama out of letting one's family duty "sleep" (4.4.58). Whether or not *we* are moved by Hamlet depends on our patience with this delay, our tarrying with it over the course of the performance. How badly do we want to see in Hamlet something more than the fulfillment of social pretense—his mother's obedient son, his father's bloody avenger? If we in the audience feel moved by Hamlet's fate (and I think we can

---

22. Tzachi Zamir suggested to me in correspondence that, perhaps, the Ghost's return itself hints at what makes a life less than full, at what more fully living one's life might require, at dying with things left "undone."

23. In this sense, Shakespeare's *Hamlet* might be said to present a problematic—that of "becoming" or "failing to become" oneself—that has been helpfully analyzed in Robert Pippin's essay on Proust: "On Becoming Who One Is (and Failing)" in *The Persistence of Subjectivity* (Cambridge: Cambridge University Press, 2005); and in Robert Pippin, "Self-Interpreting Selves," *Journal of Nietzsche Studies* 45.2 (2014): 118–33.

be) then—to tweak the Aristotelian thought with which I began—it is because we regard Hamlet's sense of leading his own life as important, beyond whatever he objectively does or leaves undone, beyond any *particular* practical identity he might achieve, and yet *as* a kind of commitment (Hamlet *does* avenge his father, for instance, and repeatedly states his commitment to doing just that). That is to say, we must see Hamlet's own *sense* of himself as an agent—his deliberation on his courses of action, his uncertainty about what he has done or might yet do—as themselves of potentially "objective" (universal) significance for all of us who might similarly lead (or fail) to lead a life in a complicated, fractured social world.[24]

By "complicated," I mean that Hamlet's *other* social duties (beyond revenge) are in fact not so easy to grasp. As far as his life at Elsinore is concerned, and as a practical matter, it is far from obvious just what he is supposed to do with himself, as a matter of practice; other than be proximate to Claudius and Gertrude—"Here in the cheer and comfort of our eye, / Our chiefest courtier, cousin, and our son" (1.2.116–17). In being passed over for the kingship, after all, it could be said that Hamlet—rather than delaying—is himself deferred. After all, just what being "most immediate" to the throne means is not at all clear (1.2.109). Hamlet is asked to "obey" without being give any clear duty or responsibility. Of course, courts of the period had names for such figures: courtiers, lieges, noblemen. More on this in a moment. For the time being, I want merely to signal that we are presented with a form of life in which participation through the reflective endorsement of a "norm" or "duty" appears practically implausible.

More generally—to move explicitly to the third social principle under consideration—Claudius's accession shows that matrilineal

---

24. This, I think, is why Hamlet has generated more intense reflection over the years than, say, Thomas Kyd's Hieronimo.

descent and the right of primogeniture have been emptied of unquestioned authority. Denmark is now an elective monarchy.[25] And this matters, in the context of my brief discussion here, because it implies that social inheritance has been at least partially severed from the "natural" devolution of generations—the bearing of children. So, while Hamlet's relation to Gertrude is necessary for his place at court, it is not sufficient to define or stabilize the significance of that place. In this way, an elective monarchy makes explicit—at the level of state organization—what is implicit in modern forms of civil society: that living as an "individual" (a legal person) means being entitled to property, to a sphere of possession irrespective of any claims of parentage. By establishing a kind of collaboration between the state structure and civil society (as in the postfeudal relation between the king and courtiers that one sees in Claudius' interactions with Hamlet, or with Laertes late in the play) property rights effectively render the "natural" family less and less relevant to the maintenance of the social structure of which it is a part. So, again, although the play shows the lingering force of Gertrude's maternal bonds, it also shows those bonds to be anachronistic and insufficient for the reflective endorsement of any "norm," for living out any clear practical identity.[26] And, by the same token, state-sanctioned property rights start to replace care for the dead as the organizing claim of the social itself.

In such a situation, the (natural-blood) family starts to appear increasingly incestuous, doomed to close in on itself in an antigenerative spiral. So, we watch Hamlet and Laertes (whom Hamlet calls "brother," 5.2.230)—the living ends of their bloodlines—struggle to

---

25. For context, see de Grazia, *Hamlet without Hamlet*, 87–89, especially her discussion of William Blackstone.

26. In this, as in other respects, Laertes's fate mirrors that of Hamlet (as does Fortinbras's or Pyrrhus's). Consider, Laertes does not waste time, upon returning to Elsinore, in describing his predicament in just these terms: "That drop of blood that's calm proclaims me bastard, / Cries 'Cuckold!' to my father, brands the harlot / Even here between the chaste unsmirched brow / Of my true mother" (4.5.117–20).

see who can be buried deepest in the grave of the young Ophelia, from whose "fair and unpolluted flesh" one can expect at best an off-spring of "violets," but no children (5.1.228–29).

Indeed, Ophelia's funeral shows us the image of a social world in which funerary rites are becoming confused, not just with marriage (as we saw earlier), but with the act of taking up possession and residence. The gravesite has become a bit of terrain to be appropriated and expropriated; so, one by one, the skulls are tossed back up— "There's another!" (5.1.93). Hamlet, of course, imagines these bones to be those of landowners—politicians, landlords, lawyers; and he sees these objects as having become, themselves, signs of ownership and entitlement. Ophelia, after all, is being given a "Christian burial" because she is a "gentlewoman" (5.1.24–25). Grave and funeral mark property and wealth. Following Ophelia's corpse, Laertes complains twice, "What ceremony else?" (5.1.212, 214). His concern is not that of, say, Antigone—whose maternal blood-ties obligate her (she thinks) to bury her dead sibling's body. Rather, they express Laertes's anxiety over the fragility of his own nobility and wealth—especially in the wake of Polonius's "obscure funeral" held with "[n]o trophy, sword, nor hatchment o'er his bones / No noble rite, nor formal ostentation" (4.5.206–7).

This erosion of (ancient, traditional-Christian) funerary rites, I take it, prompts Laertes to improvise *some* action that would help him assert nobility, give him access to wealth and a livable "practical identity" at Elsinore. Provoked by Gertrude's last words, which seek to bind Ophelia to Hamlet as his "wife" (5.1.233), Laertes leaps forward. "Hold off the earth awhile, / 'Till I have caught her once more in mine arms. . . . Now pile your dust upon the quick and dead / Till of this flat a mountain you have made / T'o'ertop old Pelion or the skyish head / Of blue Olympus" (5.1.238–43). Not to be outdone, Hamlet enters the scene and demands to know, "What is he whose grief / Bears such an emphasis?" I see these displays as motivated, not just by "love" of Ophelia, but by the desire for honor and prestige in the eyes of the King (who can enrich them). Both Laertes and Hamlet have provisionally concluded that without wealth, nobility, and honorable standing, no livable practical identity is open to them— although Hamlet (as we will see) remains ambivalent about this.

So, they fight, first over Ophelia's body and grave, and then again at court, ostensibly in order to satisfy the King's wish to see gentlemen play with swords.[27] Perhaps more surprising than Laertes's own efforts, is Hamlet's apparently eager participation in the social pretense. (Consider the "tongue" of noblesse that Hamlet affects, "Let the foils be brought, the gentleman willing and the King hold his purpose—I will win for him an I can; if not, I will gain nothing but my shame and the odd hits," 5.2.155–58.) To Horatio's surprise, Hamlet even remarks, "Since [Laertes] went into France, I / have been in continual practice. I shall win at the odds" (5.2.188–89). Honor, nobility, and property—our "third" principle of social organization—turn out to be perhaps the most plausible avenue open to Hamlet, at he sees it.[28]

This can be put more formulaically. To be "honorable" or "noble" in the sense under discussion, entails somehow outstripping—or actively disowning—one's own previous actions with ever newer, improvised endeavors. To be honorable, in this context, is to continually separate oneself from one's own deeds through a kind of

---

27. That, for Laertes, honor and nobility are at stake is plainly clear—not only because he says so (5.2.242), or because of what Osric says on Laertes behalf (5.2.91–97), but because the audience knows that Claudius has pushed Laertes into the poisoned duel with precise words: "Laertes," he goads, "was your father dear to you? / Or are you like the painting of sorrow, / A face without a heart?" (4.7.106–8). The point, of course, is not whether Laertes "really" grieves (since what *really* grieving, caring for the dead, *is* is what is at issue). The point, as Claudius knows, is Laertes's inheritance, his claims to nobility—and Claudius's desire to hold onto the throne, in the face of any popular uprising on Laertes's behalf.

28. Hamlet confides his misgivings about all of this to Horatio (as at 5.2.190–91), but he nevertheless goes through with the duel.

"madness" or "antic disposition," through practical self-alienation. Such "madness" would be a form of life—an attempt at living "nobly," as it were—in which one holds open an interpretive stance on what one does—all the while being a kind of fidelity *to* a practical identity, a kind of enacted nobility. Hamlet in fact articulates a kind of apology for this practical outlook.

> What I have done . . .
> . . . .
> . . . I here proclaim was madness.
> Was't Hamlet wronged Laertes? Never Hamlet.
> If Hamlet from himself be ta'en away
> And when he's not himself does wrong Laertes,
> Then Hamlet does it not; Hamlet denies it.
> Who does it then? His madness.
>
> (5.2.208–15)

One implication of these words is that nothing Hamlet does should be counted as *the* deed of Hamlet's life, the action on which he stakes of social existence or claims a practical identity. Whatever he does (or did) should rather be seen as a moment of "madness," of "getting better" at living this kind "mad," improvised life, and of getting better at "interpreting" it for himself and others along the way. Hamlet undertakes a kind of self-education, then, through this enacted madness.

To be clear, I do not see Hamlet (or Shakespeare) as merely repudiating the vanity or falsity of courtly life—or, as morally indicting the vain corruption of the world. Rather, I see Hamlet as exploring what a self-education into this "mad" way of life might entail, or make possible, or where it might lead. What Hamlet is working out, I think, is *his* place in relation to a social world in which detached, reflective endorsements (or refusals) of practical identities seem impractical, implausible. Hence, he accepts Osric's invitation, even as he seeks to sustain an interpretive-critical disruption of the whole affair in his private talk with Horatio ("Thou wouldst not think how ill all's here about my heart," 5.2.208–9).

Manifestly, Hamlet is trying to find his way under social conditions in which traditional forms of duty and obligation have broken down for him, and are being replaced by the "falsity" of courtier life. At stake in this negotiation with the new "courtly" world is whether he can nevertheless manage *some* kind of livable self-relation— without, however, being able to manage the self-constitution of a practical identity or social role through a reflective endorsement of this new courtly culture. Hence, the odd complexity of his "mad" interactions throughout the play. (Consider, as only two examples, the gratuitousness with which he gets Polonius to agree that "yonder cloud" looks "like a camel," only to then compel him to agree that it is "like a whale," 3.2.367–72), and the grammar of his self-abuse at the end of the second act: "Am I a coward? / Who calls me villain ... Why, what an ass am I!" 2.2.506–17.)

The fact that this madness, or "antic disposition," seems to be a part of Hamlet's *character*—rooted in the language Shakespeare supplies—has tempted some readers of the play to conclude, as Harold Bloom does, that this is "the grandest of consciousness as it overhears its own cognitive music."[29] But Hamlet's subjectivity is forged, not solipsistically, but within the social-historical conditions of "normative collapse" under analysis here. *That* is Hamlet's *Bildung*: the impossibility of forging a practical identity solely in view of (or wholly apart from) the normative demands of matrilineal descent, duty to his dead father (revenge), care for the dead, property rights (false courtly life). Hamlet's actions and soliloquys—his "mad" subjectivity, we might say—make that predicament actual and dramatic, as he self-consciously embodies it.

29. Harold Bloom, *Hamlet: Poem Unlimited* (New York: Riverhead, 2003), p. 36.

This is not to suggest that the individual "Hamlet" is *just* an effect or symptom of the historical breakdown of sociality into which he is born. (Had Horatio been born in Hamlet's place, no doubt a different drama would be on display.) In other words, we ought to take seriously the significance of Hamlet's singular "personality"—its "formal inevitability," as Hegel put it. But rather than conclude that Hamlet's "character" is just thereby the soul of the tragedy Shakespeare composed—as Hegel was tempted to do, and as A. C. Bradley largely did—I want to suggest that the play also shows us Hamlet's practical efforts to think through (in thought and deed) the relation between his social predicament and himself, the implications of the life he is born into *for* the self-formation of his character.

After all, we need to understand what makes Hamlet's fate *dramatic*. For if Shakespeare's play were only the tale of Hamlet's ruin—of *this* particular character's coming to ruin because of a "decisive adherence to himself" (as Hegel puts it)—then why would *we* be moved? What about the "universality" of which Aristotle spoke, and which still seems to apply to *Hamlet*?

Here, I think, it helps to recall what Shakespeare shows us over the course of the play. For we are at least shown the possibility of reflectively distancing oneself, not just from the duties one might take up, but from the certainty that duties *can* be taken up—as well as the historical crisis (the breakdowns in traditional forms of life) that make this possibility real. And this means we are shown how living a life in such a bereft social world is, at least, thinkable and perhaps possible—however, awkwardly—even if Hamlet's practical self-knowledge breaks down, even if he ultimately fails to form a coherent practical identity.

More than that, we are shown how a certain self-education (Hamlet's) can take place under these difficult and stifling, historical conditions. And this means, too, that we see how one's sense of oneself—Hamlet's self-consciousness, to use a sort of shorthand—might be achieved in the coherence of this kind of drama (I mean, the one we see in *Hamlet*). Self-awareness about the importance of living one's life, or failing to do so, stands as a genuine achievement of the play.

Admittedly, Shakespeare's *Hamlet* seems to show us this only in "negative"—but that is still a showing. Consider, to take a moment already mentioned, how Hamlet's self-alienation (his "attempt" to live like a courtier) is tested out—or, perhaps, starts to be realized— in his efforts to live an adult love-affair with Ophelia. When Ophelia's answer to Hamlet's request that he be "remembered" by her is to return his "remembrances" back to him, Hamlet's response is—like the passage cited a moment ago—to disown his prior acts: "No, not I / I never gave you aught" (3.1.95–96). Hamlet seems "mad" to Ophelia here, true enough. But where self-alienation (that form of "madness" whereby one tries to live one's life in a false world) appears like a possible form of "leading a life" (not *just* vanity or falseness, but not a traditional, practical identity either), then perhaps a new kind of love affair might yet be sparked in the denial of one's past role as "lover." "I did love you once," but then again, "I loved you not" (3.1.115, 118–19). Radical equivocation is, in other words, perhaps one way of facing up to the general inauthenticity of social bonds in a world where (Hamlet knows) they are always "playing a role for others." If only Ophelia could have taken his cue.

And as we watch such scenes, we come to better understand Hamlet—throughout all the changes his "madness" implies—not by finally arriving at the "truth" of who he really is, once and for all. (To search for a fixable essence called "Hamlet" *apart* from his improvised madness would be a mistake; perhaps the mistake made by Ophelia.) Rather, we watch the shape of Hamlet's life as he lives it under these difficult circumstances. We hear him and watch him in various situations—and we get better at hearing *him* through these changes in setting and circumstance. Hamlet, I take it, *is* what the provisional testing-out of a new, radically uncertain, "mad" practical identity (an attempt at *leading* a life) looks and sounds like. He cultivates an abiding uncertainty about who he might become, *as* a mode of self-realization.

WORKS CITED

Adelman, Janet. 1992. *Suffocating Mothers: Fantasies of Maternal Origin in Shakespeare's Plays*. New York: Routledge.

Aristotle. 1987. *The Poetics of Aristotle*. Ed. Stephen Halliwell. Chapel Hill: University of North Carolina Press.

Bloom, Harold. 2003. *Hamlet: Poem Unlimited*. New York: Riverhead.

Bradley, A. C. 2009. *Philosophers on Shakespeare*. Ed. Paul A. Kottman. Stanford, CA: Stanford University Press.

Gjesdal, Kristin. 2017. "Literature, Prejudice, Historicity: The Philosophical Significance of Herder's Shakespeare Studies." *The Insistence of Art: Aesthetic Philosophy after Early Modernity*. Ed. Paul A. Kottman. Bronx, NY: Fordham University Press. 91–115.

Grazia, Margreta de. 2007. *Hamlet without Hamlet*. Cambridge: Cambridge University Press.

Hegel, G. W. F. 1977. *The Phenomenology of Spirit*. Trans. A. V. Miller. Oxford: Oxford University Press.

Herder, Johann Gottfried. 2009. "Shakespeare." *Philosophers on Shakespeare*. Ed. Paul A. Kottman. Stanford, CA: Stanford University Press. 21–38.

Jardine, Lisa. 1996. *Reading Shakespeare Historically*. New York: Routledge.

Korsgaard, Christine. 1996. *The Sources of Normativity*. Cambridge, MA: Harvard University Press.

Kottman, Paul A., ed. 2009a. *Philosophers on Shakespeare*. Stanford, CA: Stanford University Press.

———. 2009b. *Tragic Conditions in Shakespeare*. Baltimore: Johns Hopkins University Press.

———, ed. 2017. *The Insistence of Art: Aesthetic Philosophy after Early Modernity*. Bronx, NY: Fordham University Press.

Lear, Jonathan. 1992. "Katharsis." *Essays on Aristotle's Poetics*. Ed. Amélie Oksenberg Rorty. Princeton, NJ: Princeton University Press. 315–40.

———. 2011. *A Case for Irony*. Cambridge, MA: Harvard University Press.

Pippin, Robert. 2005. "On Becoming Who One Is (and Failing)." *The Persistence of Subjectivity*. Cambridge: Cambridge University Press.

———. 2014. "Self-Interpreting Selves." *Journal of Nietzsche Studies* 45.2: 118–33.
Rorty, Amélie Oksenberg. 1992. "The Psychology of Aristotelian Tragedy." *Essays on Aristotle's Poetics*. Ed. Rorty. Princeton, NJ: Princeton University Press. 1–22.
Wilson, John Dover. 1959. *What Happens in Hamlet*. 3rd ed. Cambridge: Cambridge University Press.

Chapter 5

Hamlet's "Now" of Inward Being

SANFORD BUDICK

PREAMBLE

I propose that though *Hamlet* is a revenge tragedy, Hamlet's pursuit of revenge "with wings as swift / As meditation" (1.5.29–30) is purely secondary to his disclosure, to himself, *in meditation*, of the *presentness* or *now* of his inward self—"that within which passes show" (1.2.85).[1] For Hamlet-the-meditator, meditation is lived experience within language. It lives for him as self-reflection in what may be called verbal acts of theatricalization. Of this kind the Mousetrap is for him only the tip of the iceberg. We are given an early sense of this tight conjunction of thinking and theatricalization in his exhortations to the player about "playing" in act 3. Considering all the other matters that by that point command his attention—murder, revenge, the possible incest of his mother, usurpation of the throne of Denmark—his outbursts to the player about acting technique seem to edge toward

---

1. The much debated question of whether "a conception of personal inwardness . . . existed at all in Renaissance England" is considered in detail (specifically with regard to Hamlet's claim to having "that within which passes show") by Katharine Eisaman Maus, *Inwardness and Theater in the English Renaissance* (Chicago: University of Chicago Press, 1995), pp. 1–34, where she provides numerous contemporary attestations to its lively existence.

derangement. With sustained anger, virtual rage, Hamlet intermittently shouts out that his preoccupation with *reforming* the activity of *playing* comes from the depth of his *soul*: "O, it offends me to the soul"; "O, there be players"; "O, reform it altogether" (3.2.8, 27, 36). These exclamatory O, O, O's about play-acting point to something that is of colossal significance for Hamlet's being. When, in the same set of injunctions, Hamlet says that "the purpose of playing . . . both at the first and now, was and is to hold as 'twere the mirror up to Nature" (3.2.20–22) he is not merely thinking of how to expose misdeeds but, we shall see, of the mirror form and function of his verbal acts of theatricalization. These acts both reproduce and (as in a mirror) reverse patterns that, at first sight, seem to be only natural. We will soon see how these acts of mirroring make possible the initiating step of Hamlet's procedure for disclosing his inward self. The three steps of that procedure are as follows: first, momentarily suspending consciousness of the external world and of its temporality; second, discovering, in what remains to consciousness, the inward self that abides in its own temporality or special *now*; third, recurring to consciousness of the external world and its temporality while retaining consciousness of one's inward being in its *now*.

"BRACKETING" AND THE NOW

My main effort in this essay is to show how Hamlet's language of the *now* gives life and meaning to his claim for inward being. Yet I will frequently refer to a corresponding philosophical or, more accurately, meditative model that has been available in modern thought, in various forms, roughly from Shakespeare's era. According to the broad outlines of this model the meditative mind goes (1) from suspension—often called a "reduction"—of consciousness of the external world to (2) a residual consciousness of self that is independent of experience of the world—often, in this sense, called "transcendental"—and even to a special temporality or "now" to (3) reclaiming consciousness of the external world and its temporality. The principal builders of the elements of this model are the Descartes of the *Meditations*, with his methodological skepticism or hyperbolic doubt, and the Husserl of the *Cartesian Meditations*, with his "bracketing" or "universal *epoché*," although other philosophers provided bridging elements between Descartes's and Husserl's models of this kind. Via the "transcendental deduction" Kant contributed profoundly to understanding the workings and products of the mind's a priori categories. In complex ways his argument, in the transcendental deduction, for the applicability of the categories to all empirical objects cued Husserl's own naming of a "transcendental reduction"—itself usually referred to, in shorthand, as "the reduction."[2] Husserl deepened Kant's distinction between consciousness of external, empirical *reality* and consciousness of an internal a priori *actuality* that Husserl called the "transcendental ego."[3] Going further than either Descartes or Kant, Husserl explained how consciousness of an internal actuality can be systematically disclosed in

2. In viewing Kant's transcendental deduction and the inward actuality of a transcendental ego, an important way station and provocation to Husserl was Johann Gottlieb Fichte's view of the actuality of an "original," "productive" "I" laid down in *The Science of Knowledge*, trans. Peter Heath and John Lachs (Cambridge: Cambridge University Press, 1982), 206–8 (I, 232–34) and elsewhere. On these relations see Thomas M. Seebohm, "Fichte's and Husserl's Critique of Kant's Transcendental Deduction," *Husserl Studies* 2 (1985): 53–74.

3. *Critique of Pure Reason*, A 225, B 273; A 182, B 224 –A 218, B 265. I will return to this point near the close of this essay. Citations of Kant in German are from *Kants Werke: Akademie-Textausgabe* (Berlin: de Gruyter, 1968). Quotations from Kant in English translation are from the *Critique of Pure Reason*, trans. Norman Kemp Smith (London: Macmillan, 1993) and *Critique of the Power of Judgment*, trans. Paul Guyer and Eric Matthews (Cambridge: Cambridge University Press, 2000). Page numbers for citations within my text are according to the Akademie edition. For suggestive remarks on Kant's and Husserl's overlapping conceptions of a transcendental ego, see Karl Ameriks, "From Kant to Frank: The Ineliminable Subject," in *The Modern Subject: Conceptions of the Self in Classical German Philosophy*, ed. Karl Ameriks and Dieter Sturma (Albany: SUNY Press, 1995), 223–24.

a transformed "now" by "bracketing" the "natural attitude" toward spatial and temporal reality. In other words, the momentary bracketing of external reality transforms our sense of time into an internal "now" or "presence" that is outside the temporal and spatial continuity in which we are usually embedded.[4] Husserl makes clear that this *epoché* (literally a "withholding") is no automatic or painless matter; that it is even a chosen ordeal.[5] My goal here is to understand how Hamlet, in his own way, chooses to go the route of very much the same ordeal.

4. Edmund Husserl, *Ideas: General Introduction to Pure Phenomenology*, trans. W. R. Boyce Gibson (London: George Allen & Unwin, 1952), 110–11, 116–19. In *Being and Time*, trans. John Macquarrie and Edward Robinson (Oxford: Blackwell, 1962), 62 and 65, Heidegger highlights his disagreement with Husserl's conception of the now by pointedly commencing his exposition of the now of Dasein exactly as does Husserl his exposition of the now of inner human consciousness that is disclosed by the *epoché*. Thereafter Heidegger's claims for the now of Dasein as a "primordial" or originary temporality work to displace Husserl's human now. Derrida's well-known critiques of a "metaphysics of presence" underlie much of his work. They are set out in a large variety of deconstructive contexts, for example, extensively in *Margins of Philosophy*, trans. Alan Bass (Chicago: University of Chicago Press, 1982). Derrida's views of temporality are heavily influenced by Heidegger's disagreements with Husserl but Derrida is even critical of Heidegger for his implicit affirmation of vestigial elements of a metaphysics of presence. On these issues see Frank Schalow, *The Renewal of the Heidegger-Kant Dialogue: Action, Thought, and Responsibility* (Albany: SUNY Press, 1992).

5. To be sure, not everyone will agree that such a bracketing, antecedent to a reaffirmation and reclaiming of the world, is either credible or possible. Jacques Maritain, for example, remarked that Husserl's *epoché* involved the flat contradiction of "*thinking of being while refusing to think of it as being.*" See *Distinguish to Unite, Or, The Degrees of Knowledge*, trans. Gerald B. Phelan (South Bend: University of Notre Dame Press, 1995; first English language edition 1937), 108. Yet we should recall that a large part of the thinking of both Heidegger and Derrida directly begins with Husserl's *epoché* or bracketing. Quite late in his career Derrida remarked, "for me Husserl's work, and precisely the notion of *epoché*, has been and still is a major indispensable gesture. In everything I try to say and write the *epoché* is implied": from the interview titled "Hospitality, Justice, and Responsibility: A Dialogue with Jacques Derrida," in *Questioning Ethics: Contemporary Debates in Philosophy*, ed. Richard Kearney and Mark Dooley (London: Routledge, 1999), 81. Derrida, following Heidegger, parted ways with Husserl on what the *epoché* leaves behind. Derrida's many engagements with Husserl's philosophy refer frequently to Eugen Fink's Husserl-approved presentation of Husserl's philosophy in his highly influential article "Die Phänomenologische Philosophie Edmund Husserls in der gegenwärtige Kritik," in *Kant-Studien* 38 (1933): 319–83; translated by R. O. Elveton

I wish to emphasize that my aim in laying out a philosophical model of the reduction is not to argue for one-to-one correspondences with Shakespeare's procedures but only to help awaken our sense of the depth and richness of human possibility that is at stake in *Hamlet*. Awareness of a procedure of reduction of this kind fills in a very different part of a picture of proto-Cartesian skepticism that can illuminate Shakespeare's plays.[6] The parallels between Shakespeare's and Husserl's meditative models for disclosing the actuality of the self are mutually illuminating, though Shakespeare may be said to surpass Husserl in Husserl's own enterprise. Remarkably enough, that is, Shakespeare's poetic procedures enact, in practice, a fulfillment of the claims for the *epoché* and the "transcendental ego" that Husserl—despite wishing otherwise—made only in theory. To be specific: Shakespeare shows how the experience of an inward now of subjectivity is a crucial aspect of the life of the subject as such. This constructed experience internally marshals forces of alienation (times out of joint) in verbal, meditative figures that ultimately overgrow solipsistic closure and reach out to the world. Thus Shakespeare's procedures of reduction in *Hamlet* already fulfill insights into concrete artistic practice, antecedent to the reduction, that Kant was to provide, also only in theory, in the "Analytic of the Sublime" of the third *Critique*. Shakespeare's fulfillments of this Kantian kind even solve a profound problem in the very possibility of initiating the procedures of a reduction that can disclose the now of inward being. The mind's performance of the *epoché* seems

as "The Phenomenological Philosophy of Edmund Husserl and Contemporary Criticism," in Elveton, ed., *The Phenomenology of Husserl: Selected Critical Readings* (Seattle: Noesis Press, 2000), 70–139.

6. Proto-Cartesian epistemological doubt has preeminently been brought to bear on Shakespearean tragedy in Stanley Cavell's groundbreaking essays, culminating in the updated edition of *Disowning Knowledge in Seven Plays of Shakespeare* (Cambridge: Cambridge University Press, 2003).

to come out of nowhere. Nothing seems to occasion or enable it.[7] Shakespeare—actually performing what Kant describes—shows otherwise.

I suggest that Kant's description, in the third *Critique*, of an experience of "a momentary inhibition [or restraint]" ("einer augenblicklichen Hemmung") of consciousness runs parallel to his account of a transcendental deduction in the first *Critique*. It, too, amounts to a transcendental reduction in that, after the "inhibition" or "restraint" (anticipating Husserl's "withholding" of *epoché*) the mind recovers an "immediately following and all the more powerful" consciousness of its independent powers, particularly of its freedom and moral feeling (5:245, 313, 318).[8] Judgment on the sublime, he says, "*a priori*" and "immediately contains the deduction" (5:280). He explains that the suspension of consciousness of the external world in the sublime is occasioned by a particular kind of aesthetic encounter, namely, of trying to grasp the totality of an effectively endless progression of items in the field of consciousness (5:250). Encounters of this kind, he argues, are most familiar in experiences of natural phenomena but he makes clear that they are also to be found in experiences of works of art such as the Pyramids, St. Peter's Cathedral, or Milton's *Paradise Lost*. In other words, in such aesthetic encounters the mind's chosen act of momentarily bracketing consciousness of the world is prepared by the momentary inhibition of consciousness that results from attempting to grasp the totality of an infinite progression. Kant

---

7. On this problem see David Carr, "Transcendental and Empirical Subjectivity: The Self in the Transcendental Tradition," in *The New Husserl: A Critical Reader*, ed. Don Welton (Bloomington: Indiana University Press, 2003), 193.

8. As Richard Eldridge has pointed out to me, for Cavell, too, there is an experience of inhibition that produces a heightened experience of the self. Within skepticism this is an experience of alienation or estrangement from the demands and expectations of others that haunt ego formation. Eldridge elaborates on these matters in his paper for the Shakespeare Association, "'This Most Human Predicament': Cavell on Language, Intention, and Desire in Shakespeare."

does not try to specify the degree of blockage in this inhibition of consciousness. Yet it is clear that in the momentary condition that is produced in this way the mind experiences a suspension of the world's spatio-temporality, in effect, a negativity in which the residual self abides in its own temporality.

In *Hamlet*, I propose, recurring aesthetic encounters of this kind occur in Hamlet's pervasive use of a particular rhetorical figure. This is the figure of crosswise repetition that is called chiasmus, the elements of which are mapped AB:BA. Hamlet's use of this figure requires detailed explanation, such as I will attempt to provide in a moment. At the outset, however, we should remind ourselves that Hamlet, perhaps more than any other of Shakespeare's protagonists, conducts his primary battles not so much in physical skirmishes as in his own mental combats, which is to say, with language in a world of ideas. In literature—preeminently in the great war that Hamlet wages—ideas can be yoked into framing verbal formations that represent a disarranged set of ideas whose internal dynamics are more prominent than any simple stateable content. An order and ordering of ideas of this rhetorical kind can constitute a meditative action that furthers the mind's deepest aims, such as, say, the realization of a Cartesian or Kantian or Husserlian reduction.[9] Shakespeare's

9. In "The Death of Hamnet and the Making of Hamlet," *New York Review of Books*, October 21, 2004, Stephen Greenblatt has compellingly argued that "With *Hamlet* Shakespeare made a discovery by means of which he relaunched his entire career. The crucial breakthrough . . . had to do . . . with an intense representation of inwardness by a new technique of radical excision," by which Greenblatt means "occluding the rationale, motivation, or ethical principle that accounted for the action to be unfolded." Side by side with this "excision," "suspension," and creation of a "strange interim" Greenblatt notes Shakespeare's employment of a variety of poetic strategies: "Tearing away the structure of superficial meanings, he fashioned an inner structure through the resonant echoing of key terms, the subtle development of images, the brilliant orchestration of scenes, the complex unfolding of ideas, the intertwining of parallel plots, the uncovering of psychological obsessions." As a complement to Greenblatt's argument, the present essay locates Shakespeare's instrument of excision—and of suspension and creation of a strange interim—within the structure of Hamlet's theatrical language.

frequent use of the figure of chiasmus in his sonnets as well as his plays, including *Hamlet,* has been amply documented.[10] Yet the workings of chiasmus, in Shakespeare and indeed in literature in general, remain largely obscure. In *Hamlet* Shakespeare shows the innermost conflicts and potentialities of chiasmus.[11]

HAMLET'S CHIASMUS OF THEATRICALIZATION

The key to seeing the extent and significance of chiasmus in Hamlet's language is to recognize that he finds himself, throughout, in an agonizing condition of cross-purposes that takes chiastic form. Shakespeare shows how a chiasmus of theatricalization lies in wait within the human imagination itself and how, by facing its challenges, that chiasmus can be harnessed to produce consciousness of an inner atemporality where inward being is disclosed. By the imagination's inherent theatricalization I mean the back-and-forth movements between role-playing consciousness and a would-be non-role-playing consciousness that is never free from role playing. Hamlet's meditative employment—his productive thinking—of chiasmus, right to left and left to right, AB:BA, ad infinitum, is his mirror held

---

10. Joel Fineman, *Shakespeare's Perjured Eye: The Invention of Poetic Subjectivity in the Sonnets* (Berkeley: University of California Press, 1986), explored chiasmus as the psychoanalytic master trope of Shakespeare's sonnets. Fineman briefly notes the devolution of ideas about chiasmus from Husserl's "reduction and a transcendental ego" to Sartre and Merleau-Ponty to Lacan (p. 45). A sampling of the great extent of Shakespeare's use of chiasmus in the plays is available in articles by William L. Davis that also note earlier discussions of the subject: "Better a Witty Fool Than a Foolish Wit: The Art of Shakespeare's Chiasmus," *Text and Performance Quarterly* 23 (2003): 311–30 and "Structural Secrets: Shakespeare's Complex Chiasmus," *Style* 39 (2005): 237–58. More recent is Chris Scholten-Smith's "Some Chiastic Structures in Shakespeare's *Hamlet,*" *Idiom* 46 (2010): 39–44.

11. Twenty years ago I believed I had arrived at an understanding of how chiasmus works. In *The Western Theory of Tradition: Terms and Paradigms of the Cultural Sublime* (New Haven: Yale University Press, 2000) I focused repeatedly on the figure of chiasmus but I had not seen the power of chiasmus that Shakespeare reveals, especially in *Hamlet.*

up to nature. The elements of chiasmus necessarily form an effectively infinite progression because, as Lisa Freinkel has nicely put it, "Repetition becomes inversion and inversion takes us back to where we started," so that chiasmus initiates "an exchange that seems to have no beginning and no end."[12] Hamlet's representations, to himself, of his chiastic condition constitute repeated attempts to grasp the totality of infinite progressions, and they repeatedly produce momentary inhibitions or suspensions of consciousness of the immediate external world. In other words, in Hamlet's hands chiasmus becomes a compact, portable engine of infinite progression and of experiencing the impossibility of grasping the totality of such a progression. Judging by the intensity of his recurring to chiasmus we may well conclude that he knows, or at least senses, the blessings it can confer. He knows or senses that the failure it entails can somehow leave him with the residual consciousness of a self in an inward *now*. He knows, or senses as well, that paradoxically, the use of this instrument of momentary suspension can ultimately furnish the grounds for his experience and action in the world. Indeed, one of the abiding, creative paradoxes of Hamlet's thinking (and his grasp of his—of humanity's—condition) is centered in the back-and-forth movements of his theatrical chiasmata: these repeatedly disclose a resolute purposiveness within apparent vacillation. This paradox reaches a climax in his "If it be . . ." clauses concerning the *now*, in act 5. I will yet return to these clauses, but I note already that they, too, are tightly driven by the effects of chiasmus: "If it [A] be now, 'tis [B] not to come. If it be [B] not to come, it will [A] be now" (5.2.198–99).[13]

Hamlet's most significant use of the chiasmus of theatricalization— serving virtually as a template for all his other employments of this

12. Lisa Freinkel, *Reading Shakespeare's Will: The Theology of Figure from Augustine to the Sonnets* (New York: Columbia University Press, 2002), 22–23.
13. The first occurrence of the word "now" in these lines is absent at this point in the second quarto but appears there in both the First Quarto and the Folio.

figure—is his self-accusatory question concerning the player's capacity to feel and to express emotion. After asking about that emotion,
"all for nothing—For Hecuba?" he asks further:

> What's [A] Hecuba to [B] him, or [B] he to [A] her,
> That he should weep for her?
>
> (2.2.494–95).

Horatio says more than he knows when he describes the language
of Hamlet's retreat into theatrical disguise as "whirling words"
(1.2.132). These chiastic whirling words consist of a layering of play-
acting upon would-be non-play-acting upon play-acting, ad infinitum. The many chiasmata that Hamlet generates create a continual
whirling spiral of this kind. The configuration of the Hecuba chiasmus encompasses the mind's, the imagination's, interminable interchange between kinds of role playing in the quest for authenticity:

> *play-acting* (experiencing Hecuba in the fiction) to *would-be non-
> play-acting* ("him," the live actor, in real existence) // *would-be
> non-play-acting* ("he" the live actor) to *play-acting* ("her" in the
> fiction).

The interminability of this interchange, and the mind's inability to
grasp it whole, produces a powerful *epoché*. This, in turn, opens the
space of the atemporal *now*.

I suggest that Hamlet has here formulated the theatrical chiasmus that hovers over all the moments of theatrical representation
that, collectively, we call *Hamlet*. In Freinkel's analysis of a primary
exhibit of chiasmus she notes that it "precludes a *present*. . . . The
now itself . . . is lost," leaving, she says, an "odd temporality."[14]
I believe that this observation is both correct and important; and

---

14. Freinkel, *Reading Shakespeare's Will*, 30.

that it is generalizable to all usages of the figure of chiasmus. Yet what Freinkel has seen here pertains to the precluded *present* and lost *now* of worldly temporality. From the perspectives of Kant's analysis of the inhibition of consciousness in confronting the infinite progression, as well as the perspective of Husserl's *epoché*, we see that it is exactly the suspension of worldly temporality that opens the uniquely odd temporality that is the *presence* and *now* of inward being.

It is consonant with Hamlet's concealment of the sources of his suffering that he camouflages the centrality of chiasmus in his thinking. Chiasmus comes so trippingly, so wittily, from his tongue that it hides the laborious inward struggle that it harbors. We may not imagine that he is revealing anything very important about himself when, for example, he says, chiastically, "The body is with the King, but the King is not with the body" (4.2.25–26); or "We fat all creatures else to fat us, and we fat ourselves for maggots" (4.3.21–22). Yet Shakespeare has unmistakably signaled the importance of the figure of chiasmus in *Hamlet* by assigning Polonius an explicit statement about its *un*-importance. Speaking to Claudius and Gertrude about Hamlet's alleged madness, he says, chiastically, "'tis true 'tis pity, / And pity 'tis 'tis true: a foolish figure!" (2.2.97–98). Of course there is nothing foolish about the rhetorical figure called chiasmus, except when it is used by a fool. Hamlet is no such fool. Chiasmus is his figure for approaching as nearly as possible the actuality of his inner being as well as its relation to the world. In the chiastic play of "The body is with the King, but the King is not with the body" Hamlet is once again driven to find a way out of the cross purposes of theatricalization that can doom the human condition to perpetual inauthenticity—such as his addressee, Claudius, represents. The power to unsettle wielded by this chiasmus is increased by its allusion to the theory of the King's two bodies (i.e., the King as both a person and an embodiment of the national community), which comes with its own intensity of role playing.[15] Hamlet here adds dangerous insult to lethal injury. Intertwined with his cat-and-mouse riddle is his public announcement that within the walls of Elsinore no true body of a king, of any kind, is to be found. There is an especially dislocating undecidability to this chiasmus. Yet, among other things, it insinuates that the body of Polonius is in the true King's domain, but the true King (Hamlet's father) has been deprived of his body—both as living man and as living embodiment of Denmark's community. In Hamlet's chiastic hands the permutations of what "seems" and what "is" multiply open-endedly and dizzily.

Hamlet's theatrical chiasmus frequently informs even the minutiae of his theatrical language. When, for example, he addresses the player as "old friend" (2.2.360, 473–74) he makes an effort to step up, as it were, to the real world and to find a stable place to stand there while simultaneously sustaining his recognition that theatricalization always threatens to swallow the present moment. Neither the age of the player (who has only recently grown a beard) nor Hamlet's acquaintance with him is truly "old." Rather the young actor is a player located in the theatrical world that exercises an irresistible attraction for Hamlet and upon which he is about to gamble with his life in the real world. Here, too, this unsettling state of affairs can be mapped as AB:BA: "What's Hamlet (entering into play-acting) to the real-life actor called the 'old friend,' or that 'old friend' to that Hamlet?" A variety of the same shadow chiasmus is offered in Hamlet's whirling words about the player of the King, words that, at the same time, once again point at the unwelcome man on the throne who is only an impersonator of the King: "He that plays the King shall be welcome—his majesty shall have tribute on me" (2.2.285).

15. Both the chiasmus and the likely allusion to the theory of the king's two bodies have been noted here by various editors, yet the workings of the allusion within the chiasmus have seemed obscure. For the theory itself, see Ernst Kantorowicz, *The King's Two Bodies: A Study in Mediaeval Political Theology* (Princeton, NJ: Princeton University Press, 1957).

In this contorted moment of violently displaced authority, Hamlet's chiasmus is itself acutely contorted. The (B) impersonal royal presence of the rightful heir to the throne (would-be non-play-acting Hamlet) shall welcome (A) the player-King: (A) the player-majesty shall have tribute from (B) Hamlet (would-be non-play-acting). Behind this chiasmus is the chiastic question, "What's Hamlet to the player-King, or the player-King (majesty) to Hamlet?" so that we realize once again that we are never far from Hamlet's arch chiasmus of theatricalization concerning Hecuba.

Given the piling up of hints of futility or helplessness in these chiasmata, we should confront the fact that Hamlet introduces the Hecuba chiasmus with a negating phrase that describes the rhetorical upshot of the movements of chiasmus itself, namely, that they are "all for nothing" (2.2.492–94). At this moment one of Hamlet's meanings in this phrase is that, indeed, it records the potential meaninglessness of theater and acting. This meaning is totally transformed, however, by the figural implications of the phrase "all for nothing" within the productive potentiality of chiasmus, namely, that this nothing is generated as a space of negativity where the *now* of inward being may emerge.[16]

In Hamlet's ordeal of theatricalization we repeatedly see him at first resisting, then embracing, the deeper implication of his own

16. With chiasmus, too, a swerve from Husserl's understanding of what follows from the *epoché* has vast consequences. On Heidegger's applications of his view of negativity to chiasmus, among other things, in order to disclose Dasein or nonhuman being, see Jean-François Mattéi, "The Heideggerian Chiasmus," in *Heidegger: From Metaphysics to Thought*, ed. Dominique Janicaud and Jean-François Mattéi, trans. Michael Gendre (Albany: SUNY Press, 1995), 39–150. Paul de Man, *Allegories of Reading: Figural Language in Rousseau, Nietzsche, Rilke, and Proust* (New Haven: Yale University Press, 1979), 49, offered the oft-quoted (though largely unexplained) observation that "chiasmus ... can only come into being as the result of a void, of a lack that allows for the rotating motion of the polarities." De Man's location of a terminal void within chiasmus has been questioned by Brian Vickers, "Deconstruction's Designs on Rhetoric," in *Rhetoric as Pedagogy: Its History, Philosophy, and Practice—Essays in Honor of James J. Murphy*, ed. Winifred Bryan Horner and Michael Leff (London: Routledge, 1995), 304, and Frank B. Farrell, *Why Does Literature Matter?* (Ithaca, NY: Cornell University Press, 2004), 88–90. For a survey of thinking about chiasmus in

whirling words. A parallel manifestation of this resistance, giving way to deeper recognition, is to be seen in his usages of whirling language as a weapon against the camp of his adversaries. There, again and again, one meaning is meant to mislead his interlocutor while, at the same time, the very same words contribute to his evolving inner meditation—with its momentary bracketing of the world and his place in it. Such moments are in one sense intentional misrepresentations of a would-be surrender of being. Yet the same moments also bespeak Hamlet's struggle to effect a productive *epoché*. The latter is the meaning, for himself, that, for example, he keeps from Polonius (who has offered to take his leave from Hamlet) when he plays the suicidal melancholic, saying: "You cannot take from me anything that I will not more willingly part withal—except my life, except my life, except my life" (2.2.210–12). Parallel to this usage, in the previous scene Ophelia misses Hamlet's doubleness (it is far more than duplicity) when she recounts his "sigh so piteous and profound / As it did seem to . . . end his being" (2.1.91–93).

Shakespeare has even gone to considerable lengths to inscribe his personal identification with Hamlet's ordeal of theatrical chiasmus. He does this by having Hamlet elaborate a theatrical chiasmus that depends upon topical references to the London children's companies that were damagingly competing with the established companies, including, he explicitly informs us, the players at the Globe Theatre. This is seen in the Folio text where Hamlet asks Rosincrance (the spelling of his name in the Folio), "Do the boys carry it away?"—meaning, are the children's companies winning in this competition—to which Rosincrance answers, in a series of near perfect chiastic reversals, "[A]

poststructuralism, especially in de Man and Derrida, see Rodolphe Gasché's "Reading Chiasms," his introduction to Andrzej Warminski's *Readings in Interpretation: Hölderlin, Hegel, Heidegger* (Minneapolis: University of Minnesota Press, 1987), ix–xxvi as well as Warminski's own comments on the topic.

Ay, that they do, [B] my lord—[B] Hercules [A] and his load too [i.e., the sign of the Globe Theatre]" (2.2.358–60). Not only do *Ay* (confirmatory) / *too* (replicative) and *they do [carry it away]* / *his load [carried away]* mirror each other in reverse order, but in the apposition of *my lord /Hercules* the chiasmus levies upon Hamlet's earlier comparison of himself with Hercules. Claudius, Hamlet said, is "no more like my father / Than I to Hercules" (1.2.152–53). This self-belittling comparison will be redeemed by Hamlet's heroic exertions, including, we may say, his cleansing of rotten Denmark's Augean stables. As a result, there is in fact a fitting match between "my lord" (Hamlet) and "Hercules." More than that, however, the behind the scenes Herculean carrier of this load of theatricalization is Shakespeare himself, the playwright at the sign of the Globe Theatre and the author of this chiasmus and all other of Hamlet's chiasmata. More needs to be said about Shakespeare's ways of identifying with Hamlet's condition of theatricalization, but I believe the suggestion is clear that Hamlet's journey toward his *now* of inward being is Shakespeare's as well.

The same may be said of the spectator of *Hamlet*. In this play there are two kinds of spectator of the problematic of would-be non-play-acting versus play-acting. One kind of spectator, the sort called "barren spectators," misses the possibility of fruitfully bracketing the world, or one's life in the world. The "necessary question of the play" that is "then to be considered" passes over their heads (3.2.39–41). But Shakespeare allows us to be aware of the presence of another kind of spectator, one who brings a muteness (and its affiliations with the nothing) to match Hamlet's rest that is silence. This is the living (non-play-acting) spectator in the theater, to whom Hamlet (play-acting) turns in the gesture of linkage or handing on that Shakespeare (from within his chiasmus of play-acting/non-play-acting) has configured. We hear an echo of Hamlet's self-accusatory "What's Hecuba to him, or he to her, / That he should weep for her?" in the chiasmus that Hamlet aims at the spectators of *Hamlet*:

[A] You that look pale [B] and tremble at this chance,
[B] That are but mutes [A] or audience to this act.

(5.2.318–19)

In their own way these spectators are caught at theatrical cross-purposes. Their trembling is a kind of horrified speech within mute-ness; they look pale, as if they are on the scene of violence, yet they remain at a safe distance from the reaches of killing. These cross-purposes cannot be rationally formed into a whole idea or feeling. On a level of ideas and feelings that is beyond the ideas and feelings that are directly described by the infinitely progressive words of the chi-asmus, we (the spectators) momentarily feint away in failure to take in fully where we are or what is happening to us. Thus for each of the spectators in this audience—each of whom is also caught, even before entering the theater, in the condition of theatrical imagination—the Hamlet chiastic question booms over him or her as well, only in a dif-ferent form: "What's the fiction of *Hamlet* to this real-life spectator, or this real-life spectator to the fiction of *Hamlet* . . . that he or she should tremble, should look pale at this act?" (Are we *in* this fiction? Are we *in* our lives?) We, as spectators, can hope that to the extent that the spectator of Hamlet's ordeal of theatricalization participates in it, he or she might also reap the reward of disclosing inward being in his or her own *now*.

HAMLET'S NOW

I wish to ask again, in somewhat amplified form, what I take to be the primary question of the play: Does Hamlet provide the grounds for his claim that he *has, presently* or *immediately*—in a dimension of *now*—experience of his inward being, "that within which passes show," even, that is, at the moment of reproaching the Queen for not having it herself (1.2.85)? Compared to this, the question of whether "to be or not to be" (3.1.55) is logically of secondary importance. Of course it is possible to contend that there is no need to demonstrate the grounds of experience of inward being because it is universally available and self-evident. Hamlet, however, insists otherwise. He claims that the experience of such a self that he is *having* even now is what distinguishes him from the *seeming* and play-acting—the soul-deep shamming—that he sees all around him. Thus nothing could be more immediately to the point than for Hamlet to make his claim for his inward being to the mother who gave him being and who, in this son's eyes, has abandoned the innermost being that she plighted to the man with whom this son was begotten:

> "Seems," madam—nay it is, I know not "seems." . . .
> These ["all forms, moods, shapes of grief"] indeed "seem,"
> For they are actions that a man might play,
> But I have that within which passes show,
> These but the trappings and the suits of woe.

$$(1.2.76–86)$$

Hamlet is telling Gertrude that what is left of her inner being is incapable of knowing *him*—this son at this moment—at all, that she has no access to anything but his outward appearances. Later, in fact, he seems almost to succeed in getting her to "throw away the worser part" of her being and to "live the purer with the other half" (3.4.155–56). If she could actually manage this, it might secure her own inner *now*. But this *now* never occurs for her. It is time to delve the emergence of Hamlet's *now*.

Of all the complex words in Hamlet's rich lexicon, one of the most complex, and also most evanescent, is the word "now." Hamlet's journey toward an ultimate location of the *now* is traced throughout the play but his arrival in that location takes place only in his last moments. Each of his usages of the *now* carries with it the shadow awareness of a demand not only for action but for consolidating the inner self that can freely choose such action. All of his thirty-two uses of the *now* are keyed to his first, apparently perfunctory use of the word. "What hour *now*?" he asks, when he is awaiting his first sight of the Ghost at the hour expected from Horatio's report (1.4.3; emphasis added). Hamlet's hour of the *now* is here already splitting apart. At this witching hour a chasm opens between the world and Hamlet as well as between the spatio-temporal *now* of the spinning world and the non-spatio-temporal *now* and *presence* in which he must find his inner being. In other words, from the time of his waiting upon this hour of *now* his life is riven between these two species of temporality, the second of which requires a sworn bonding with the whole of his innermost being. We hear this in his very next usages of the *now*. Upon concluding his interview with the Ghost, he says, "So, uncle, there you are. *Now to my word. / It is 'Adieu, adieu, remember me.' / I have sworn't*" (1.5.110–12; emphases added). He turns again from a worldly temporality to the ghostly *now* to make his friends swear, from their presumed innermost beings, not to reveal what they have witnessed: "And *now*, good friends, / As you are friends, scholars, and soldiers, / Give me one poor request.... Never make known what you have seen tonight.... *swear't*" (1.5.139–44; emphases added). In the middle three acts of the play Hamlet trembles uncomprehendingly on the verge of this nonworldly *now* in which he would—but cannot yet—fulfill his sworn bond, as in the following failed attempts: "*Now* I am alone. / O what a rogue and peasant slave am I!" (2.2.484–85); 'Tis *now* the very witching time of night . . . *Now* could I drink hot blood" (3.2.377–80); "*Now* I might do it. But *now* 'a is a-praying. And *now* I'll do it" (3.3.72–73; emphases added). All of these *now*'s elude Hamlet because he has not yet found his own *now*, on which he might then act in the world. We could profitably explore each of his usages of *now* from this and closely related points of view, but

I proceed to his usages of the *now* in act 5. Hamlet's transformed *now* finally emerges there, thus realizing the potential that awaits within his theatrical language, even in his apparent drifting.

In the two scenes of act 5 Hamlet goes through two distinctive stages in making his way to a *now* of immediate self-presence. In the first stage, that of the graveyard scene, he sees the corruption of the self's *now*, the virtual degradation of the time of the self in the arrogance of mortality. The tone of these usages of the worldly *now* is set, and then sustained, from its first appearance: "This might be the pate of a politician which this ass *now* o'erreaches—one that would circumvent God, might it not?" (73–75; emphasis added). There are seven more instances of the degraded *now* in this scene (83, 94, 96, 176, 179, 181, 182). In the second scene, having bracketed the world's *now*–in what we will see is his chiasmus of theatricalization— a Hamlet who is both within and beside (looking in on) the time of his own life takes charge of the *now*. As if he is now suddenly capable of dispensing with the play-acting of his imagination, Hamlet tumbles into his final phase of being in his excited account to Horatio of his resolute acts of survival in the sea voyage. His *now* within has become the lever for his self-related experience of the temporality of the world. Among other ways, his internal *now* emerges in a storytelling in medias res that shifts the past time of *now* to a present medias res that is, in his individual *now*, inseparable from it: "So much for this, sir. *Now* shall you see the other" (5.2.1), "But wilt thou hear *now* how I did proceed?" (27), "*Now* the next day / Was our sea-fight" (53), "Does it not, think thee, stand me *now* upon?" (62) (emphases added). Hamlet's *now*, we may say, now occupies that medias res within the world.

The full emergence of Hamlet's inward *now* takes place as he prepares for being fully present, fully ready, for the close of his journey. This *now* is registered in phrases that are among the most cryptic and elliptical that Shakespeare ever wrote. Something is being revealed

opaquely—wrenchingly—in these words, though it is unmistakable
that they bind Hamlet to the present time of a threatening world, and,
side by side, allow him to stand in the perpetual "readiness" of an inward,
atemporal *now*. This readiness of being is not altered by the change or
becoming or forward movement of worldly time. *Now*, indeed, he can
let the world (including his fated participation in the world) simply *be*:

> We defy augury. There is special providence in the fall of a spar-
> row. If it be *now*, 'tis not to come. If it be not to come, it will be
> *now*. If it be not *now*, yet it will come. *The readiness is all* . . . Let
> be. (5.2.198–202; emphases added)

Twenty lines earlier Hamlet seems to explain, in advance, this *now* of
readiness, but his words there are only slightly less gnomic:

> If his [the King's] fitness speaks, mine is ready. [A] *Now* or [B]
> whensoever, [B] provided I be so able [A] as *now*. (5.2.180–81;
> emphases added)

Taken together these chiasmata of the explicit *now* form the endgame
of Hamlet's meditative, theatrical bracketing and its products. The
effect of these chiasmata is to displace all merely temporal *now*'s into
the internal atemporal *now* of the readiness that cannot be touched
by the world's time.

CONCLUSION

"The purpose of playing," says Hamlet, "both at the first and *now*, was
and is to hold as 'twere the mirror up to Nature" (3.2.20–22; emphasis added). For the full playing out of this dramaturgy Shakespeare
counted on the fact that the spectator never forgets that within the

play called *Hamlet* Nature is itself only a play-acting of Nature. As a result, the mirroring of Nature that fulfills the purpose of this playing is necessarily reflexive and unstoppable. In other words, apparent non-play-acting ("Nature") is mirrored by play-acting, while, in its turn, play-acting mirrors back to us apparent non-play-acting ("Nature"), and so on forever because we only know any one of these items within the mirroring process that is endless and infinite. The mirror workings of chiasmus deploy left-to-right (BA) in the face of right-to-left (AB). Shakespeare has already set all of these chiasmata into motion in the third line of the entire play, in the watchmen's life-or-death password: "Long live the King," of which the unspoken counterpart that hovers, mirror-wise, over the entire play is that *The King still lives*—whether in the Ghost who still walks abroad or in Hamlet who is the true successor to the throne.

Thus Hamlet's rhetorical use of mirroring mobilizes the crisis of the human imagination in its play-acting and would-be non-play-acting among different spatio-temporal moments. His theatrical chiasmata enact a struggle that is potential in the internal life of a subject as such. These configured crises enable the emergence of the transformed *now*—the bracketing of spatio-temporal existence—and the disclosure of inward being. If spectators or readers can inwardly follow these chiasmata for themselves they may be precipitated into the same struggle and they may experience, for themselves, the same kind of disclosure.

If my account of Shakespeare's achievement of the *now* contains a measure of practical truth, it may not be too much to suggest that when we experience "the magic of theater" in *Hamlet* many of us may be accessing far more than intense make-believe. We may also be gaining glimpses of recognition into our innermost beings, in our own individual *now*. Such momentary glimpses of the self are achieved, that is, in the struggles of a dramaturgy that concentrates the back-and-forth theatrical motions of everyday human existence.

The *now* of inward being that emerges, in silence, from Shakespeare's chiasmus of theatricalization, as from Husserl's reduction, finally turns, I have suggested, toward rejoining the world. How this rejoining actually takes place is perhaps beyond the scope of this essay. I submit, however, that Shakespeare and Kant come close to sharing the same detailed insight into the condition that at this culminating juncture defines inward being and its possibility of turning to the world. As a result of the actions of clearing away in the Kantian deduction, the individual's residual being is left with only the a priori categories of understanding. For Kant the three categories that make possible what he calls "relation" to the world are "permanence of substance," "succession," and "community."[17] By act 5 Hamlet, in a similar way, has not only disclosed to himself his inward being but has unlocked the same avenues of relation to the external world. In a single concatenated insight he lays claim—swift as meditation—to all three of Kant's indispensable categories of relation between self and world. "This is I, Hamlet the Dane" (5.1.246–47), he announces. "This is I" unequivocally, immovably, declares his *permanence of substance* (no longer fearful that his self will melt away together with his too sallied, or sullied or solid, flesh); "Hamlet" establishes his *succession* to his father's name and virtue (and, incidentally, the claim to his throne); "the Dane" reaches to the bond of *community* that always locates the individual life within the human species. At the edge of the grave (Ophelia's as well as his own) his inward being stands in this readiness that has opened all avenues of outreach to the world, *now*.

---

17. For Kant these three categories of relation have a special power in defining inward being. He says that these are the grounds, "comparatively speaking," of the inward or a priori "actuality" that can reach out to the world for "perceptions, in accordance with the principles of their empirical connection (*the analogies*)" (A 225, B 273; emphasis added). "The analogies" refers of course to Kant's immediately preceding lengthy exposition of the three "Analogies of Experience": permanence of substance, succession, and community (A 176, B 218-A 218, B 265).

ACKNOWLEDGMENTS

For valuable comments on this essay I am indebted to Richard
Eldridge, Shaul Hochstein, and Michael Kaufman.

WORKS CITED

Ameriks, Karl. 1995. "From Kant to Frank: The Ineliminable Subject." *The Modern
    Subject: Conceptions of the Self in Classical German Philosophy*. Ed. Karl Ameriks
    and Dieter Sturma. Albany: SUNY Press. 217–30.
Budick, Sanford. 2000. *The Western Theory of Tradition: Terms and Paradigms of the
    Cultural Sublime*. New Haven: Yale University Press.
Carr, David. 2003. "Transcendental and Empirical Subjectivity: The Self in the
    Transcendental Tradition." *The New Husserl: A Critical Reader*. Ed. Don Welton.
    Bloomington: Indiana University Press. 181–98.
Cavell, Stanley. 2003. *Disowning Knowledge in Seven Plays of Shakespeare*. Cambridge:
    Cambridge University Press.
Davis, William L. 2003. "Better a Witty Fool Than a Foolish Wit: The Art of
    Shakespeare's Chiasmus." *Text and Performance Quarterly* 23: 311–30.
———. 2005. "Structural Secrets: Shakespeare's Complex Chiasmus." *Style* 39:
    237–58.
de Man, Paul. 1979. *Allegories of Reading: Figural Language in Rousseau, Nietzsche,
    Rilke, and Proust*. New Haven: Yale University Press.
Derrida, Jacques. 1982. *Margins of Philosophy*. Trans. Alan Bass. Chicago: University
    of Chicago Press.
———. 1999. "Hospitality, Justice, and Responsibility: A Dialogue with Jacques
    Derrida." *Questioning Ethics: Contemporary Debates in Philosophy*. Ed. Richard
    Kearney and Mark Dooley. London: Routledge. 65–83.
Eldridge, Richard. 2016. "'This Most Human Predicament': Cavell on Language,
    Intention, and Desire in Shakespeare." Lecture to the Shakespeare Association.
Farrell, Frank B. 2004. *Why Does Literature Matter?* Ithaca, NY: Cornell
    University Press.
Fichte, Johann Gottlieb. 1982. *The Science of Knowledge*. Trans. Peter Heath and John
    Lachs. Cambridge: Cambridge University Press.
Fineman, Joel. 1986. *Shakespeare's Perjured Eye: The Invention of Poetic Subjectivity in
    the Sonnets*. Berkeley: University of California Press.
Fink, Eugen. 1933. "Die Phänomenologische Philosophie Edmund Husserls in
    der gegenwärtige Kritik." *Kant-Studien* 38: 319–83. Trans. R. O. Elveton as
    "The Phenomenological Philosophy of Edmund Husserl and Contemporary

Criticism," *The Phenomenology of Husserl: Selected Critical Readings*, ed. Elveton (Seattle: Noesis Press, 2000), 70–139.

Freinkel, Lisa. 2002. *Reading Shakespeare's Will: The Theology of Figure from Augustine to the Sonnets*. New York: Columbia University Press.

Gasché, Rodolphe. 1987. "Reading Chiasms." Introduction to *Readings in Interpretation: Hölderlin, Hegel, Heidegger*, by Andrzej Warminski. Minneapolis: University of Minnesota Press. ix–xxvi.

Greenblatt, Stephen. 2004. "The Death of Hamnet and the Making of Hamlet." *New York Review of Books*, October 21. Incorporated in Stephen Greenblatt, *Will in the World: How Shakespeare Became Shakespeare* (New York: Random House, 2012).

Heidegger, Martin. 1962. *Being and Time*. Trans. John Macquarrie and Edward Robinson. Oxford: Blackwell.

Husserl, Edmund. 1952. *Ideas: General Introduction to Pure Phenomenology*. Trans. W. R. Boyce Gibson. London: George Allen & Unwin.

Kant, Immanuel. 1968. *Kants Werke: Akademie-Textausgabe*. Berlin: de Gruyter.

———. 1993. *Critique of Pure Reason*. Trans. Norman Kemp Smith. London: Macmillan.

———. 2000. *Critique of the Power of Judgment*. Trans. Paul Guyer and Eric Matthews. Cambridge: Cambridge University Press.

Kantorowicz, Ernst. 1957. *The King's Two Bodies: A Study in Mediaeval Political Theology*. Princeton, NJ: Princeton University Press.

Maritain, Jacques. 1995. *Distinguish to Unite, or, The Degrees of Knowledge*. Trans. Gerald B. Phelan. South Bend, IN: University of Notre Dame Press. First English-language edition 1937.

Mattéi, Jean-François. 1995. "The Heideggerian Chiasmus." *Heidegger: From Metaphysics to Thought*. Ed. Dominique Janicaud and Jean-François Mattéi. Trans. Michael Gendre. Albany: SUNY Press. 39–150.

Schalow, Frank. 1992. *The Renewal of the Heidegger-Kant Dialogue: Action, Thought, and Responsibility*. Albany: SUNY Press.

Scholten-Smith, Chris. 2010. "Some Chiastic Structures in Shakespeare's *Hamlet*." *Idiom* 46: 39–44.

Seebohm, Thomas M. 1985. "Fichte's and Husserl's Critique of Kant's Transcendental Deduction." *Husserl Studies* 2: 53–74.

Vickers, Brian. 1995. "Deconstruction's Designs on Rhetoric." *Rhetoric as Pedagogy: Its History, Philosophy, and Practice. Essays in Honor of James J. Murphy*. Ed. Winifred Bryan Horner and Michael Leff. London: Routledge. 295–315.

Warminski, Andrzej. 1987. *Readings in Interpretation: Hölderlin, Hegel, Heidegger*. Minneapolis: University of Minnesota Press.

Chapter 6

To Thine Own Selves Be True-ish

Shakespeare's Hamlet *as Formal Model*

JOSHUA LANDY

If you're one of the many people who have the sentence "to thine own self be true" tattooed on their arm, wrist, or ankle, or one of the several who have used it as the title of a book, you may want to stop reading right now. Here's the thing: Shakespeare never said it. Shakespeare *wrote* it, but he wrote it as something for a character named Polonius to say. And Polonius, it turns out, is a grade-A nincompoop.

Yes, he's the guy who says "to thine own self be true"; but he's also the guy who tells Ophelia that Hamlet isn't really in love with her (thanks, *Dad*).[1] A handful of scenes later, he decides—equally confidently—that Hamlet loves her *too much*, and that this explains all of his weird behavior.[2] He is so pompous and long-winded that he gets lost in the middle of his own speech.[3] Too dense to understand

---

1. 1.3.100–130.
2. 2.1.99–109.
3. 2.1.48–50.

metaphorical insults, he thinks Hamlet is literally mistaking him for a fishmonger.[4] He finds the actors boring.[5] He dangles his own daughter as bait. He sends a lackey off to spy on his own son.[6] Hamlet calls him a "great baby," a "foolish prating knave," and (three times over) a "fool."[7] Why on earth have we taken him so seriously all these years?[8]

You might think that none of this matters: a smart idea is a smart idea, regardless who we hear it from. Unfortunately, however, "to thine own self be true" is *not* a smart idea. It's not wrong, exactly, but it's so simplistic as to be almost useless. How should Hamlet, for example, apply it to his life? Hamlet is the son of a king. He's also the son of a usurper's wife. He's a courtier. He's a scholar (thirty years old and still in school!). He's a mourner. He's a man in love. He's an avenger. He's a poet and playwright and theatrical director.[9] If Hamlet overheard Polonius's injunction "to thine own self be true," his only rational answer would be: "which one?"

This, I think, is the key question of *Hamlet*. How exactly can we be who we are? Being authentic sounds like a good thing, but it turns out to be massively complicated. Shakespeare is not offering us the potted aphorism "to thine own self be true" as a lesson to be learned, but as an invitation to think hard. For those who do think hard, a solution is available within the parameters of the play, one that

---

4. 2.2.171–72, 184–86.

5. "This is too long" (2.2.436).

6. 2.1.1–70.

7. 2.2.319; 3.4.213; 2.2.214; 3.1.131–31; 3.4.29. I realize, of course, that there are wise fools in Shakespeare. Polonius, however, is not one of them.

8. I was delighted, on reading Paul Woodruff's chapter in this volume, to see how much agreement there is between our positions. Anyone who is interested in the question of Polonius's untrustworthiness, and in the question of what follows from it, should look at that wonderful essay.

9. For the various selves, compare Harry Levin, "The Antic Disposition," *Shakespeare, Hamlet: A Casebook*, ed. John D. Jump (Nashville: Aurora Publishers, 1970), 122–36, pp. 134–35. And compare Lionel Trilling's discussion of *Rameau's Nephew* in *Sincerity and Authenticity* (Cambridge, MA: Harvard University Press, 1972), 44.

involves giving each part of the self its day in the sun. And something even more important is on offer: the opportunity to explore, through the very act of spectating, the kind of thing we need to do in order to pull it off.

We'll get to that solution, and to that exploration, at the end. Along the way, we'll see how this line of questioning helps us to resolve a number of tantalizing puzzles set by the play. Why is Hamlet already suicidal before he knows his father has been murdered? Why does he suddenly decide "we will have no more marriage"? Why does he have a play performed in which the ear-poisoner is a nephew, not a brother? Why is so much of that inset play about remarriage? Why does Horatio, the Stoic, lose faith in Providence? Why does Hamlet at one moment say he'll beat Laertes and at another that he won't? And why on earth does Hamlet force Claudius to drink the poisoned wine when he's already stabbed him with the poisoned sword? For all of this, stay tuned.

WHY SHOULD HAMLET KILL CLAUDIUS?

Let's start, though, by returning to the core issue: "to thine own self be true" is easier said than done. Some people might think, I suppose, that this doesn't matter very much; those people probably reckon that authenticity is a luxury, a narcissistic value invented by a decadent civilization, a "First World problem" if ever they saw one. But that's not how it looks to Hamlet. Hamlet has a monumental decision in front of him. He's been told his uncle killed his father, and he's been told he needs to make it right by killing the uncle back. If he does it, he'll have blood on his hands—the blood of the King, the blood of his uncle, the blood of his mother's new husband. And he may very well end up dead himself. So, should he do it? How can he decide? I'm going to try to convince you that he can only decide on the basis of his own values. And if I'm right about that, then the only way for him to make a good decision is by being true to himself. And if I'm right about *that*, then being many things is a potentially paralyzing obstacle, not a First World problem.

Hamlet wouldn't need to appeal to his own values, of course, if there were something else that could settle the question for him. For example, maybe he should kill Claudius because, well, everyone else is doing it. Fortinbras is getting revenge for *his* father;[10] Laertes is about to dole out rough justice for his;[11] and even the story told by the traveling players is one of a son (in this case Pyrrhus) taking up arms for a dead dad (in this case Achilles).[12] So, avenging one's father is simply the Done Thing. It's tradition. As a young Englishman said in the 1970s when asked why he mugged old ladies, "it's the *fing*, innit?"

That's all well and good, but "it's the *fing*, innit?" is not an entirely compelling argument. Very early on in the play, we hear of a local custom that is "more honoured in the breach than the observance":[13] just because something is the done thing, that doesn't make it desirable. And let's not forget that traditions aren't always internally consistent. Enthusiastic smiting in return for ancestral wrongs does seem to be part of Hamlet's local culture, but Hamlet's local culture is also Christian, and Christianity is (at least officially) not too big on revenge; you know, "turn the other cheek" and all that. It's no coincidence that when Hamlet confesses a list of sins to Ophelia, being "revengeful" is one of the top three.[14] (Isn't it fascinating that Hamlet sometimes feels guilty about wanting to kill Claudius and sometimes

10. 1.1.79–103.
11. 4.5.130–35; 4.7.26–30.
12. "After Pyrrhus' pause / A roused vengeance sets him new a-work" (2.2.425–26).
13. 1.4.15–16.
14. "I am myself indifferent honest but yet I could accuse me of such things that it were better my mother had not borne me. I am very proud, revengeful, ambitious . . ." (3.1.121–24).

feels guilty about not going through with it?) So Hamlet's tradition is telling him to do some smiting, and Hamlet's tradition is also telling him to *refrain* from doing any smiting. Way to go, tradition: you're a fat load of good.

In fact, the "Denmark" we see in the play—which is, of course, really a version of England in 1600—is an unusually big mess, culturally speaking. Hamlet and Horatio have been studying in Wittenberg, a place made famous in Shakespeare's time by Martin Luther, leader of the Protestant Reformation. As John Dover Wilson brilliantly argued, Hamlet seems to have brought back with him a Protestant way of thinking about ghosts.[15] And in case we miss these subtleties, Shakespeare has Hamlet drop the brilliant line "your worm is your only emperor for diet,"[16] making absolutely sure we're thinking about Luther. Anachronistically, there are two different conceptions of Christianity floating about the twelfth-century Denmark of *Hamlet*, in addition to the residue of pre-Christian ways of doing things. Even if Hamlet wanted to follow tradition, then, which tradition should he pick?

The world of *Hamlet* is a world in which the sanction of authority no longer carries the weight it once used to. We don't have to believe any more that the sun turns around the earth, just because the Bible and Aristotle and Dante say so.[17] We don't have to believe any more

15. As Wilson shows, *Hamlet* stages three different responses to the question of apparitions. The Ghost himself says he is on a visit from Purgatory (1.5.9–13), returning to the world of the living in order to right a wrong; that's the Catholic position on ghosts. Hamlet, however, worries that "The spirit that I have seen / May be a de'il" (2.2.533–34): if, as Protestants believe, there is no Purgatory, then no sinners are coming back from the afterlife. (Death, remember, is the "country from whose bourn / No traveller returns," 3.1.78–79.) And Horatio simply thinks the Ghost is an "illusion" (1.1.126). See John Dover Wilson, *What Happens in Hamlet?* (Cambridge: Cambridge University Press, 1951), 61–70.

16. 4.3.21. The Diet of Worms was the meeting convened by Holy Roman Emperor Charles V in 1521 to try Martin Luther for heresy.

17. There is a subtle allusion in the play to the Copernican revolution. Whereas Claudius says that "the star [sun] moves not but in his sphere" (4.7.16), Hamlet, perhaps archly, invites Ophelia to "Doubt that the sun doth move" (2.2.115). The decline of traditional belief systems is on everyone's mind.

that the communion wafer really contains the body of Christ.[18] There is more than one way of thinking about life, and more than one "done thing"; everything is potentially up for grabs. We are free, and perhaps obliged, to take our own stand on which version of physics, which version of religion, and which version of morality actually have it right about the world.

A WORLD WITHOUT JOINTS

Here's a second potential reason why Hamlet should kill Claudius: because the universe needs him to.[19] "The time is out of joint," says Hamlet.[20] What Hamlet means is that things have fallen out of their natural resting-places. Your humerus is supposed to be inside your shoulder-socket; if it's not, you've got yourself a dislocated shoulder, and you really need to pop that thing back in. Similarly, Denmark is supposed to be ruled by an elected monarch; if it's not, you've got yourself a dislocated kingdom, and you really need to pop that guy back out.

I think Hamlet is seriously tempted by this kind of idea. He's seriously tempted by the thought that there's a way the world is meant to be, with a proper place for everything. Hamlet Senior *belonged* on the throne of Denmark; Gertrude *belonged* with Hamlet Senior;

---

18. There is a hint of this debate, perhaps, in the line "The body is with the King, but the King is not with the body" (4.2.25–26).
19. An additional candidate, of course, could be Hamlet's love and respect for his father (1.5.23–25). Hamlet's father has asked him for a favor, and Hamlet loves him: shouldn't he do what he asks? Maybe, but maybe not. It would not be morally right, for example, for Laertes or Ophelia to follow the instructions of *their* father, that prating knave Polonius. (Never lend anything to anyone? That's a bit cheap!) And it's not at all clear, even in the case of the vastly superior Hamlet Senior, that his paternal wishes are enough to justify murder. In the world of *Hamlet*, a parent's charge is no more binding than the injunctions of religion and custom.
20. 1.5.186.

Claudius *belongs* in the ground. When things fall out of their proper places, the world goes out of joint, and our job is to "set it right." If that's true, then Hamlet's decision is easy. There's no need for him to inspect his soul; all he needs to do is answer the call of the universe. So, is it true? Does everyone have a place she's meant to occupy and a partner she's meant to be with? Does the world have joints? Is there such a thing as setting right the times in which we live?

LOVE AND (RE-)MARRIAGE

No, there isn't. And Hamlet knows it. And it's precisely his knowledge of this fact that has sent him into a tailspin. What drives him most profoundly to despair, as he famously says in the "To be" speech, is "outrageous fortune," with its endless "slings and arrows."[21] (In fact it's remarkable how often the word "fortune" crops up in the play: some eighteen times, including four within the space of six lines.)[22] Hamlet *wishes* the world were an orderly place, only troubled every now and then by villains like Claudius; the reality, however, is that outrageous fortune is running the show, and that there are no joints for things to fall out of. The depth of his current dejection shows us just how much he needed to believe the opposite.

We see the same thing, though more indirectly, in the *other* reason Hamlet gives for his suicidal despondency. His very first soliloquy expresses a desire to be dead, and the explanation he offers is—astonishingly perhaps—that his mother has remarried.[23] That

21. 3.1.57.
22. 3.2.195–200.
23. "Oh that this too too sallied flesh would melt, / Thaw and resolve itself into a dew, / Or that the Everlasting had not fixed / His canon 'gainst self-slaughter. . . . A little month, or e'er those shoes were old / With which she followed my poor father's body / Like Niobe, all tears. Why, she . . . married with my uncle" (1.2.129–32, 147–51).

could well strike us as, to put it mildly, a bit of an overreaction. Why shouldn't a widow find a new husband, if that's what she wants? And why should it affect Hamlet? The answer, I think, is that it obliterates his view of love, and with it his sense that there's a way things are meant to be. Gertrude's remarriage demolishes a picture of life in which each of us has an "other half," a person we are uniquely suited to, perhaps even destined to be with; once we have found our other half, an encounter with anyone else should seem insipid, drab, even pointless. If Gertrude found her other half in Hamlet Senior,[24] and if Gertrude nonetheless went on to fall for Claudius, then Hamlet must have been massively wrong in his initial assumption.

If you don't believe that Hamlet has theories of love on his mind, consider *The Murder of Gonzago*, the play he stages in act 3. I know, this play-within-the-play is supposedly all about "catching the conscience of the King": when Claudius sees a monarch having poison poured in his ear while he sleeps, his face will reveal whether he did something like that to Hamlet Senior. And yes, that's part of what Hamlet is using it for. But considering that it's officially about poisoning, there's an awful lot about warm fuzzy feelings. Seventy-five whole lines about them, in fact.[25]

"I'm getting old," Gonzago says, "and I want you to find a new husband after I'm gone." (I'm paraphrasing.) No, says his wife Baptista: "Such love must needs be treason in my breast." "In second husband let me be accurst," she continues; "None wed the second but who killed the first."[26] Note the use of the word "love" here: the

---

24. We know that Gertrude and Hamlet Senior loved each other, because the Ghost tells Hamlet "I had love for Gertrude" (1.5.48) and Gertrude doesn't deny it when Hamlet says she reciprocated with "an innocent love" (3.4.41). According to Hamlet, indeed, Hamlet Senior was "so loving to my mother / That he might not beteem the winds of heaven / Visit her face too roughly" (1.2.140–42); as for her, "Why, she would hang on him, / As if increase of appetite had grown / By what it fed on" (1.2.140–42, 143–45).
25. The seventy-five lines in question are 3.2.148–222.
26. 3.2.172–74.

only reason Baptista can imagine for marrying a second husband is if she falls in love with him. (Follow me to the footnote if you want to quibble.)[27] But she can't possibly do that, because, she says, she loves her current husband—really, *really* loves him. (The word "love" crops up a staggering fourteen times in forty-nine lines, including a stretch where it's mentioned four lines in a row.)[28] Remarriage is inconceivable because marrying twice means loving twice, and there is no such thing as loving twice.

And if there is no such thing as loving twice, that is because the world has joints: for every individual, there is one and only one partner he or she is meant to be with. No one else in the world could elicit the overwhelming feelings that he or she stirs up in us. If you fall in love with someone new, that can only mean one thing: *your original partner was not your other half*. To marry again is to reach back and destroy the romance of the original match; "none wed the second but who killed the first."

Guess what happens after Gonzago is killed . . . Yes, Lucianus, the murderer, "gets the love of Gonzago's wife."[29] Again, note the wording. Gonzago's wife doesn't just *marry* Lucianus; she *loves* Lucianus. And if she loves him, according to her own logic, that means she never really loved Gonzago. The lady did indeed protest too much.

---

27. It's true that Gonzago's wife says, at another point, "The instances [motives] that second marriage move / Are base respects of thrift [gain], but none of love" (3.2.176–77). But this does not appear to be her settled view. In addition to the line we started with ("Such *love* must needs be treason in my breast"), there's also the fact that she ends up falling in love with Lucianus ("You shall see anon how the murderer gets the *love* of Gonzago's wife"), not just coveting his property; and then again, it's not clear why remarrying for convenience would be such an affront to one's first husband, let alone prove that one did not love him. One thing is for certain: Hamlet does not think *Gertrude* remarried for money. He berates her for everything under the sun, but not once does he so much as insinuate that she's in it for the cash.

28. 3.2.148–222; 3.2.164–66.

29. 3.2.256–57; cf. 3.2.128.

Now Hamlet probably wrote some or all of these lines himself,[30] and he is extremely pleased with them. They are designed to catch the conscience of the *Queen*, not that of the King; if the ear-poison scene is a replaying of his crime, the remarriage scene is a replaying of hers.[31] Hamlet has Baptista fall in love with Lucianus because he takes his mother to have fallen in love with Claudius.[32] And (to say it again) if Gertrude has fallen in love with Claudius, after also being in love with Hamlet Senior, then Hamlet's view of love is utterly bankrupt.[33]

30. "You could for need study a speech of some dozen lines, or sixteen lines, which I would set down and insert in't, could you not?" (2.2.476–78)
31. For the play as "all-purpose mousetrap," compare Francis Fergusson, *The Idea of a Theater: A Study of Ten Plays* (Princeton, NJ: Princeton University Press, 1949), 122–23.
32. Here's what Hamlet *doesn't* say to his mother in the Closet Scene: (1) that she remarried for political or financial reasons; (2) that she married the murderer of her husband; (3) that it would all have been fine if she had just waited a little longer. Here's what Hamlet *does* say to his mother: (1) that she finds Claudius attractive (3.4.84); (2) that she is having sex with Claudius on a regular basis, and enjoying it (3.4.89–91); (3) that in private the two of them are "honeying and making love" (3.4.91), i.e., speaking sweet nothings to each other; and (4) that he knows it will take real effort on her part to keep her hands off him (3.4.157–58, 163–68). It's true that Gertrude could merely be infatuated with Claudius, but (a) that goes against what we learn in *The Murder of Gonzago* (if you remarry, that must mean you *love* the guy) and (b) this subtle distinction probably wouldn't matter much to Hamlet (if you've found your other half, you shouldn't even be able to become infatuated with anyone else).
    There's an interesting moment when Hamlet tells Gertrude she cannot possibly be in love with Claudius. "You cannot call it love," he says, "for at your age / The hey-day in the blood is tame, it's humble, / And waits upon the judgment: and what judgment / Would step from this [Hamlet Senior] to this [Claudius]?" (3.4.66–69). But of course Gertrude *has* stepped from this to this. And as Hamlet is about to admit only a handful of lines later, the hey-day in her blood is *not* tame: "Rebellious hell, / If thou canst mutine in a matron's bones, / To flaming youth let virtue be as wax" (3.4.80–82). Clearly it's just wishful thinking on Hamlet's part when he says it isn't love. If the only reason it can't be love is a lack of desire, and if desire is present, then—isn't it love?
33. A note for pedants: it is of course true that someone in Gertrude's position *could* marry someone in Claudius's position for reasons of expediency. But nobody in the play claims that this is what's going on here. The Ghost doesn't say it: he tells Hamlet that Claudius won Gertrude over "with witchcraft of his wit, with traitorous gifts— / O wicked wit and gifts that have the power / So to seduce" (1.5.43–45). Hamlet doesn't say it: he blames demonic possession rather than Claudius's smooth-talking charm, but he too thinks Gertrude has the hots for him. And Gertrude doesn't say it either: when Hamlet points out that she and Claudius are constantly "honeying and making love" (3.4.91), all she says is "Thou turn'st

That's why Hamlet is suicidal from the very first soliloquy. That's why he devotes so much of the play-within-the-play to Gertrude. (He's watching her reaction, by the way, much more than he's watching that of Claudius.) That's why he prefaces it with a snide quip about the brevity of "woman's love."[34] That's why he keeps hounding Gertrude after the play is over, badgering her into admitting her betrayal. (The Ghost, at one point, has to remind him to get back on uncle-stabbing track.)[35] That's why Hamlet ends up turning against lifelong partnerships—"I say we will have no more marriage"[36]—and driving Ophelia away, with fatal consequences. What's the point of relationships, after all, if love is never true?[37] ("How should I your true-love know," Ophelia asks, "From another one?"[38] Answer: you can't, because there's no difference, because there's no such thing as a "true-love," because the world has no joints.)

If Hamlet is deeply troubled by his mother's second marriage, then, it is not for absurd Freudian reasons; it is because the possibility of remarriage has exposed the vanity of the idea that couples are destined to be together. There is no necessity ruling human affairs. There are no proper places for things to occupy. There is no such thing as the world falling out of joint. So putting things back in their proper places cannot be a sufficient reason for him to take Claudius's life. Once again, he is entirely on his own.

---

my very eyes into my soul / And there I see such black and grieved spots / As will leave there their tinct" (3.4.87–89). In other words, "guilty as charged." This is clearly a marriage of mutual affection, not a union of reciprocal convenience.

34. 3.2.147.

35. 3.4.103–7.

36. 3.1.146.

37. Compare to some extent G. Wilson Knight, "The Embassy of Death: An Essay on *Hamlet*," *Hamlet (Bloom's Major Literary Characters)* (New York: Chelsea House, 1990), 80–94, p. 87 and Levin, "The Antic Disposition," 124.

38. 4.5.23–24.

THE DIVINE RIGHT OF KINGS

We are slowly but surely working our way back to the idiocy of Polonius. Authenticity is going to turn out to be vital—and divided-ness a critical problem—because Hamlet has nothing else on which to base his decision. The fact that revenge is the done thing is not sufficient reason for him to kill Claudius; nor can he convince himself that he needs to put things back into their proper places, since there simply *are* no proper places.

Everything would be OK, of course, if only God were around to tell us what to do. What, for example, if God were responsible for deciding which monarch belongs on which throne? If that were the case, then again Hamlet's decision would be easy. Potential reason three: Hamlet must kill Claudius because God hates usurpers.

There's a fascinating hint in this direction in act 4, when Laertes storms into the castle accompanied by an insurrectionary mob. Claudius tells Gertrude not to worry: "there's such divinity doth hedge a king," he reassures her, "that treason can but peep to what it would."[39] Claudius is here alluding to the "divine right of kings," which is to say the idea that kings and queens are chosen by God. Since kings and queens are put on their thrones by God, Claudius is saying, they are also protected by God; so we really don't have to worry about a pesky little revolution.

Now this is a pretty standard thing for someone to claim in the twelfth century (when the play is set) or even in the early seventeenth century (when it was first performed). But it's a wildly strange thing for *Claudius* to be saying. He of all people—the guy who murdered Hamlet Senior—should know that God does not protect kings. He of all people should know that treason can be exceedingly effective.[40]

39. 4.5.123–24.
40. In Shakespeare's time, some considered regicide compatible with the "divine right of kings," on condition that the ruler be despotic. Many, however, did not sanction rebellion even

Claudius telling Gertrude "don't worry, God protects kings" is a bit like Don Corleone telling his henchmen "don't worry, God protects mobsters. Now go kill the Tattaglias."

Kings and queens are not protected by God, because kings and queens are not chosen by God. There is no natural, necessary, preordained relation between monarch and country, any more than there is between lover and beloved. In the political domain as in the romantic, there are no natural joints to the world. Who ends up ruling a country comes down to a pinch of human agency and a heaping spoonful of chance.

"A DIVINITY THAT SHAPES OUR ENDS"

I think I know what you're going to say at this point. (If I'm wrong, and you don't care about objections, please feel free to skip to the "Reasons Must Come from Within" section; I won't be offended. On the other hand, you'll miss some fun stuff about sparrows and Satanists.)

Here's what I think you're going to say: I'm forgetting about Providence. How can I pretend that God is not operating in the world of *Hamlet* when Providence is so clearly all around us? Doesn't H. D. Kitto say "we are made to feel that Providence is working in the events"? Doesn't Francis Fergusson agree that "we are returned, with the healthy rhythms of young Fortinbras, to the wider world of the order of nature, with the possibility . . . of divine sanction"? And doesn't David L. Edwards find that "'Providence' has established justice through this apparently total confusion"?[41]

---

then. And in any case there is no evidence within *Hamlet* to suggest that Claudius's victim was a tyrant.

41. H. D. F. Kitto, *Form and Meaning in Drama: A Study of Six Greek Plays and of Hamlet* (London: Methuen, 1956), 527; Fergusson, *Idea of a Theater*, 137–38; David L. Edwards,

Prominent scholars such as these are, of course, taking their lead from Hamlet himself, who appears to have undergone some kind of conversion between acts 4 and 5. "There's a divinity that shapes our ends," he tells Horatio, "rough-hew them how we will"; "there is special providence," he adds, "in the fall of a sparrow."[42] Specifically, when it comes to having his father's signet ring in his purse while on the boat, "even in that was heaven ordinant."[43]

But hang on—really? *Was* heaven ordinant? *Is* there a divinity shaping Hamlet's ends? Did Providence prompt Hamlet to rummage through Rosencrantz and Guildenstern's luggage late one night? Did God put Dad's signet ring in his purse? Not on your life.

> I must to England—you know that . . . .
> There's letters sealed and my two schoolfellows—
> Whom I will trust as I will adders fanged—
> They bear the mandate, they must sweep my way
> And marshal me to knavery. Let it work.
> For 'tis the sport to have the enginer
> Hoist with his own petard, and't shall go hard
> But I will delve one yard below their mines
> And blow them at the moon.[44]

This is Hamlet speaking to Gertrude in act 3, scene 4. Two whole acts earlier than his conversation with Horatio, then, Hamlet is already telling his mother that he knows Rosencrantz and Guildenstern are up to no good; that he knows they have a deadly letter; and that

Poets and God: Chaucer, Shakespeare, Herbert, Milton, Wordsworth, Coleridge, Blake (London: Darton, Longman, & Todd, 2005), 74.

42. 5.2.10–11, 197–98. This is an allusion to the Gospel of Matthew (10:29).
43. 5.2.48.
44. 3.4.198, 200–207.

he has every intention of destroying them by means of their own weapons. Heaven? Providence? Divinity? Come on. God did not do this: Hamlet did.[45] *He* stashed the ring in his purse (if you want to unseal an envelope, you'd best carry something to reseal it with); *he* got himself up at night to find the letter, which he already knew was there; *he* had Rosencrantz and Guildenstern killed, as he had planned to all along. There is no Providence at work in this play; there is a battle between chance and human agency, and there is nothing else.

HAMLET AND HORATIO, PROVIDENCE-DENIERS

At the end of the play, Fortinbras enters to find a huge pile of dead bodies, and naturally enough asks what on earth he's missed. Horatio offers to fill him in. Now Horatio is a Stoic,[46] and Stoics are big believers in Providence; they think that everything happens for a cosmic reason, and that we should be happy even if our dog dies, an idiot becomes emperor, or our legs fall off. Thus when Marcellus says "something is rotten in the state of Denmark," Horatio immediately responds "Heaven will direct it"; and when Hamlet says "There's a

---

45. Compare to some extent Maynard Mack, "The World of Hamlet," in *Hamlet," Shakespeare, Hamlet: A Casebook*, ed. John D. Jump (Nashville: Aurora Publishers, 1970), 86–107, p. 105.

46. For Horatio as Stoic, see for example D. G. James, "Moral and Metaphysical Uncertainty in Hamlet," in *Shakespeare, Hamlet: A Casebook*, ed. John D. Jump (Nashville: Aurora Publishers, 1970), 78–85, p. 82; Charles and Michelle Martindale, *Shakespeare and the Uses of Antiquity: An Introductory Essay* (London: Routledge, 2005), 166. Horatio describes himself as "more an antique Roman than a Dane" (5.2.325), and elsewhere Hamlet admiringly describes him as "A man that Fortune's buffets and rewards / Hast ta'en with equal thanks." "Blest are those," he continues, "Whose blood and judgement are so well co-meddled / That they are not a pipe for Fortune's finger / To sound what stop she please. Give me that man / That is not passion's slave and I will wear him / In my heart's core—ay, in my heart of heart— / As I do thee" (3.2.62–70).

divinity that shapes our ends," Horatio says (in so many words) "amen, brother."[47] So, does Horatio begin his speech to Fortinbras by saying "let me tell you an amazing story about God's Providence working through human beings"? Not in the slightest. Instead he says his story will be full

> Of carnal, bloody and unnatural acts,
> Of accidental judgments, casual slaughters,
> Of deaths put on by cunning, and for no cause,
> And in this upshot purposes mistook
> Fallen on th'inventors' heads.[48]

Horatio then goes on to say they should hurry up with the coronation, in case yet more bad stuff goes down:

> let this same be presently performed,
> . . . lest more mischance
> On plots and errors happen.[49]

Mischance? Errors? Accidents? These are not the words of a believer in Providence. Fascinatingly, *Horatio has changed his mind*. What he has seen, especially in the last five minutes or so, has disabused him of the idea that there is a Divine Plan working for the ultimate good of human beings, making sure that the good prevail and the bad are punished.[50]

Nor do I think Hamlet would accuse Horatio of getting the story wrong, if he were to show up at this point as a second ghost. "In this

---

47. 1.4.90–91; 5.2.11.

48. 5.2.365–69.

49. 5.2.377–79.

50. *Pace* Andrew Hui, who says accidents are consistent with Providence as long as one is a Neostoic like Justus Lipsius ("Horatio's Philosophy in Hamlet," *Renaissance Drama* 41.1–2 [2013]: 151–171, pp. 164–66).

harsh world draw thy breath in pain," he has just begged Horatio, "to tell my story."[51] He has not said "in this great world draw thy breath in bliss, / To tell my story of how everything worked out for the best in the end / Thanks to, you know, that Divine Providence we talked about earlier." At least in act 5, scene 2, Hamlet does not appear to be a believer in the Grand Cosmic Plan.

So what about the fall of a sparrow, heaven being ordinant, and all that stuff? Well, yes, Hamlet does say that. But then, Hamlet says all kinds of things. In the very same scene, Hamlet tells Laertes that he, Laertes, will beat him at fencing. ("I'll be your foil, Laertes. In mine ignorance / Your skill shall, like a star i'th' darkest night / Stick fiery off indeed.") He then says the same thing to Claudius: "Your grace has laid the odds o' th' weaker side." That is all very gallant, but consider this: *Hamlet has just told Horatio exactly the opposite.* "Since he [Laertes] went into France," he says, "I have been in continual practice. I shall win at the odds."[52]

Hamlet cannot possibly believe that he is going to win *and* that he is going to lose. Maybe he is telling Laertes what Laertes wants to hear, to put him off his guard; or maybe Hamlet is telling Horatio what Horatio wants to hear, to set his mind at rest. Either way, Hamlet is using a little bit of rhetoric. Why not think this applies to the Providence chatter too? Hamlet knows full well that he deliberately brought the signet ring with him on the boat; surely he cannot actually imagine it was an act of God. There is no reason for us to assume he is giving his honest opinion. When Hamlet says he'll lose the bout, he is telling Laertes what Laertes wants to hear; when he deploys a string of fifty-dollar words to the puffed-up Osric, he is telling Osric what Osric wants to hear.[53] And when he says the world is ruled by

51. 5.2.332–33.
52. 5.2.232–34, 238, 189.
53. For the string of fifty-dollar words, see 5.2.98–105.

Providence, he may well be telling Horatio, the Stoic, what Horatio wants to hear.

I don't think Hamlet ever really believes in Providence. As for Horatio, we saw a moment ago that he learns to let go of the idea. And surely they are both right. The play we have actually seen is Horatio's version—the "casual slaughters" version—not the one told by all those starry-eyed scholars. Why does Polonius die? Because he's in the wrong place at the wrong time. Why does Fortinbras succeed? Because he's in the right place at the right time. Why do Rosencrantz and Guildenstern die? Because they are caught in the crossfire.[54] Why does Gertrude die? Because she drinks from the wrong cup. Why does Laertes die? Because the foils get swapped in the confusion. Why does Claudius die? Because the poison works too slowly on Hamlet. (Note to the vengeful: when buying poison, spend the extra dollar for the fast-acting kind.) Above all, why does Hamlet die? If it's Providence that kept him alive on the boat, where is Providence now?

DESPERATE DEFENSES OF
THE PROVIDENCE VIEW

Over the years I've made these arguments to a number of people, and it's been surprising to me how many still want to make a case for Providence being operative in *Hamlet*. For some of them, it's sufficient that the usurper meets a sticky end. But taking out the usurper is only half of the job; the other half is putting a rightful

---

54. Hamlet says so himself: "'Tis dangerous when the baser nature comes / Between the pass and fell incensed points / Of mighty opposites" (5.2.59–61). As pawns in the battle between Hamlet and Claudius, they arguably don't deserve what happens to them. And even if *they* merit death, surely Gertrude doesn't (despite her bad taste in men) and neither does Polonius (despite his idiocy and intrusiveness).

ruler in his place. And that's not what happens here. Fortinbras is a Norwegian, which means that the Danish kingdom has fallen to one of its enemies—hardly what Hamlet Senior had in mind when calling for action. What's more, Fortinbras is a bit of a lunk, compared to Hamlet. True to his name, he is a strong commander, but he is hardly the smart, thoughtful, charismatic leader Hamlet would have been. The throne of Denmark has fallen to Norwegian GI Joe; Providence apparently fell asleep halfway through the planning meeting.

Other fans of the Providence theory prefer the Mysterious Ways defense. "Yes," they'll say, "Hamlet is dead and Fortinbras the Norwegian has seized the throne. Ophelia is drowned. And Gertrude is poisoned. But who knows: maybe all these calamities are going to lead to something amazing later on. The Lord moves in mysterious ways, in *Hamlet* as in real life." Well, maybe. But using that logic, I can prove that the entire plot—including the apparently happy moments—was masterminded by *Satan*, who presumably moves in equally mysterious ways. Why does Ophelia die? Because the Devil is in control, of course. Why does Hamlet live? Because the Devil wants as many violent deaths as possible. If Hamlet were to die too soon, Laertes and Gertrude would probably live to a ripe old age and expire in their sleep—and that would be no fun at all. So why not think that Hamlet's survival is the work of the Devil? Who is to say? The same arguments that can be used to show that bad events turn out for the best can also be used to show that good events turn out for the worst. At the end of the day, nothing we see in the play proves that there's a providential design (whether divine or satanic) behind the massive heap of bodies.

THE UNDISCOVERED COUNTRY

The theodicy-believer is now left with only one card to play: the afterlife card. Doesn't the Ghost return from purgatory? If there's a purgatory, mustn't there be a hell and a heaven (that place Hamlet worries he'll send Claudius to if he kills him at prayer)? And if so, doesn't that mean that God is, after all, making sure the wicked are punished and the virtuous rewarded?

Well, yes, God is indeed doing that; but only in the afterlife. Providence means God acting *in the world* and *for our good* and *in a way we can understand*. It doesn't mean God doing whatever he wants and calling it good; it doesn't mean God intervening at random in the world; and it doesn't mean God waiting until the afterlife to take action. It means God acting now, here, in the realm of the living.[55] Surely God isn't doing that when he lets Ophelia sink to her watery grave, Gertrude drink the poisoned cup, and Fortinbras ascend the throne. (Gertrude's recent choices may have been in poor taste, but they hardly warrant death.) Indeed, one might wonder why God would *bother* doing any of that, given that he's got the whole afterlife in which to settle accounts. The Ghost tells Hamlet to leave Gertrude to heaven; why not leave *everyone* to heaven, Claudius included?

No, this is not a play in which a benevolent God reaches down into the human realm to make sure that everything works out for the best in the end. There's a word for plays like that: comedies. *Hamlet*, by contrast, has the word "tragedy" right in the title. And whatever else the word "tragedy" means, it does not mean God making sure good people get rewarded and bad people get punished. (That's poetic justice, not tragedy.) The very existence of tragedy depends on

---

55. A note for pedants: I know that the term "Providence" has been used in all kinds of different ways. But when Claudius says "there's such divinity doth hedge a king," he means God protects us *now*, not in the afterlife. When Hamlet says "even in that was heaven ordinant," he means heaven was ordinant *now*, not in the afterlife. And again: when Claudius talks of God protecting kings, he is referring to God doing something that is good for us, in ordinary human terms. When Hamlet talks of heaven saving his life on the boat, he is referring to heaven doing something that is good for us, in ordinary human terms. There's no need for fancy footwork here: when Hamlet and Claudius and Horatio paint a portrait of divine Providence, they mean God operating *in the world* and *for our good*, where this means *good by everyday human standards*. They're wrong.

a belief that bad things happen to good people—which is to say, on a belief that Providence does not operate in the world of the living.

So let's not get confused: in *Hamlet*, God is not intervening in the lives of mortals. The only two forces at work are human agency and blind luck. Hamlet would *love* there to be a divinity shaping our ends, but there isn't one; instead, as Horatio comes to realize, the world is full of "mischance" and "errors," of "accidental judgments and casual slaughters." The world is a "harsh" place, one where bad things happen to good people, like Hamlet, and where good things happen to mediocre people, like Fortinbras. Human agents can work against that randomness, to try to control it; but God appears to be entirely out of the picture.

REASONS MUST COME FROM WITHIN

That, then, is what Hamlet has come to understand: the earth is a giant swarming chaos, marginally tamed in a few places by human decision-making. And so Hamlet's position, after hearing the Ghost's injunction to dispose of Claudius, is not as straightforward as it may initially appear. It's easy to imagine that Hamlet's task is blindingly obvious: do the thing, stab the king. It's easy to be puzzled—maybe even a little impatient—at the fact that Hamlet doesn't start stabbing right away. But his hesitation really shouldn't be so baffling. He cannot feel like an agent of Providence, because he has no evidence that God intervenes in the human realm. He cannot feel like a dutiful follower of tradition, because his tradition is internally contradictory. And he cannot feel like a restorer of order, since there was never any order to begin with. It's not open to Hamlet to inspect the state of the universe, notice a "disturbance in the Force," and automatically feel compelled to fix it. Maybe there's no way that things absolutely need to be. Maybe there are no "joints" to experience.

TO THINE OWN SELVES BE TRUE-ISH

No wonder Hamlet hesitates. No wonder he *keeps* hesitating, even after he is sure that the Ghost is telling the truth.[56] It's simply not enough for him to know that his murdered father calls for revenge; Hamlet needs to find his *own* reason for doing it. He needs to make sure that it is what *he* wants, not just what the Ghost wants. If you can't rely on tradition or divine sanction, you are going to have to get your reasons from within.

HAMLET'S MANY SELVES

We are back, finally, to the hopelessly vague advice of prating Polonius. Hamlet, it turns out, desperately *needs* to be true to himself; not so that he "cannot be false to any man" (ridiculous),[57] and not just for his own satisfaction, but because it is the only way to move forward. It's the only way he can make decisions about vitally important questions, such as whether or not to take revenge on Claudius. It's the only kind of grounding he can give to his actions, now that Providence and tradition have proven themselves ineffectual resources. It's the only guarantee that he won't keep doing things

56. A note for pedants: yes, Hamlet does delay; we know this because he beats himself up about it. In act 2, Hamlet calls himself a coward, explaining that he must be "pigeon-livered . . . or ere this / I should ha' fatted all the region kites / With this slave's offal" (2.2.512–15). In act 3, when the Ghost shows up in Gertrude's room, Hamlet asks him "Do you not come your tardy son to chide . . . ?" (3.4.102). (Yes, says the Ghost: "this visitation / is but to whet thy almost blunted purpose," 3.4.106–7.) In act 4, after Hamlet has had a chat with Fortinbras's captain, he feels renewed pangs of remorse. "How all occasions do inform against me / And spur my dull revenge!" he exclaims. "I do not know," he continues, "Why yet I live to say, 'This thing's to do,' / Sith I have cause, and will, and strength, and means / To do't" (4.4.31–32, 42–45). Uncertainty about the murder of Hamlet Senior isn't a factor in any of these speeches, especially not the last two, which come after the moment when Hamlet says he'll "take the Ghost's word for a thousand pound" (3.2.278–79).

  Of course, Hamlet isn't completely idle during this time, and he even manages to kill Polonius, taking him (so he claims) for Claudius. And the refusal to kill Claudius at prayer (3.3.76–86) is probably not a case of delay. But Hamlet must have had other opportunities to do the deed, otherwise he wouldn't be feeling so guilty about it.

57. As Polonius sees it, honesty is an inevitable consequence of authenticity: "This above all, to thine own self be true, / And it must follow, as the night the day, / Thou canst not then be

he regrets—reckless, impulsive quasi-actions like the stabbing of Polonius—and will, instead, do things he can be proud of.

But, to say it again, Hamlet has multiple selves to which he could be true. He is a mourner, an avenger, a lover, a son, a scholar, a poet. And no single one of these facets *defines* him. He isn't *just* a mourner. He isn't *just* a poet. And crucially, he cannot give up everything else and become an avenger, in spite of what he tells the Ghost in act 1:

> Remember thee?
> Yea, from the table of my memory
> I'll wipe away all trivial fond records . . .
> And thy commandment all alone shall live
> Within the book and volume of my brain . . .[58]

Hamlet does no such thing, of course—and that is exactly as it should be. To forget everything else and become pure Avenger would be an enormous, brutal reduction. Each of his various roles captures a genuine part of who he really is; none of them, however, can lay claim to constituting the whole truth of his being, an essence next to which the others are mere sideshows. Hamlet has many, many selves to which to be true. *Pace* Polonius, he has a major problem on his hands.

LIVING LIKE AN ACTOR

The predicament is clearly a very bad one, but there is an ingenious solution on offer, one that allows Hamlet to move forward in the brief

---

false to any man" (1.3.77–79). But is that really true? Setting aside the ironic fact that Polonius himself is a bit of a fibber (3.2.367–73), and that he tells his own son in the very same speech (!) not to reveal his true thoughts to anybody (1.3.58), let's consider the case of a diplomatic soul, a compulsive liar, or a natural-born Machiavellian schemer (like Claudius, perhaps). For people such as these, being true to themselves is perfectly compatible with being false to anyone else they please. Indeed it may at times *require* them to lie. "As the night the day?" Not so much.
58. 1.5.97–103.

time he is allotted. That solution is, in a nutshell, to *live like an actor.* It is to take what actors do on stage and import it into your everyday life. It is, in a way, to *play at being yourself.*[59]

Think about what many actors do (the "method" ones, at least). When they want to convince us that they're feeling sad, they draw on a genuine source of sadness in their own heart. (Who, after all, has never known adversity?) They magnify it, intensify it, amplify it, until they are melancholy through and through. Maybe sadness is only 5% of what they are feeling right now, but they take that 5% and inflate it to 100%.

Now think about your own life. You're someone's son or daughter; you are, perhaps, someone else's parent; you're someone's employee (or student), maybe someone's boss (or teacher); you're someone else's best friend, someone else's life partner, someone else's squash buddy . . . At any given moment, you are mainly called upon to be just one of these things. At work, you're called upon to be the employee; at home, the child or parent; at squash, the fearsome but gracious opponent. And you have a choice. You can bring all of yourself to each moment, thinking about your kids while reaching for the drop shot, practicing your backhand while listening to Jimmy talk about his day at school, and worrying about emails while kissing your beloved; or you can attend fully to what's in front of you, relegating everything else to the deep background. While helping with homework you can be *just* the parent. While hitting a cross-court volley you can be *just* the squash buddy. While writing an essay you can be *just* the student.

---

59. Self-fashioning was of course a topic of considerable interest in the Renaissance: think of Montaigne ("I have no more made my book than my book has made me"), Erasmus ("homines non nascuntur sed finguntur"), Pico della Mirandola, and so on. Stephen Greenblatt's examples are More, Tyndale, Wyatt, Spenser, Marlowe, and Shakespeare; see *Renaissance Self-Fashioning from More to Shakespeare* (Chicago: University of Chicago Press, 1980).

JOSHUA LANDY

That's what it means to live like an actor: it means taking your many parts and giving each its day in the sun. It means identifying completely with one aspect of yourself at any given time. For as long as the moment lasts, you take that 5% and inflate it to 100%, living it to the full, giving it your undivided concern. You *pretend* that it defines you; you act *as if* it defines you; you *make believe* that it defines you.

Here are some things this kind of life is *not*. It is not, first of all, a matter of inventing a persona for the benefit of other people; we're talking here about the part that "passes show."[60] It is not, second, a matter of picking a single aspect and calling it "the real you." (Hamlet tries that with The Avenger, remember, and it doesn't work.) It is not, third, a matter of combining all the parts into a unified super-self. (It's not at all clear, for example, how Lover and Avenger and Scholar could go together.) And it is certainly not a matter, lastly, of inventing yourself out of nothing: *each of those roles is a genuine part of you*, even if none of them exhausts who you are. (To say "I'm a scholar" is not a *lie*; it's just a *simplification*.) This may be acting, but it's not *performance*. Instead, it is a matter of taking the many things you already are and giving each of them a proper run-out when its moment comes around.

WHAT HAMLET LEARNS FROM THE PLAYERS

This, it seems to me, is what Hamlet learns from the actors when they come to town. Hamlet, you'll recall, is fascinated by their ability to get all worked up over a long-gone and probably legendary figure.

60. 1.2.85. My argument here has nothing, for example, to do with Erving Goffman's fascinating discussion of performance in *The Presentation of Self in Everyday Life* (New York: Anchor Press, 1959). Goffman is talking about (intended) effects on an audience; I am talking about effects on one's own psyche.

("For nothing— / For Hecuba!").[61] Somehow the man playing Hecuba has managed to "force his soul . . . to his own conceit"[62]— to convince himself, in other words, that he actually is the Trojan queen, complete with her sorrows and fears. And if the actor can do that, Hamlet reasons, then surely he can convince himself that he is Hamlet. All he needs to do is to borrow the technique.

Sure enough, what we see in act 5 is Hamlet playing at being himself.[63] In the graveyard scene, he inflates his love for Ophelia into something truly gargantuan: "Forty thousand brothers / Could not with all their quantity of love / Make up my sum."[64] (He really *does* have strong feelings for Ophelia—he is not lying—but he is inhabiting that affection to the greatest degree possible, with the full commitment of his entire being.) With Horatio he is pure friendship, even to the point, as we saw above, of pretending that his masterful jujitsu with Rosencrantz and Guildenstern was all a stroke of luck sent from Heaven during a fortuitously sleepless night on shipboard.[65] With Osric, he is all courtier. And with Claudius, at last, he is pure revenge.

The death of Claudius is an extraordinary moment, one whose weirdness has not, I think, been fully appreciated. Yes, revenge heroes always kill the bad guy. But they don't usually do it *twice*. And yet that's exactly what Hamlet does: after stabbing Claudius with the poisoned rapier, he turns around and forces him to drink from the poisoned cup. Why do both? Why not let the wound do its work, as it

---

61. 1.5.97–103.
62. 2.2.488.
63. For this idea, compare Eric R. Boyer, "*Hamlet* and Absurd Freedom: *The Myth of Sisyphus* as Commentary on Shakespeare's Creation," *Ball State University Forum* 16.3 (1975): 54–66, pp. 62–63 and, to some extent, L. C. Knights, *Some Shakespearean Themes: An Approach to Hamlet* (Stanford, CA: Stanford University Press, 1966), 231. Boyer's essay is inspired by Albert Camus's *Myth of Sisyphus*, and mine is too, to some extent; I am thinking in particular of the section on "Don Juanism" (*Le mythe de Sisyphe* [Paris: Gallimard, 1942], 99–107).
64. 5.1.258–60.
65. Note that he is being true to himself (as good friend) precisely by being "false" to Horatio; sorry, Polonius.

just did on Laertes? On Laertes it took a mere thirty lines.[66] Is Hamlet really in that much of a hurry?

No. Hamlet needs to give Claudius the cup because he killed him the wrong way the first time. When he ran at Claudius with the rapier, he was moving impulsively (just as he had been earlier, when Polonius stirred behind the arras); he was reacting, not acting; he was simply getting his own back for the plot against his life. And his one-line avenger speech—"The point envenomed too? Then venom to thy work!"[67]—was a serious disappointment, a crashing anticlimax. Four and half acts of waiting for him to stand triumphantly over Claudius's corpse, and then *this*? It is hardly "you killed my father, prepare to die."

Everything changes, however, when Hamlet forces the wine down Claudius's throat. His gloating, for one thing, is vastly improved: "Here, thou incestuous, murd'rous, damnèd Dane, / Drink off this potion." (Not bad.) And this is a sign that Hamlet is remembering why he is *supposed* to be killing Claudius. Claudius is "murd'rous" not just because he has plotted against Hamlet Junior but also because he plotted against Hamlet *Senior*, going on, "incestuously," to seduce and marry the latter's widow. Hamlet is picking up from where he left off in the chapel, when his aim was to avenge his father. As though regretting his rush of blood, Hamlet is making up for it by killing Claudius a second time: no longer for himself but for his father and mother; no longer absent-mindedly but with full premeditation; no longer as an impulse but now as an *action*.

HOW HAMLET USES THE THEATER

How did Hamlet get to this point? How did he get from observing the actors to turning in such a bravura performance of his own? The

66. 5.2.285–315.
67. 5.2.206.

bridge, I think, is *The Murder of Gonzago*, that same play with which, as we saw, he aimed to catch the conscience of both King and Queen.

In *The Murder of Gonzago*, one man (Lucianus) kills another (Gonzago) by pouring poison into his ear. This, of course, is supposed to remind Claudius of his own dastardly crime: "I'll have these players / Play something like the murder of my father / Before mine uncle"; "If his occulted guilt / Do not itself unkennel in one speech / It is a damned ghost that we have seen."[68] But there's one enormous difference between the two scenarios. Whereas Claudius is the brother of the man he kills, Lucianus is the nephew. Lucianus is to Gonzago, that is, as Hamlet is to Claudius.

Why, then, does *The Murder of Gonzago* suit Hamlet's purposes so well? It's not just because of the ear-poison. And it's not just because of the remarriage subplot that we talked about earlier. It's also because the killer looks a bit like Hamlet. So the play-within-the-play is more than a repetition of a past act of violence; it is also a preview of (and practice for) a *future* act of violence. It's a way for Hamlet to imagine what it will be like to take up arms against his uncle. It's a way for him to act out the murder in his imagination.[69]

Kenneth Branagh's film version captures this beautifully. Not content to remain within the audience and observe his mother (with Horatio keeping an eye on Claudius), Hamlet dashes onstage and stands right next to the actor playing Lucianus, yelling "the croaking raven doth bellow for revenge"[70] (fig. 6.1). (Notice, incidentally, how weird this line is: Lucianus is a murderer, not an avenger! Unless, of course, Lucianus is a figure for Hamlet . . .) Then, when Lucianus

---

68. 2.2.529–31; 3.2.76–78.

69. In *The Spanish Tragedy*, too, the protagonist (Hieronimo) writes a play and gives himself the role of the killer. But here it is so that he can actually take his revenge: Hieronimo makes sure that the swords used on stage are real. Hamlet, by contrast, uses the play in order to prepare himself, psychologically, for the task ahead.

70. 3.2.247.

Fig. 6.1 Hamlet and "Lucianus"

Source: Hamlet, directed by Kenneth Branagh (1996; Burbank, CA: Warner Home Video, 2007), DVD.

Fig. 6.2 Hamlet *as* Lucianus

kneels, Hamlet kneels along with him; and finally Hamlet goes so far as to take the vial of poison in his own hand, holding it menacingly beside the head of sleeping Gonzago (fig. 6.2).

What we are seeing here is the third and most important function of the play-within-the-play. It's not just a trap for the conscience of the King (thanks to all the talk of ear-poison); it's not just a trap for the conscience of the Queen (thanks to all the talk of remarriage); it's also a model for the prince, allowing him to imagine his way into the skin of a full-blown avenger. Hamlet sees himself as Lucianus, and indeed as the actor playing Lucianus. He is learning, by example, how to be the actor—the honest but amplifying actor—of his own multifarious selves.

WHAT REALLY CHANGES IN *HAMLET*

So, is there a transformation in *Hamlet*? Yes. But it's not the one we might imagine. It's not that Hamlet has found a way to act; it's that he's found a way to act in the right manner. (He is already perfectly capable of killing as early as act 3—but impulsively, not deliberately.)[71] It's not that Hamlet has found Providence; it's that he's found a way to live without it. And above all, it's not that Hamlet has found himself; it's that he's found a way to be true to his various selves.

Hamlet has learned how to live like an actor, taking the 5% and inflating it to 100%, letting each component have its day in the sun. That's how he's able to play the role of the lover, which he is in part but not entirely; that's how he's able to play the role of the friend, which he is in part but not entirely; and that's how he's able to play the role of the avenger, which he is in part but not entirely. When he kills Claudius for the second time, he is absorbedly inhabiting that last position, in the clear awareness that it does not completely define him. To Polonius's glib "to thine own self be true," I like to think of Hamlet countering "to thine own *selves* be true-*ish*."

---

71. Up to this point, Hamlet has only been able (a) to think without acting (as, say, in the Dull Revenge speech) or (b) to act without thinking (as when he kills Polonius). Authentic action requires both. Hamlet's problem is not that he thinks too much, and his solution is not to stop thinking: that's a recipe for a whole bunch of additional dead bodies. (It's worth remembering that Hamlet comes to regret the murder of Polonius; impulsive action often leads to remorse.) The proper solution is to connect actions up to intentions.

HOW *WE* SHOULD USE THE THEATER

Being the actor of your life, living with full commitment to whatever part of yourself you are being at any given moment, inflating the 5% to 100%—that's a pretty good way to live with intensity. It's a pretty good way to be everything you are. And it's a pretty good way to be true to yourself (or rather, to your selves). Although the terms "acting" and "performance" may suggest deceit and invention, let's not be confused: these selves really are part of you. You really are the parent, the child, the coworker, and the squash buddy.

It is not, however, a solution to all the problems of life. It won't protect you from failure, from sickness, from death. It won't protect you from fiendish plots hatched against you; for that you need a bit of prudence, a few friends, and a whole lot of luck. Hamlet, of course, isn't so fortunate: he inhabits his roles for a heartbreakingly short time, and the play remains a tragedy. We should not be misled by this into thinking that he must be getting it wrong, since Shakespeare would have let him live longer if he had been getting it right. (Great literature doesn't work that way.) But we should be aware that cultivating our many selves is not sufficient to guarantee us a long life safe from danger.

It is also not sufficient to guarantee us a *moral* life. Perhaps many of the parts of your personality are altruistic: you are the *caring* parent, the *dutiful* child, the *inspiring* boss. (For most of us there's a moral self in there, and that self too needs her day in the sun.) But some parts are no doubt morally neutral, and one or two may be positively antisocial. In that case, again, you will need something else beyond a desire to live your components out to the full.

Finally, it won't help you choose which self to bring online in cases where it's not obvious. It won't help you make a hierarchy out of the selves (should your status as CEO trump your status as parent? should you skip your grandchild's wedding to attend your weekly squash game?). It won't help you organize the various components into a single mass; you may at times feel fractured, scattered, at odds with yourself.

But who knows: perhaps this fascinating option could still find its place within a well-lived life. And if it is, then our time spent with *Hamlet* is as worthwhile as Hamlet's time with *The Murder of Gonzago*. What we learn from the play is not some two-bit piece of folk wisdom from a doddering fool but a technique, a practice, a method.[72]

Armed with our understanding of what life might require of us, we too can examine the activity of the performers, wonder what it would take to do the things they do, imagine ourselves imbuing our day-to-day experience with that special state of mind. All that talk about the importance of theater; all that discussion of the miracle of imagination; all those indications that Hamlet is using dramatic performance as a formal model for self-fashioning—everything invites us to engage with the play before us in a similar spirit, learning not its "lessons" but its techniques. Maybe we won't live longer, but we surely will live more.

ACKNOWLEDGMENTS

It has been my good fortune to lecture on *Hamlet* on many occasions. At different times, I have team-taught the play with Lanier Anderson, Andrea Nightingale, Rush Rehm, and Ken Taylor; each offered feedback on my lecture as well as brilliant ideas of their own, and it was a pleasure and an honor to work with them. The students, too, have

---

72. For the difference between knowledge and know-how, see Gilbert Ryle, "Knowing How and Knowing That," in *Collected Papers 1929–1968* (New York: Barnes and Noble, 1971), 2:212–25. For a book-length elaboration of the idea that some literary works are designed to transmit techniques, rather than to deliver lessons, see my *How to Do Things with Fictions* (New York: Oxford University Press, 2012).

been phenomenal. (Those in the Structured Liberal Education program, in particular, are off all possible charts.) And I have learned a tremendous amount, about *Hamlet* and countless other things, from the SLE team: Michael Bogucki, Beth Coggeshall, Lisa Hicks, Peter Mann, Jeremy Sabol, and Greg Watkins. The same is true for Noël Carroll, Jonathan Dancy, Cynthia Freeland, Kathleen Higgins, Andrew Huddleston, Hans Kamp, Alexander Nehamas, Galen Strawson, and Paul Woodruff, who provided gracious and insightful commentary after a lively conference session at UT Austin in February 2016. My gratitude to everyone is greater than I can express here.

WORKS CITED

Boyer, Eric R. 1975. "*Hamlet* and Absurd Freedom: *The Myth of Sisyphus* as Commentary on Shakespeare's Creation." *Ball State University Forum* 16.3: 54–66.

Branagh, Kenneth, dir. 1996. *Hamlet*. Warner Brothers.

Camus, Albert. 1942. *Le mythe de Sisyphe*. Paris: Gallimard.

Edwards, David L. 2005. *Poets and God: Chaucer, Shakespeare, Herbert, Milton, Wordsworth, Coleridge, Blake*. London: Darton, Longman, & Todd.

Fergusson, Francis. 1949. *The Idea of a Theater: A Study of Ten Plays*. Princeton, NJ: Princeton University Press.

Goffman, Erving. 1959. *The Presentation of Self in Everyday Life*. New York: Anchor Press.

Greenblatt, Stephen. 1980. *Renaissance Self-Fashioning from More to Shakespeare*. Chicago: University of Chicago Press.

Hui, Andrew. 2013. "Horatio's Philosophy in Hamlet," *Renaissance Drama* 41.1–2: 151–71.

James, D. G. 1970. "Moral and Metaphysical Uncertainty in *Hamlet*." *Shakespeare, "Hamlet": A Casebook*. Ed. John D. Jump. Nashville: Aurora Publishers. 78–85.

Kitto, H. D. F. 1956. *Form and Meaning in Drama: A Study of Six Greek Plays and of "Hamlet"*. London: Methuen.

Knight, G. Wilson. 1990. "The Embassy of Death: An Essay on *Hamlet*." *Hamlet (Bloom's Major Literary Characters)*. New York: Chelsea House. 80–94.

Knights, L. C. 1966. *Some Shakespearean Themes: An Approach to Hamlet*. Stanford, CA: Stanford University Press.

Landy, Joshua. 2012. *How to Do Things with Fictions*. New York: Oxford University Press.

Levin, Harry. 1970. "The Antic Disposition." *Shakespeare, Hamlet: A Casebook*. Ed. John D. Jump. Nashville: Aurora Publishers. 122–36.

Mack, Maynard. 1970. "The World of Hamlet." *Shakespeare, Hamlet: A Casebook*. Ed. John D. Jump. Nashville: Aurora Publishers. 86–107.

Martindale, Charles, and Michelle Martindale. 2005. *Shakespeare and the Uses of Antiquity: An Introductory Essay*. London: Routledge.

Ryle, Gilbert. 1971. "Knowing How and Knowing That." *Collected Papers, 1929–1968*. New York: Barnes and Noble.

Trilling, Lionel. 1972. *Sincerity and Authenticity*. Cambridge: Harvard University Press.

Wilson, John Dover. 1951. *What Happens in Hamlet?* Cambridge: Cambridge University Press.

Chapter 7

"Unpacking the Heart"

Why It Is Impossible to Say "I Love You"
in Hamlet's Elsinore

DAVID SCHALKWYK

That Shakespeare's *Hamlet* represents the forging of a new subjectivity of "inwardness" fully characteristic of a postfeudal, and therefore a "modern," bourgeois sense of the self, has long been argued. But it has also been challenged. The locus classicus of the argument is Francis Barker's 1984 monograph, *The Tremulous Private Body*.[1] Versions of this historicist view, that proto-Cartesian modern subjectivity focused on an authentic and ultimately inexpressible interiority, are evident in Catherine Belsey's *The Subject of Tragedy* (1985), Jonathan Dollimore's *Radical Tragedy* (1984), and Stephen Greenblatt's New Historicist books, *Renaissance Self-Fashioning* (1980) and *Shakespearean Negotiations* (1988).[2]

---

1. Francis Barker, *The Tremulous Private Body: Essays on Subjection* (Ann Arbor: University of Michigan Press, 1995). The 1984 edition was published by Methuen, London.
2. Catherine Belsey, *The Subject of Tragedy: Identity and Difference in Renaissance Drama* (London: Routledge Kegan & Paul, 1985); Jonathan Dollimore, *Radical Tragedy: Religion, Ideology and Power in the Drama of Shakespeare and His Contemporaries* (Durham, NC: Duke University Press, 2004); Stephen Greenblatt, *Renaissance Self-Fashioning: From*

These interventions are clustered within a signal period of literary critical history and theory: they all appeared in the 1980s, when a new concern with theory and politics in early modern studies manifested itself in a bifurcated historicism. The one, predominant in the United States and influenced by Michel Foucault, replaced causal explanation with a looser, analogical method that emphasized the interpenetration of what was formerly regarded as "work" and "background" and, more pressingly, sought to use arguments from history to displace the naturalized politics of what was derided as "liberal humanism." In its British, cultural materialist form this argument was driven by a new politics that sought to displace what was considered a reactionary, complacent reading of Shakespeare that entrenched a conservative cultural politics. Such politics was thought to depend upon an Enlightenment philosophy that rested upon an uncritical assumption about the givenness of an isolated, autonomous, and individual subjectivity untrammeled by any essential social relations, and blessed with free choice.

This belief in the sanctity of individual free choice was exemplified in popular terms in Britain by Margaret Thatcher's notorious pronouncement, in 1987, that there is no such thing as society, only individual men and women.[3] The new political activism against such individualism countered with a contrary philosophical and political argument to the effect that all people are subject to and therefore subjects of social forces that they do not control. In its structuralist and poststructuralist versions this argument took a linguistic turn by which the interior self of the liberal humanist individual was held to be a fantasy—no more than a product of language as a social system

---

More to Shakespeare (Chicago: University of Chicago Press, 2005); Stephen Greenblatt, Shakespearean Negotiations: The Circulation of Social Energy in Renaissance England (The New Historicism: Studies in Cultural Poetics) (Berkeley: University of California Press, 1989).

3. Women's Own magazine, October 31, 1987, http://briandeer.com/social/thatcher-society. htm (accessed February 21, 2016).

of arbitrary differences through which the self is always displaced by the continuous movement of signifiers without any anchoring signifieds.

This philosophical argument was mobilized in a pincer movement with a historicist one: that the supposedly given or natural selfhood of liberal humanism is the product of a very particular historical cusp, when social and political forces engendered the chimera of bourgeois subjectivity which was shaped by a protocapitalist movement that required only apparently autonomous subjects for its ideological purposes. The historical foundry of such a subjectivity was claimed to be Shakespeare's *Hamlet* and its peculiar, enigmatic protagonist. In Barker's words, "In the name, not of the body, but of the secular soul, an interior subjectivity begins to speak here. . . . An early embarrassment for bourgeois ideology, and one of which Hamlet is in part an early victim, was that even as it had to legitimize the active appropriation of the world, it also had to encode its subject as an individual, privatized and largely passive 'consciousness' systematically detached from the world" (Barker, 32).

David Hillman offers a somewhat different historical account of this division by tracing the early modern replacement of a Galenic notion of bodies open to the world by a newly enclosed and therefore interiorized body, exemplified by William Harvey's account of the circulatory system. "The founding moment of modern subjectivity," he argues, "is the moment the body is shut up, confined in solitude."[4] Such confinement has important implications for the possible relationship between such an enclosed subjectivity and the society of others. Hamlet's world-weariness is attributable to the fact that his "own body mirrors the sealed bodies around him. This lack of any open bodies to turn to or identify with, a lack of 'visceral matching,'

---

4. David Hillman, *Shakespeare's Entrails: Belief, Scepticism and the Interior of the Body* (Houndmills, Basingstoke, Hampshire: Palgrave MacMillan, 2007), 89.

appears to leave Hamlet with a sense of corporeal and spiritual isolation" (*Shakespeare's Entrails*, 91). This isolation, Hillman holds,
gives rise to the kind of other-mind skepticism that forms the core of
Stanley Cavell's earlier philosophical argument that a proto-Cartesian
skepticism lies at the heart of Shakespeare's tragedies and late plays.[5]

By the 1990s the historicist argument against inwardness was
being subjected to fierce criticism. In 1995, Katharine Maus argued
that the historicist and philosophical arguments of this pincer attack
do not entail each other. One can hold it as a transhistorical philosophical truth that human selfhood is constituted publicly, through
language or social forces, while simultaneously acknowledging that
certain historical moments held opposite, but mistaken, beliefs. Nor
does one have to argue for the invention of an interiorized subjectivity at the moment of incipient capitalism: one might concede, as
many have argued, that the invention of an essentially inward self
does *not* begin with Shakespeare's *Hamlet*, but is evident in many
other earlier writings: to take some random examples, in Myrrha's
internalized contest within herself about sleeping with her father in
Book X of Ovid's *Metamorphoses*, through the instances of interiorized consciousness in William Langland's *Piers Plowman*, Geoffrey
Chaucer's *Troilus and Creseyde*, and Petrarch's *Secretum*.

This is the burden of David Aers's scathing argument against
those who assume that Shakespeare invented interiority. He accuses
the proponents of this argument of inexcusable ignorance and blindness to especially medieval forms of such consciousness: "There is
no reason to think that the languages and experiences of inwardness,
of interiority, of divided selves, of splits between outer realities and
inner forms of being, were unknown before the seventeenth century, before capitalism, before the 'bourgeoisie,' before Descartes,

---

5. Stanley Cavell, *Disowning Knowledge: In Seven Plays of Shakespeare*, 2nd ed. (Cambridge: Cambridge University Press, 2003).

before the disciplinary regimes addressed in Foucault's *Discipline and Punish*."[6] Aers is deliberately expanding on Lee Patterson's prior argument against Shakespeare's supposed invention of the interior self.[7] And in his magisterial study of the development of the concept of selfhood in Western societies, Charles Taylor argues that the figure who "invents" the modern notion of inwardness as the essence of selfhood is not Shakespeare but rather St. Augustine, who precedes the English playwright by some twelve centuries: "Augustine's turn to the self was a turn to radical reflexivity, and that is what made the language of inwardness irresistible. The inner light is the one which shines in our presence to ourselves . . . it was Augustine who introduced the inwardness of reflexivity and bequeathed it to the Western tradition of thought."[8]

INWARDNESS AND THE THEATER

The theater, and especially the early modern stage, highlights this reflexivity in ways that Maus finds paradoxical. She argues that "inwardness as it becomes a concern for the theatre is always perforce inwardness displayed: an inwardness, perforce, that has already ceased to exist."[9] In the theater inwardness becomes the opposite

6. See David Aers, "A Whisper in the Ear of Early Modernists," in *Culture and History: 1350–1600: Essays on English Communities, Identities and Writing*, ed. David Aers (Detroit: Wayne State University Press, 1992), 177–202 (186).

7. Lee Paterson, "On the Margin: Postmodernism, Ironic History and Medieval Studies," *Speculum* 65 (1990): 87–108. Myrrha's inward debate in Book X of the *Metamorphoses*, or Piers Plowman's discovery of "crist . . . never smoothly but in myself in a Mirrour," or the split Petrarchan self in the *Secretum* seem to express a sense of inwardness long before Shakespeare. But it could be argued that in the history of the representation of inwardness, Shakespeare gives full expression to its self-reflexivity—when the self becomes explicitly the object of reflection and aware of its own interiority.

8. Charles Taylor, *Sources of the Self* (Cambridge, MA: Harvard University Press, 1992), 131.

9. Katharine Eisaman Maus, *Inwardness and Theater in the English Renaissance* (Chicago: University of Chicago Press, 1995), 32.

of itself; in being displayed the essential character of inwardness is destroyed, for the stage *displays* outwardly something intrinsic to inwardness that may be passed over in something like the novel or even a confession. Inwardness on the stage of necessity has to show itself in a publicly available discourse: it has to be conveyed in language, as "that which passes show," as Hamlet declares. But the theater also shows that inwardness is a crucial component of human life, and that the very language that displays it also preserves a critical distinction between the public and the private as concepts. This means, *pace* Maus, that it does not "cease to exist" in the displayed language of the theater. The theater allows us to put inwardness in it its proper place: not destroy or deny it or make it "vaporize like the Wicked Witch of the West, under Dorothy's bucket of water" (Maus, 28).

As Maus expresses it, and generally as all other commentators consider the matter, there either is or there isn't such a thing as "inwardness" or "interiority." These words appear to designate something that exists, Maus intimates, but whatever that may be, it evaporates the moment it is brought outward, through expression or representation. If there isn't such a thing as inwardness, then the words that are meant to designate it are empty. The moment they touch whatever is inexpressibly interior, that interiority as some*thing* dissolves. This reveals a specificity of the theater that lies in more than merely generic or formal peculiarity: its philosophical charge. The capacity of theater to engage in a self-reflexive, metatheatrical mode, combined with the distance between actor and character, means that, as Wittgenstein notes, the public nature of language and meaning is made palpable in the theater—it is open, shared, precisely through the capacity of the stage to reflect on its own public conditions of meaning, even when it gestures toward something ostensibly private and hidden: "The contexts of a sentence are best portrayed in a play. Therefore the best example for a sentence with a particular meaning is the quotation from a play. And whoever asks a person in a play what he's experiencing when he's speaking?"[10]

If we can understand everything the actor says on behalf of the character, if it makes sense *without* the presence of the character or the actor's inwardness, then it means that such inwardness as a place or *thing* is irrelevant to the meaning of what is claimed by the character through the actor. But that doesn't mean that inwardness as a *concept* is empty. Our language games distinguish between the public and the private, the intimate and the exposed. And those distinctions play a role in our language as a reflection of our forms of life. The point is not that the actor or character has no interior state, but rather that such a state is irrelevant to the grounding or constitutive sense of the language that the actor uses on behalf of the character. Hamlet's words express a state of deep mourning, but the language he uses does not depend on *the actor's* referring to an actual interior state to convey their sense; the actor does not have to be in a state of deep mourning to make the words meaningful. Indeed, it would be very strange if every actor who played Hamlet had to be in such a state to convey the meaning of the character's grief.

"I KNOW NOT 'SEEMS' "

Let us look at the famous speech in which Hamlet disavows "outward show" and what "seems" for that which "is," that "within which passes

---

10. Ludwig Wittgenstein, *Last Writings on the Philosophy of Psychology I* (Chicago: University of Chicago Press, 1982), para. 38. Actors and directors of a particular acting school, especially Stanislavskian "method acting," ask this question all the time, but Wittgenstein would argue that the inward state of the actor has no internal connection with the meaning of the words uttered. That is to say, we can understand them whatever the internal state of the actor.

show" which has become the crux for critical disagreements about inwardness and interiority in Shakespeare and beyond:

> QUEEN: If it be
> Why seems it so particular with thee?
> HAMLET: "Seems," madam? Nay, it is. I know not "seems."
> 'Tis not alone my inky cloak, cold mother,
> Nor customary suits of solemn black,
> Nor windy suspiration of forced breath,
> No, nor the fruitful river in the eye,
> Nor the dejected haviour of the visage,
> Together with all forms, moods, shapes of grief,
> That can denote me truly. These indeed "seem,"
> For they are actions that a man might play;
> But I have that within which passes show,
> These but the trappings and the suits of woe.
>
> (1.2.74–86)

A Wittgensteinian analysis of these claims would argue that the interiority to which Hamlet refers may or may not exist (the question is not ontological but logical or grammatical, in Wittgenstein's sense)—but it has no bearing on the intelligibility of language, speech, or bodily expression. It has the character of Wittgenstein's "beetle in the box":

> Now someone tells me that he knows what pain is only from his own case!—Suppose everyone had a box with something in it: we call it a "beetle." No one can look into anyone else's box, and everyone says he knows what a beetle is only by looking at his beetle.—Here it would be quite possible for everyone to have something quite different in his box. One might even imagine such a thing constantly changing.—But suppose the word "beetle" has a use in these people's language?—If so it would not be

used as the name of a thing. The thing in the box has no place in the language-game at all; not even as something: for the box might be empty.—No, one can "divide through" by the thing in the box; it cancels out, whatever it is.[11]

Let's replace Wittgenstein's reference to "pain" with Hamlet's claim to his own inexpressible interiority. Such inwardness is like Wittgenstein's beetle: each person has his or her own; no one else has any access to the other beetles. But the words "that within" have a use in English: we can understand the language Hamlet uses. Following Wittgenstein, we can see that, contrary to appearances, "that within" does not refer to any *thing*, or for that matter, to *anything* inside actor or character. It's not that it disappears or vaporizes, as Maus puts it, when it is spoken of. It's simply that it can be no kind of "thing" that plays any role in the constitution of the language, not even one that disappears. When Wittgenstein says, of an interior state, that "it is not a something but not a nothing either" (*PI*, 304), he is not denying the possible existence of such a state; rather he is trying to find its proper place in the language games of interiority that we do actually play. He is asking us to focus on the word or concept, not anything we may think it designates.

The word "interiority" ("*that within*"), as Wittgenstein puts it, has a use in the language game, which means that it has a meaning. But that doesn't mean that it inevitably has a referent. Its grammar as a substantive makes us look for some thing that it designates or to which it refers. This common inclination or habit always to assume that a substantive refers to an object (from which it derives its meaning) is one of the major targets of Wittgenstein's therapeutic approach to philosophical clarification. He is not claiming, like

11. Ludwig Wittgenstein, *Philosophical Investigations*, trans. G. E. M. Anscombe (Oxford: Blackwell, 1973), para. 293.

cultural materialist critics, that the notion of inwardness has no sense or did not exist until Descartes. "Am I saying something like 'and the soul itself is merely something about the body?'" he asks. "No. (I am not that hard up for categories)."[12] Rather, as Paul Johnston puts it, "the notion of the Inner brings into play a whole network of concepts which could otherwise have no place." Consciousness is not a kind of experience: "Seeing and consciousness are not experiences—they can therefore not be described—only taught within a language-game."[13]

Let's be clear about the usefulness of the concept of inwardness—about the role it plays in our language games. Without the notion of inwardness we would find it difficult to draw a distinction between a human being and automaton, for instance; we would be hampered in our distinction between intending to do something and doing so by accident or unconsciously; we would find it hard to draw a distinction between sincerity and hypocrisy, for which the words that are ready to hand are seeming or pretending or acting, on the one hand—mere show—and really being on the other. And we would have great difficulty (more than the difficulties we already have), in negotiating the language of love. The notion of an *inside* is thus a placeholder not for a hidden thing inside, but rather for a network of language games about what it means to be human, to be moral, to have intentions, to express emotions. It needs no actual hidden inside *thing* from which to derive its meaning.

Once we accept Wittgenstein's caveat that inwardness does not refer to any interior object that, like the beetle in the box, can by definition not be shown, and adopt the position that it is a point around which concepts of personal integrity, moral being, perhaps humanity

---

12. Ludwig Wittgenstein, *Remarks on the Philosophy of Psychology* 2 (Chicago: University of Chicago Press, 1980), para. 690.
13. Paul Johnston, *Wittgenstein: Rethinking the Inner* (London: Routledge, 2014), 198 and 200.

itself, are organized, we can recognize the different ways in which Gertrude and Hamlet use the word "seem" in her question and his answer. And we might also recognize that *love* is a concept around which the concepts of the inner and the outer circulate in a network of *public* uses meant to capture or express a *private* emotion.

The philosophical contours of this speech have been traced often enough. Asked by his concerned mother why the quotidian fact of death and its necessary acceptance seems to have passed him by, Hamlet turns her *ordinary*, everyday use of the word "seems" into a *philosophical* signifier. As far as I know, this Wittgensteinian point about the shift in use between mother and son has not been made. But for the philosophical significance of Hamlet's speech it is crucial. The "seems" in Gertrude's question does not carry the same meaning as the "seems" in Hamlet's response. Wittgenstein would argue that, as Hamlet uses it, "seems" has gone on holiday, it has ceased to do its ordinary work, it is no longer bolstered by its place at home—the language game that gives it sense. He takes a concept that has an ordinary use, in which the difference between appearance and reality is discernible or discoverable, and collapses that distinction into something imponderable. To the ordinary question: *Why do you seem inordinately sad?* an ordinary answer might be: *Because I am grieving for my father, whom I admired and loved deeply—can't you see?* But Hamlet offers a concept of "seems" in which the contrasting concepts, "apparent" or "real," have been emptied: for which there is no possible mode of discovery or confirmation.

Hamlet thus rejects his mother's use of the word "seems" by claiming that the word has been emptied of significance for him. *I do not "seem,"* Hamlet claims, *I simply am.* This is a curious assertion. For it places Hamlet beyond language. He is saying, *I inhabit a domain that lies beyond the possibility of seeming, of pretending, of acting, of lying (which you clearly do not).* But how would representation or language work in such a domain? We are asking ourselves to imagine a language in which it would impossible to lie—to entertain any possibility beyond the immediacy of self-presence, to put it in Derridean terms. This means not only that one would be unable to "say the thing which is not" (i.e., to tell lies),[14] but one would also be unable wish, hope, speculate about the future, invent fictions, or create characters like Hamlet. Such a language would be severely restricted, if not impossible. It would be reduced to the philosophers' language in Book III of Swift's *Gulliver's Travels*, in which its proponents converse simply and solely by carrying the objects of their intercourse on their backs, and confine themselves to gesticulating with such objects without the intervention of mediating signifiers.

As it is usually read, Hamlet's diatribe against "seems" posits an ineffable interior realm of the real sense that lies beyond representation. Such a realm is an ultimate instance of what Jacques Derrida calls the total presence of consciousness to itself. Hamlet insists that what he really feels or is—his "being" rather than mere "seeming"—cannot possibly touch the "forms" or "actions" of representation. This is curiously similar to Husserl's notion of a language filled with the full presence of intention, but untrammeled by any of the outward forms of representation.[15] Hamlet's exclusion embraces not only what we might consider the prosthetics of bodily expression— "the customary suits of solemn black"—but also every way in which the *body itself* signifies—tears, facial expressions, sighs. *Nothing* can denote Hamlet truly because by definition all forms of representation and expression alike are open to *possibility* of pretense.[16] This is in fact the burden of Derrida's notoriously acerbic disagreement with John Searle over J. L. Austin's supposed exclusion of "nonserious" (i.e. fictional) speech acts from his theory.[17] *No* "action that

14. Jonathan Swift, *Gulliver's Travels*, Bk. IV.

15. Jacques Derrida, *Speech and Phenomena* (Evanston, IL: Northwestern University Press, 1972).

16. Note that for Hamlet forms of expression, which are not the same as forms of representation, also fall under the category of "show" that he excludes.

17. Jacques Derrida, *Limited Inc.* (Evanston, IL: Northwestern University Press, 1975).

a man may play" can be counted as an expression of "that within" which denotes Hamlet "truly." But all the resources of the body and all its appurtenances, including language, may be used by anybody as such "actions" of "play" or pretense because of the independence of expressed language from intention.

The "radical reflexivity" of Hamlet's speech is doubled (as it is not in Augustine, for example) by the metatheatrical position of the actor on the stage. For if the character Hamlet claims an interiority beyond representation, the actor performing the part and saying the words has no such interiority to offer—or hide. Recall Wittgenstein's remark about the theater as the exemplum of the nature of meaning, because of the separation of the actor's interior state from that of the words s/he speaks. Hamlet the character claims a deep inwardness that not only constitutes the true being but is also the space in which the core or life of representation proper lies, but which paradoxically exists beyond representation: it "passes show." But this claim to an interiority that "passes" the "show" of *all* "forms, moods, shapes of grief" is made by an *actor*, who has none of the inwardness peculiar to Hamlet the character (whatever inwardness of his own he might have). The actor is indeed nothing but "show": he is, as actor, merely the forms, shapes, moods, and signifiers so passionately repudiated by the character he represents. This means that representation in the form of the character's claims to an inaccessible interiority does not depend on the inwardness claimed by the actor on behalf of that character.

"A DREAM OF PASSION"

This is a paradox that Hamlet encounters when he is confronted by the expression of passion by an actor—one of the troupe of players who visit Elsinore, and whose "show," first meant to distract Hamlet from his "antic disposition," is turned by the prince into the "thing

wherein [he'll] catch the conscience of the king" (2.2.539–40).
Almost immediately after Hamlet's repudiation of "actions that a man
might play," he encounters the quintessence of playing in the actor
who "in a fiction, in a dream of passion, / Could force his soul so to
his own conceit / That from her working all his visage wanned, / —
Tears in his eyes, distraction in his aspect, / A broken voice, and his
whole function suiting / With forms to his conceit" (2.2.487–92).
Not surprisingly, he finds the intensity of the player's passion "mon-
strous," for it is based not on a foundation of ineluctable inwardness,
but rather on "nothing"—on a fiction—"Hecuba": "What's Hecuba
to him, or he to her, / That he should weep for her?" (494–95).

This is a profound question. How, Hamlet asks in bewilderment,
can anyone express or show intense passion for *nothing*—what has
no existence, and therefore no direct connection with the heart? So
he tries to imagine what the player would do, "Had he the motive and
the cue for passion / That I have?" He responds with the projection
of redoubled histrionics on the part of the player—all the "forms,
moods, shapes of grief":

> He would drown the stage with tears
> And cleave the general ear with horrid speech,
> Make mad the guilty and appal the free,
> Confound the ignorant, and amaze indeed
> The very faculties of eyes and ears.
>
> (2.2.497–501)

Hamlet moves from the player's behavior to his own actions, specifically to the way in which, despite his interior motivation, he *seems* to
be unmoved:

> Yet I,
> A dull and muddy-mettled rascal, peak
> Like John-a-dreams, unpregnant of my cause,

And can say nothing. No, not for a king
Upon whose property and most dear life
A damned defeat was made.

(501–6)

Hamlet is now concerned not with his inexpressible, interior self but rather with how he *appears* to others—specifically to the audience watching his performance, to whom he addresses this direct, meta-theatrical appeal:

Am I a coward?
Who calls me villain? breaks my pate across,
Plucks off my beard and blows it in my face,
Tweaks me by the nose, gives me the lie i' th' throat
As deep as to the lungs—Who does me this . . . ?

(506–10)

The direction of genuineness or authenticity has been inverted: the audience can tell from Hamlet's lack of public show that his protestations of interior authenticity are vacuous—indeed, it is by seeing himself reflected in their evaluation of his behavior that the prince recognizes his own inauthenticity:

Ha! 'Swounds, I should take it. For it cannot be
But I am pigeon-liver'd and lack gall
To make oppression bitter, or ere this
I should ha' fatted all the region kites
With this slave's offal.

(511–15)

There is worse to come. For when Hamlet tries to express his inward being, when he tries to display his deeply felt "cause" as much to himself as to his observers, he descends into pure histrionics, into the worst kind of excessive, ham acting:

> bloody, bawdy villain,
> Remorseless, treacherous, lecherous, kindless villain.
> Why, what an ass am I: this is most brave,
> That I, the son of a dear father murdered,
> Prompted to my revenge by heaven and hell,
> Must, like a whore, unpack my heart with words
> And fall a-cursing like a very drab,
> A stallion! Fie upon 't, foh!
>
> (515–22)

This self-reflexive turn runs counter to Hamlet's earlier diatribe against "seeming" by displaying the impossibility of his earlier claim. It is the attempt to "unpack [his] heart with words" that disgusts the prince here, expressed in terms of his characteristic aversion to female sexuality in its assumed promiscuous openness to the world. But what alternatives are there? An "antic disposition," the quintessence of deceitful playfulness, hiding a putatively genuine "heart of [his] mystery" (3.2.357–58), immediate, unreflecting revenge? Or does the real test of Hamlet's skeptical philosophy come when he feels the urgent need to show his love for Ophelia in the "forms, moods, shapes of grief"?

"I DID LOVE YOU ONCE"

The question of Hamlet's desire has exercised a wide range of writers, especially psychoanalytic thinkers like Sigmund Freud, Ernest Jones, and Jacques Lacan. The first two famously read Hamlet's condition as anticipating the Freudian Oedipus complex, whereby the prince displays all the symptoms of desiring to kill his father. His lack of resolution in taking revenge on his uncle is the result of his unconscious recognition that Claudius has done precisely what lies at the heart of his deepest desires: to kill his father and sleep with his mother.[18] Lacan offers a more complex explanation of Hamlet's desire, not as being *for* the mother but rather, as Jonathan Gill Harris puts it, "his fixation *within* his mother's desire, from which he cannot separate himself."[19] But these meditations on the role of desire in *Hamlet* pay no attention to the (dis)place(d) force of love.

Love lies at the heart of this enigmatic play. And it straddles precisely the realms of the interior and exterior, the inner and the outer, the private and the social. Love differs from desire insofar as it is always amenable to doubt. One may doubt whether one loves another, or whether one is loved, but one is hardly uncertain of one's desire.[20] And Shakespeare's plays, including the romantic comedies from the early *Two Gentlemen of Verona* to *Twelfth Night*, the lacerating *Troilus and Cressida*, and the plays overtly concerned with groundless male jealousy, *Much Ado About Nothing*, *Othello*, *The Winter's Tale* and *Cymbeline*, seek constantly to find the heart of love's mystery, especially when it is beset by doubt. Cavell's Shakespeare criticism focuses exclusively on skepticism in the plays, especially the degree to which love is thwarted by the corrosive doubt that cannot

18. See Sigmund Freud, *The Interpretation of Dreams: Annotated*, trans. Abraham Arden Brill (CreateSpace Independent Publishing Platform, 2015), V, and Ernest Jones, "The Œdipus-Complex as an Explanation of Hamlet's Mystery: A Study in Motive," *American Journal of Psychology* 21 (1910): 72–113.
19. Jonathan Gil Harris, *Shakespeare and Literary Theory* (Oxford: Oxford University Press, 2010), 97 (my emphasis).
20. Of course, this distinction runs counter to the central tenet of psychoanalysis, especially in its Lacanian forms, where the uncertainties of desire are central. In the light of the work already done on Hamlet and desire, I remain with this "common-sense" conceptual distinction between love and desire.

either acknowledge the other's love or acknowledge one's own need for the love of the other.

Hamlet presents us with a range of situations in which love is in question. Do Gertrude and Claudius love each other? What kind of love exists between Hamlet and Horatio? Does Hamlet love his mother or his father? And does Hamlet love Ophelia? Here there is doubt—not only in our minds, but also in Hamlet's own mind, despite his supposed access to his own indubitable, interior state of being.

The first evidence presented to us is Ophelia's distressed account of the prince's invasion of her innermost, most private space, in a strikingly theatrical action:

> OPHELIA: My lord, as I was sewing in my closet
> Lord Hamlet, with his doublet all unbraced,
> No hat upon his head, his stockings fouled,
> Ungartered, and down-gyved to his ankle,
> Pale as his shirt, his knees knocking each other,
> And with a look so piteous in purport
> As if he had been loosed out of hell
> To speak of horrors, he comes before me.
> POLONIUS: Mad for thy love?
> OPHELIA: My lord, I do not know,
> But truly I do fear it.
>
> (2.1.74–84)

The description echoes the revenant about whose true nature Hamlet is ultimately left uncertain: his father's ghost "loosed out of" Purgatory "to speak of horrors." Hamlet's action and dress (or undress) conform to a thoroughly conventional, early modern stereotype of the unrequited or thwarted lover. And it is precisely for that reason that, against the assumptions of Ophelia and her father, we might be inclined to doubt that "This is the very ecstasy of love." At best we are left uncertain, with access to no more than a secondhand account of Hamlet's behavior and appearance.

We thus have no access to Hamlet inwardness nor are we presented with behavior that would provide what Wittgenstein calls criteria for Hamlet's love. For Wittgenstein, "an 'inner process' stands in need of outward criteria" (*PI*, 580), which depend on a social agreement in judgments:

> Wittgenstein's insight . . . [is] that all our knowledge, everything we assert or question (or doubt or wonder at . . .) is governed not merely by what we understand as "evidence" or "truth conditions," but by criteria . . . (Without the control of criteria in applying concepts, we would not know what counts as evidence for any claim, nor for what claims evidence is needed.) And that suggests . . . that every surmise and each tested conviction depend upon the same structure or background or necessities and agreements that judgements of value explicitly do.[21]

The crucial points here are the background agreement that judgments of value presuppose and require and that criteria are about the use of words and the applicability of concepts. It may well be that the behavior that Ophelia describes would have constituted indubitable criteria for "the ecstasy of love" that Polonius diagnoses to an Elizabethan audience or reader. But they offer no such certainty to us. Criteria are not fixed: they change historically and culturally. It is thus very difficult for us to decide, not whether there is sufficient evidence for Hamlet's love as an interior state, but rather whether there are sufficiently agreed-upon criteria for us to use the word "love" in relation to the actions we see Hamlet play—from what he says and

21. Cavell, 1979, 14.

does. This is closely connected to the point I make above, that the notion of inwardness does not refer to anything "within" that "passes show," but, rather, to a network of concepts and the rules for their use. Criteria do not determine the existence of anything; they concern the applicability of concepts: are we going to call this kind of behavior "love"?

What makes Shakespeare's *Hamlet* delight, intrigue, and puzzle us in equal measure is precisely its unsettling questioning of the criteria that enable some kind of consensual agreement in judgments of value. Wittgensteinian criteria are always defeasible: Hamlet may be pretending—"one may [always] smile and smile and be a villain"—he may reduplicate the criteria by which we judge authenticity or genuineness, as Claudius does for most of the play. But criteria play out over time, judgments about their applicability are not made instantaneously, they are cumulative. Nor are they systematic, in the way that mathematical calculations are. The criteria for love do not form a checklist, nor is there necessarily agreement about what would count as criteria. "There is," Wittgenstein writes, "in general complete agreement in the judgement of colours by those who have been diagnosed normal. *This is characteristic of the concept of colour*. But there is in general no such agreement over the question whether an expression of feeling is genuine or not . . . It is certainly possible to be convinced by evidence that someone is in such-and-such a state of mind" (*PI*, p. 227). Wittgenstein distinguishes between "ponderable" and "imponderable" evidence, the latter including "subtleties of glance, of gesture, of tone" (228). It is thus characteristic of the concept of love that it requires a whole range of subtle, nuanced, and unsystematic judgments of fine shades of behavior made over time. Love is not purely some thing or state that lies within; but nor is it a set of purely external actions open to the view. It is in a liminal position—it lies in between the concept of inwardness and the culturally embedded, learned forms of human action, expression, and feeling. Love indubitably involves feeling or emotion, but it also judged by the ways in which it expresses itself in and through action.

The fact that such forms of behavior and the finest nuances they entail are necessarily culturally embedded signals a further complexity in their representation in *Hamlet*—what happens to them in a *rotten* state, such as Denmark under Claudius? Criteria hold only in society in which values and concepts like love, both as modes of public behavior and marks of personal identity, are relatively stable and recognizable—and can be recognized, passed on, duplicated. What Hamlet's radical uncertainty reveals is the rottenness of his society: the degree to which it has made it impossible to know, to recognize, to identify what love is, even in oneself.

"NEVER DOUBT I LOVE"

We may explore this by considering Hamlet's poem to Ophelia, brought to the royal couple by Polonius as indubitable evidence of Hamlet's love for Ophelia:

> [Reads.] To the celestial, and my soul's idol, the most beautified
> Ophelia—that's an ill phrase, a vile phrase; "beautified" is a vile phrase,
> but you shall hear—Thus in her excellent white bosom, these, etc.
> QUEEN: Came this from Hamlet to her?
> Polonius: Good madam, stay awhile: I will be faithful.
> [Reads.] Doubt thou the stars are fire,
> Doubt that the sun doth move.
> Doubt truth to be a liar,
> But never doubt I love.

O dear Ophelia, I am ill at these numbers. I have not art to reckon my
groans, but that I love thee best, O most best, believe it. Adieu. Thine
evermore, most dear lady, whilst this machine is to him. Hamlet.

(2.2.108–21)

There are two points to make about the cultural embeddedness of
Hamlet's poem. First, an intimate declaration of love between two
people is here circulated publicly for scrutiny and critical commentary by others: in the most exposed, public sphere of the court.
Polonius plays the literary critic when he deplores Hamlet's use of
"beautified," and the prince's private declaration is theatricalized: it is
one more reiterable linguistic form that may be wrenched out of one
context into another that is inimical to its spirit and intent. This is a
violation of personal integrity that is characteristic of the society as a
whole. May love be expressed under such circumstances? What kind
of evidence, imponderable or otherwise, would count in this kind of
society?

Second, in the Elizabethan context the poem is an entirely *conventional* expression of love: its artifice—and the complex public
relationships that it seeks to negotiate as a display of supposedly private emotion—multiplies the imponderability of evidence required
to judge its genuineness. Shakespeare elsewhere writes of "truth tired
with iteration" (*Troilus and Cressida*, 3.2177), while in his groundbreaking sequence of sonnets, *Astrophel and Stella*, the poet Philip
Sydney asks despairingly of the capacity of poetry to offer any kind
of genuine testimony: "What may words say, and what may words
not say / When truth itself must speak like flattery?" (sonnet 35).
Consequently, Hamlet feels the need for a metacommentary that will
attest to the genuineness of expression that escapes the poem itself.
The "groans" as expressions of inward desire and torment require
"art"; but the artifice of the poem's disquisition on *doubt* (the word
is reiterated four times in as many lines) finally involves the merely
banal plea for belief.

It is part of the language game of belief that it is not necessarily secured by assertion. If Hamlet's metacommentary is required to attest to the genuineness of the original expression, then that need goes all the way down, in an infinite regress; nothing that Hamlet can add to his poem would necessarily secure the belief in his love for which he asks. He may indeed allude to an interior condition to which his "numbers" and his "groans" are supposed to attest, as a form of aposiopesis, but such allusions or gestures are not sufficient to secure the belief that he does in fact love Ophelia.

The poem ends with the conventional pledge of eternal love, which, as Jean-Luc Marion argues, is a *necessary* component of the language game of love. One cannot love with qualifications: "I cannot give myself over to loving if I restrain my intention and its signification in a finite lapse of time. Loving for a predetermined amount of time . . . does not signify loving provisionally, but loving not at all—not even having begun to love."[22] Marion is not arguing that people do not fall in and out of love, or transfer their love from one person to another. He is saying that at the moment one opens oneself to another in love one cannot qualify that openness as in, *I love you, but only provisionally, for a while.* The failure or transfer of love is something that infects a love that must be made without conditions or limits.

Marion's argument that one cannot love for a predetermined amount of time takes us to the scene in which Hamlet encounters Ophelia alone, after he has delivered his "To be or not to be" speech. Supposedly an encounter between two lovers, it is again complicated by its theatricality: by the fact that Ophelia has been set up to perform a part by Claudius and Polonius to enable them to judge Hamlet's true condition from his reaction to her. This adds a further complexity to

22. Jean-Luc Marion, *The Erotic Phenomenon*, trans. Stephen E Lewis (Chicago: University of Chicago Press, 2008), 185.

Hamlet's about-turn, when he first declares "I loved you once" before negating that statement with the blunt "I loved you not."

> HAMLET: I did love you once.
> OPHELIA: Indeed, my lord, you made me believe so.
> HAMLET: You should not have believed me. For virtue cannot so inoculate our old stock but we shall relish of it. I loved you not.
> OPHELIA: I was the more deceived.

(3.1.114–19)

Hamlet's violent rejection of Ophelia and his denial of his love for her may, as some directors think, result from his suspicion that she has been set up by her father and he may sense the eavesdroppers nearby. Certainly, Ophelia's return of his gifts, presumably including other poetic declarations of love, "words of so sweet breath composed / As made the things more rich" (97–98), shocks the prince. She alludes to other evidence, perhaps imponderable, that he has done something "unkind" that has emptied his earlier words of truth or sincerity: "Their perfume lost / Take these again; for to the noble mind / Rich gifts wax poor when givers prove unkind" (98–100). For the audience, this is enigmatic. Is she referring to an event or series of events in which Hamlet has indeed been unkind to her? Perhaps the closet scene? Or is she simply mouthing words given to her by her father? We do not know. And there is no way of knowing.

Hamlet's contradiction of his statement of love acts again as a metacommentary on the problem of belief or faith in making judgments of value. Why should she not have believed him? Because he was insincere or lying? And which of his statements is actually true? "I loved you once" or "I loved you not"? They are both in the past tense. He is not saying "I loved you once but I now no longer love you." Does *he* know whether he loved her or still loves her? If he has access to that within which passes show, then surely he should know!

One way of reading the contradiction is to see it in the context of love as an inescapably political and therefore public concept for members of royalty and the aristocracy, alluded to again and again in Polonius's and Laertes's concerns that in love Hamlet's will is bounded by public expectation—his love is not his to give:

> Perhaps he loves you now,
> And now no soil nor cautel doth besmirch
> The virtue of his will; but you must fear,
> His greatness weigh'd, his will is not his own,
> For he himself is subject to his birth:
> He may not, as unvalued persons do,
> Carve for himself, for on his choice depends
> The safety and the health of this whole state.
>
> (1.3.14–21)

Laertes's reference to Hamlet's "will" resonates, as do sonnets 123 and 136, with multiple senses that include Hamlet's autonomy, his desires, his love, and his genitals. Hamlet's love is not a product of an inward intention or disposition, Laertes warns—it belongs to the public sphere of the state. And that means that he is not permitted to love Ophelia in the full social sense that it entails the honorable intention of marriage, although he may indeed, as a young man of privilege, take advantage of her, as Polonius so clearly fears. What Hamlet may be struggling with through his contradiction, then, is the fact that it is impossible, for public reasons, for him to love Ophelia—that all his love could turn out to be is mere desire, no matter what he may feel inwardly.

"I LOVED OPHELIA"

In 5.1, when a newly animated Hamlet has escaped from the clutches of Claudius by sending Rosencrantz and Guildenstern to their deaths in his place, but before he has adopted the Stoic fatalism that "there is special providence in the fall of a sparrow" (5.2.197), the prince is shocked to encounter not only Ophelia's funeral, but also her brother's exhibitionist display of love and grief. How does he respond? By first subjecting Laertes's "show" to ironic questioning:

> HAMLET: What is he whose grief
> Bears such an emphasis, whose phrase of sorrow
> Conjures the wandering stars and makes them stand
> Like wonder-wounded hearers? This is I,
> Hamlet the Dane.
>
> (5.1.243–47)

Here is a prince whose newly confident affirmation of his identity and status "bears . . . an emphasis," not merely in his unprecedented assertion of his royal status, "Hamlet the Dane," but also in his interrogation of Laertes's social station: "*what* is he?" (rather than "who is he"?).[23]

But he soon loses control and decorum, plunging, kicking, and screaming, after Laertes into Ophelia's grave—according to the Q1 stage direction. There, grappling with Laertes—if we follow Rowe's editorial insertion and Hamlet's imprecation, "I prithee take thy fingers from my throat" (249)—the prince strives to do what he professes in scene 2 is impossible: to display, to prove his love for Ophelia through the public show of bodily and linguistic representation:

> HORATIO: Good my lord, be quiet.
> HAMLET: Why, I will fight with him upon this theme
> Until my eyelids will no longer wag.

---

23. For a discussion of the relation between these two forms regarding social identity, see Sylvia Adamson, "Questions of Identity in Renaissance Drama: New Historicism Meets Old Philology," *Shakespeare Quarterly* 61.1 (2010): 56–77.

QUEEN: O my son, what theme?

HAMLET: I loved Ophelia—forty thousand brothers
Could not with all their quantity of love
Make up my sum. What wilt thou do for her?

KING: O, he is mad, Laertes.

QUEEN: For love of God, forbear him.

HAMLET: 'Swounds, show me what thou 'lt do.
Woul't weep, woul't fight, woul't fast, woul't tear thyself,
Woul't drink up eisel, eat a crocodile?
I'll do 't. Dost come here to whine,
To outface me with leaping in her grave?
Be buried quick with her, and so will I.
And if thou prate of mountains let them throw
Millions of acres on us till our ground,
Singeing his pate against the burning zone,
Make Ossa like a wart. Nay, an thou'lt mouth,
I'll rant as well as thou.

QUEEN: This is mere madness.

(254–73)

Such histrionics are even more excessive than those at which he expresses such intense self-disgust after the player's Hecuba speech, when he "unpack[s his] heart with words / And fall[s] a-cursing like a very drab" (2.2.520–21). But Hamlet is now caught on the rack of his earlier position against seeming. For if he did indeed love Ophelia, despite all he has said and done—if he feels this in his heart of hearts—how does he express that love? How does he show it? And why should he need to show it? Why not rest assured that he has it securely wrapped up in his heart? Because however much love may be a private matter between two people at one level, it needs public expression—it has to be expressed or shown, even if that expression is only to a single person: the person who loves. In an important sense, Hamlet is talking to himself here—he is trying to convince himself of his love for Ophelia. Here Wittgenstein's argument against a private language is apposite. For Hamlet, loving Ophelia cannot be the kind of nice warm feeling so beloved of cognitive scientists who attempt to find its equivalent in neural activity or the release of dopamines. Let us assume that it is some kind of inner sensation or feeling, like the sensation "S" in Wittgenstein's private-language argument, where, without some criterion for recognizing the sensation as the *same* from day to day or moment to moment, the person experiencing such sensations has no way of knowing whether the sensation s/he had yesterday is the same one as the one s/he has today (or tomorrow, and so on) (*PI*, 258 passim):

> What reason have we for calling "S" the sign for a sensation? For "sensation" is a word in our common language, not one intelligible to me alone. So the use of the word stands in need of a justification which everybody understands.—And it would not help either to say that it need not be a sensation; that when he writes "S," he has something—and that is all that can be said. (*PI*, 270)

The point is that if we treat love as something akin to Wittgenstein's sensation—*something* which passes show—then the person who has such a sensation has no way of recognizing each sensation as being the same as the one experienced before or after. There is no public criterion available to stabilize the sensations as similar, or belonging to a single category—as falling under the concept "love."

Faced with an overwhelming sense of loss and grief, and with Laertes's capacity within the social context of Ophelia's funeral to express his own grief and love for his sister, Hamlet desperately grasps at the most overblown, conventional, stereotyped, and palpably hyperbolic criterion for true love, being prepared to undergo ridiculous tests and trials: from swearing, fasting, weeping, to inflicting self-damage, drinking unpotable liquids, eating impossible creatures, being buried alive. But all this, he recognizes, is mere ranting: histrionic, overblown, empty. Does that mean that Hamlet did not love Ophelia? Or that that love is impossible to express, in the metaphysical sense when he decries all "forms, moods, shapes" of grief? No. It means that in the context in which Hamlet finds himself, given all the shades of his other actions and behavior, and the rottenness of the Danish state, no language game is available to Hamlet to express his love and grief. Such language games require a sustaining set of social conditions and relationship to support them. And the prison that is Denmark offers no such support.

The social world of Elsinore leaches all meaning from the language games through which intimacy can flourish. It is therefore understandable that critics should have wanted either to argue that what appears to be the private in the play is in fact public, or alternatively that the "real" self resides in an interior realm that is inscrutably impervious to the ravages of the public domain. But the relationship between the private and the public, or the interior and the exterior, should not be decided via metaphysical dogmas that the one is *really* the other. Wittgenstein's argument against the possibility of a private language does not reduce the private to the public. These concepts are distinct; each has a role in the language game, even the language that Shakespeare and Hamlet speak. They are embroiled in a multitude of complex ways, but they nevertheless belong to different language games.[24] *Hamlet* shows the debilitating personal and social effects when the one is subsumed or obliterated by the other.

In short then, it is not as if Hamlet has that within himself— loving feelings for Ophelia—which cannot be expressed. Rather, he

---

24. Cf. *Philosophical Investigations*, p. 220: "Silent 'internal' speech is not a half hidden phenomenon which is as it were seen through a veil. It is not hidden *at all*, but the concept may easily confuse us, for it runs over a long stretch cheek by jowl with the concept of an 'outward' process, and yet does not coincide with it."

finds himself within a society in which it is impossible to say "I love you" because the validity conditions of that performative speech act are missing or do not exist. They have been obliterated by a world of hypocrisy and deceit, totalitarian control, and relentless spying and surveillance. That is not to claim that Hamlet has no feelings of love for her or never had, as he claims in his cruel repudiation of her in the scene in which Claudius and Polonius eavesdrop on the intimacy of his conversation with Ophelia.

"HER SPEECH IS NOTHING"

In Hamlet and Ophelia alike the feelings of love have been subjected to the cruelest forms of repression. Their only outlet for Ophelia is the public innuendo of popular song and the release through the uncontrolled discourse of insanity. Here we see the gender imbalance of the critical claim that it is in the prince of Denmark that Shakespeare invents a modern subjectivity through his claims to interiority. No such interiority is available to Ophelia. Her language is almost always spoken for her by the male figures of authority who control her life. When she does come to speak what she feels, in the moving scenes of grief and madness in act 4, there is no sense of the inwardness that Hamlet claims:

> Her speech is nothing,
> Yet the unshaped use of it doth move
> The hearers to collection. They yawn at it,
> And botch the words up fit to their own thoughts;
> Which, as her winks and nods and gestures yield them,
> Indeed would make one think there might be thought,
> Though nothing sure, yet much unhappily.

> (4.5.7–13)

"Her speech is nothing" says it all—both that she is unable to follow the rules of semantics and syntax that would present at least the show of a publicly available sense, and that there is nothing discernable behind that speech, quite contrary to Claudius's statement of Hamlet, "Nor what he spake, though it lacked form a little, / Was not like madness" (3.1.162–63). The "nothing" of Ophelia's speech and thought recalls Hamlet's vicious response to Ophelia's statement "I think nothing, my lord," that "nothing" is "a fair thought to lie between a maid's legs" (3.2.111–12). Ophelia thus says nothing because of her gendered place in the society of Elsinore, nor is that speech capable of representing anything that "might be thought," but her behavior is indeed capable, in the most poignant and moving ways, of conveying her deep unhappiness and distress. All she can finally do to convey that distress is resort to the most public, the least personal of media: the reiterated stereotypes of popular song are all she has to show "how hard true sorrow hits":

> By Gis, and by Saint Charity,
>> Alack, and fie for shame,
>> Young men will do 't if they come to 't:
>> By Cock they are to blame.
> Quoth she, "Before you tumbled me,
>> You promised me to wed."
> He answers:
>> "So would I ha' done by yonder sun,
>> An thou hadst not come to my bed."

(58–65)

The prince has it slightly easier. He can at least try to use publicly available language games to express a sense of interiority, as so many critics have noted. But I have argued that the private is not simply subsumed within and by the public, nor does the private suggest a deep sense of the self beyond social representation. What *Hamlet* demonstrates is, rather, that a society like Claudius's Denmark, in which the private is always invaded by the public, is pathological: it obliterates the possibility of the language games of inwardness—like love or grief—that are nevertheless necessarily constituted through the shared, public nature of language.

Here it is important to preserve subtle distinctions in Wittgenstein's (and my) argument. Unlike the historicists and materialist mentioned in the opening of my essay, who argue that in the early modern period the private *is* simply the public, I am arguing that the language games of a healthy society allow for a sense of inwardness, privacy, and intimacy for which a public sphere—a language and its social institutions—is necessary for its expression, recognition and reiteration. But this sense can be reduced to neither the public surveillance nor private interiority. Hamlet's society provides ways in which love may be explored and expressed—writing poetry to the beloved, offering gifts and tokens of affection, declaring one's love, mutually navigating feelings through what Cavell calls "passionate utterance," the intimacies of making love, with their own rituals, and the ritualized grief of morning. But each of these socially constituted spaces for dwelling *in* privacy and intimacy is invaded or obliterated by the exposure of Hamlet's poetry to royal scrutiny, the staging of Ophelia's return of the tokens of love and the voyeuristic gaze upon that theater of Claudius and Polonius, the invasion by Hamlet himself of Ophelia's closet and her manipulation by brother and father, and, finally, the emptiness of the funeral as a ritual expression of personal and familial love.

Hamlet can try to play the language games of love rendered virtually impossible by the world of Elsinore, or he can release the repression of his love for Ophelia in the form of his "bad dreams," which finally prevent him from counting himself "the king of infinite space." These forms of behavior are, as we know from Freud, not aspects of an inwardness that "passes show": they speak their own enigmatic language—the carnivalesque language of Hamlet's "antic disposition" and the endlessly intriguing displacements and condensations of the play that bears his name.

WORKS CITED

Adamson, Sylvia. 2010. "Questions of Identity in Renaissance Drama: New Historicism Meets Old Philology." *Shakespeare Quarterly* 61, no. 1: 56–77.

Aers, David. 1992. "A Whisper in the Ear of Early Modernists." *Culture and History: 1350–1600. Essays on English Communities, Identities and Writing*, edited by David Aers, 177–202. Detroit: Wayne State University Press.

Barker, Francis. 1995. *The Tremulous Private Body: Essays on Subjection*. Ann Arbor: University of Michigan Press.

Belsey, Catherine. 1985. *The Subject of Tragedy: Identity and Difference in Renaissance Drama*. London: Routledge Kegan & Paul.

Cavell, Stanley. 1979. *The Claim of Reason: Wittgenstein, Skepticism, Morality, and Tragedy*, New York: Oxford University Press.

———. 2003. *Disowning Knowledge: In Seven Plays of Shakespeare*. 2nd ed. Cambridge University Press.

Derrida, Jacques. 1973. *Speech and Phenomena*. Trans. David B. Allison. Evanston, IL: Northwestern University Press.

———. 1975. *Limited Inc*. Evanston, IL: Northwestern University Press.

Dollimore, Jonathan. 2004. *Radical Tragedy: Religion, Ideology and Power in the Drama of Shakespeare and His Contemporaries*. Durham, N.C.: Duke University Press.

Freud, Sigmund. 2015. *The Interpretation of Dreams: Annotated*. Translated by Abraham Arden Brill. Annotated edition. CreateSpace Independent Publishing Platform.

Greenblatt, Stephen. 1989. *Shakespearean Negotiations: The Circulation of Social Energy in Renaissance England (The New Historicism: Studies in Cultural Poetics)*. Berkeley: University of California Press.

———. 2005. *Renaissance Self-Fashioning: From More to Shakespeare*. Chicago: University of Chicago Press.

Harris, Jonathan Gil. 2010. *Shakespeare and Literary Theory*. Oxford: Oxford University Press.

Hillman, David. 2007. *Shakespeare's Entrails: Belief, Scepticism and the Interior of the Body*. Houndmills, Basingstoke, Hampshire: Palgrave Macmillan.

Johnston, Paul. 2014. *Wittgenstein: Rethinking the Inner*. London: Routledge.

Jones, Ernest. 1910. "The Œdipus-Complex as an Explanation of Hamlet's Mystery: A Study in Motive." *American Journal of Psychology* 21: 72–113.

Marion, Jean-Luc. 2008. *The Erotic Phenomenon*. Trans. Stephen E Lewis. Chicago: University of Chicago Press.

Maus, Katharine Eisaman. 1995. *Inwardness and Theater in the English Renaissance*. Chicago: University of Chicago Press.

Taylor, Charles. 1992. *Sources of the Self*. Reprint, Cambridge, MA: Harvard University Press.

Wittgenstein, Ludwig. 1973. *Philosophical Investigations*. Trans. G. E. M. Anscombe. Oxford: Blackwell.

———. 1980. *Remarks on the Philosophy of Psychology*. Ed. G. E. M. Anscombe and G. H. von Wright. Trans. G. E. M. Anscombe. Chicago: University of Chicago Press.

———. 1982. *Last Writings on the Philosophy of Psychology*. Ed. G. H. von Wright and Heikki Nyman. Trans. C. G. Luckhardt and Maximilian A. E. Aue. Chicago: University of Chicago Press.

Chapter 8

Hamlet's Ethics

SARAH BECKWITH

Consider the following case: In July 1985 in Duduza, a township thirty miles east of Johannesburg, South Africa, a man with a tire laced with gasoline around his neck is pushed and thrust into a burning car. The crowd around him are calling for his death: "Kill him! Kill him." The man is a police informer. This was his punishment in the eyes of those whose long and appalling struggle against apartheid he had betrayed. Archbishop Desmond Tutu, a small man, not much taller than me, and a gentle man, thrusts his way into the mob. While sixty or more young men are still beating the man bloody, Desmond Tutu and Simeon Nkoane pull the man from the car and drag him to safety. "Let us not use methods in this struggle that we will be ashamed of."

Did the archbishop *choose* to plow into the mob to extricate this man—as if there were two possible things to be done and not only one? Did he weigh up the pros and cons of so doing, and *decide* that he must gather his courage to enter the jostling, violent mass because saving this man's life was the greater good, overriding both the risk to himself and the idea that he might then be perceived as undermining the struggle to end the supremacy of self-styled whites? There is something ridiculous about such a description of his actions. For there was no choice at all involved for Desmond Tutu. Had there been such a choice he would have not been the man he showed himself to be. He acted on what he saw, *responded* immediately—but not thereby thoughtlessly—not simply to the man being kicked and stomped on, but to what those actions made of those doing them. "Let us not use methods in the struggle that we will be ashamed of." What he was trying to prevent was not alone the killing of the informer but what his killers would become in that act. The preciousness of the man in the car and the perception that it would be evil to kill him are here coterminous. His acts were deeply moral, not because he was choosing anything but because of what he held precious, what he valued as infinitely worth preserving.

In the following essay I will be arguing that the depth of *Hamlet* as a dramatic work of moral philosophy will only emerge if we shift the terrain of moral discussion away from the naked choosing will and toward what I articulate as the responsibilities of response.

We are all too likely to imagine that moral thinking takes place alone in decisions about what to do or what ought to be done. Moral life is not primarily a matter of choices, said Iris Murdoch.[1] Yet critics of *Hamlet* have often behaved as if the making of a choice is the sole dimension of a moral life. To be sure Hamlet's thought is often concertedly contrapuntal, oscillating poetically and intellectually between two antitheses, the most famous of which is "to be or not to be." In the same soliloquy there are other antitheses too—taking arms against a sea of troubles and in your opposition to those troubles

1. She first articulates this in her 1956 essay "Vision and Choice in Morality," where she has a broad sweep of moral philosophers in her sights (among them R. M. Hare and Stuart Hampshire). See also "The Idea of Perfection," in *The Sovereignty of Good* (New York: Routledge and Kegan Paul, 1970), 36, where she argues against the identification of the person with the "empty choosing will and the corresponding emphasis on the idea of movement rather than vision." She pursues this picture of the will through Sartrean existentialism and Kantianism, and examines the deterministic picture that emerges in opposition to it, but that is caught inside the same conception.

ending them, or merely suffering your fate, bearing it patiently in the slings and arrows of outrageous fortune. Most critics interpret this as pondering a decision whether to revenge his father in an act of regicide, or to endure his fate as the isolated and mourning son. And so we get the critical obsession with Hamlet's delay. Once the premise is granted that Hamlet is deliberating about *what to do*—this or that, the *problem* of delay becomes obligatory. For then we simply must ask why Hamlet is not doing one or the other thing. We are inside the very logic of will that the play undoes.

Hamlet does give us a picture of Hamlet deliberating about whether to kill Claudius in act 3, scene 3, and the audience is by no means invited to endorse it. Claudius has left before the ending of Hamlet's play within the play at the point when Lucianus enters the scene and pours poison in the Player King's ear. In his choric accompaniment to the action, Hamlet has introduced Lucianus as "nephew to the king" (3.2.237). It is at this point and after Hamlet's gloss on the action which supplies Lucianus's motivation, Gonzago's estate and Gonzago's wife, that "the king rises" (3.2.258) and asks for lights, as Polonius stops the action of the play. Is Lucianus a picture of Claudius or of Hamlet? How does Claudius take it? Is it as unambiguous as Hamlet takes it to be? ("I'll take the Ghost's word for a thousand pound," 3.2.278.) The King has retired "in choler" and the Queen has sent for Hamlet. That is the situation when we are given the picture of Hamlet, the Senecan revenger, deliberating on his choice: to kill or not to kill Claudius in prayer. When Hamlet stands over the praying Claudius with his sword he is indeed choosing whether or not to kill him. He chooses not to: "Why, this is base and salary, not revenge" (3.3.79). That act must be "scanned"; it is as likely as not to send Claudius on his way to heaven in his act of repentance. So the picture we are offered here, Hamlet standing behind the praying Claudius, weapon in hand, is the deliberating, choosing Hamlet as a Senecan revenger trying on the role of Lucianus in *The Murder of*

Gonzago. We are asked to recall the moment when Hamlet has asked one of the actors to play the death of Priam by Pyrrhus, "he whose sable arms / Black as his purpose, did the night resemble" (2.2.390–91). As the actor takes up the lines Hamlet remembers, he gives us an image of Pyrrhus pausing, doing nothing as the sword "which was declining on the milky head / Of reverend Priam seemed i'th' air to stick" (2.2.416–17) before he remorselessly brings down the sword on Priam's head. Prompted by the play within the play, we too will see Hamlet trying on the role of Lucianus, who in the Gonzago play is complexly both an image of Claudius himself who poisons the Player King, and, as nephew to the King, also the future specter of the revenging hero, the threat or prospect of what Hamlet might do to Claudius. In the compact doubleness of the role—what Claudius was, what Hamlet might become, the problem is now posed: how to bring about justice without, as in William Blake's formulation, becoming what you behold?

This is not, of course, how Hamlet himself necessarily perceives the question. Hamlet does not question the necessity of avenging his father's murder as an act of retributive justice. Though he regrets the accidental killing of Polonius, he has no qualms at all about arranging for the execution of Rosencrantz and Guildenstern. But this is not, I believe, how *Hamlet* the play, as opposed to Hamlet the character, works. And to collapse that distinction is to be blind to the play's tragic ironies; it is to ignore the contrast between our knowingness as spectators, say, as witnesses to Claudius's prayers to God in his confession, with Hamlet's lack of knowledge, which lack is a condition of human limitation and finitude, and source of those very tragic ironies. To resist the play's tragic ironies is almost inevitably to moralize the play, to imagine that we would be in a greater state of knowingness than Hamlet. The play is scrupulous and brilliantly original on the limits of human knowingness and the conditions of possibility of knowledge in Denmark. It provides us with several kinds of response to murder, violence, and primal human aggression and continually opens these responses out for reflection and self-reflection.[2]

In a brilliant set of remarks that gloss the "pause" in revenge tragedy, Tony Tanner cites Aeschylus's *Libation Bearers*, at the point when Orestes is finally confronting his mother, Clytemnestra. He is about to kill her and she begs for pity from him, reminding him that she gave him suck. He turns to his friend Pylades: "What shall I do, Pylades? Be shamed to kill my mother?" Tanner calls this pause the most important moment in the whole trilogy and "in the emergence of Western drama." It is so because "in this brief moment, Orestes has introduced a break in the circle." He has opened up the gap in which reflection can disrupt and interrupt action. In his soliloquy in *Julius Caesar* (2.1.61–69), Brutus says: "Between the acting of a dreadful thing / And the first motion, all the interim is / Like a phantasma or hideous dream." Hamlet's pause lasts for the whole play.[3]

So the picture of the choosing will shows us Hamlet histrionically trying out for the role of Lucianus. His intentions are thoroughly

2. I have found Nigel Alexander's discussion of these points sharply clear and helpful. See *Poison, Play, and Duel: A Study in "Hamlet"* (Lincoln: University of Nebraska Press, 1971), especially pp. 3 and 10. Although Hamlet never questions the appropriateness of revenging his father, Alexander remarks, "The play which Shakespeare wrote *does* ask its audience to examine and question the assumption made so readily by so many of Hamlet's critics—the assumption that Hamlet's only proper response to the news that his father has been murdered in secret is to become a secret murderer" (my italics). To make this assumption is to ignore the seven soliloquies and the deliberate and careful patterning of doubles and foils which invite a pointed variety of responses. Most importantly it is to moralize the play's action, dissolving the contingencies and uncertainties that lie at the very heart of the play, rather than explore its ethics. On moralism and moralization see Stanley Cavell, *The Claim of Reason: Wittgenstein, Skepticism, Morality, and Tragedy* (Oxford: Oxford University Press, 1979, 2nd ed., 1999), 326, in the important third part of this seminal book. See also Raimond Gaita's illuminating comments in the preface to his book *A Common Humanity: Thinking about Love, and Truth and Justice* (New York: Routledge, 2000), xv–xvi: "Moralizing (in the pejorative sense) goes deep in what we call morality and is, I think, one of the reasons why many keep their distance from it." A full exploration of the resistance of tragedy to moralization must await a different occasion.
3. *Prefaces to Shakespeare* (Cambridge, MA: Belknap Press of Harvard University Press, 2010), 490, 493, 499.

ironized by the fact that Claudius is in the full throes of what appears to be remorse. In the confessing prayer we overhear, Claudius realizes that he will not give up the fruits of his murder. It is the first time we know unequivocally that he is guilty; and that his guilt will inform a greater self-knowledge but not a true contrition, for that as he lucidly explains, would entail making an act of restitution of the kingdom and relinquishment of the Queen. So at the very point where Hamlet imagines he is in charge of Claudius's afterlife, acting out his part of scourge and minister, bone-setting the time back into joint, he is seen to be wholly unaware of what he is actually doing. It is a dramatic hollowing out of the role of the revenge hero/villain and it resituates Hamlet's deliberation in an altogether different moral context, one in which he does not know what he is doing. He thinks he is savoring a more just revenge in the future, one guaranteeing Claudius a place in the hell he deserves, rather than the heaven to which Claudius' prayers might bring him. He thinks this is not the best time for the real satisfactions of revenge, yet he is thus mysteriously, and despite his own overt intentions, preserved for a potentially nobler end. The problem of the play then is not the misconceived delay which merely assumes the obviousness of revenge as Hamlet's solution, but the problem of not becoming like Claudius in revenging his father. (Revenge tragedy after all, is, as John Kerrigan has said, naturally histrionic, and it relishes the dramatic exchange of roles in which it conventionally trades: "When B, injured by A, does to A what A did to him, he makes himself resemble the opponent he has blamed while he transforms his enemy into the kind of victim he once was.")[4] Yet when we have become too enamored of the deracinated idea of

4. John Kerrigan, *English Revenge Tragedy: Aeschylus to Armageddon* (Oxford: Clarendon Press, 1996), 6. Tzachi Zamir has pointed out to me (personal communication) that murder and its revenge cannot be symmetrical, if any distinction between the original act and an act of retributive justice is to be maintained. But revenge tragedy often pointedly patterns the modeling of revenge to the original act: Orestes models his murder on Clytemnestra on her

choice, we sever the will from its intrinsic connection to both memory and understanding in the Augustinian tradition.[5]

I have referred to Archbishop Desmond Tutu's act in rescuing the tire-laced man as a *response* to a man in pain, rather than a choice to rescue him or not. It was a *response* emerging out of Tutu's vision of the world (and so of this particular man in front of him) rather than a choice of what to do there and then, weighing up the possibilities for action.[6] I might now put Desmond Tutu's orientation toward the man in Platonic or Christian terms. Tutu's action involved not merely doing, but also being and loving. In a superb essay on Iris Murdoch in *Iris Murdoch and the Search for Human Goodness*, Charles Taylor says: "If we give the full range of ethical meanings their due, we can

killing of Agamemnon, for example. Characters such as Vindice in *The Revenger's Tragedy*, or Hoffman in Chettle's revenge tragedy, ruin themselves on the plot and path of revenge even as revenge plots flirt with parody and camp grotesque. Shakespeare's deep insight is to bring out the grief that underlies both mourning and revenge, where both are forms of remembrance, both ways of imagining death, but with very different consequences. The popularity of the revenge plot is explored most recently in Linda Woodbridge, *English Revenge Drama: Money, Resistance, Equality* (Cambridge: Cambridge University Press, 2010).

5. In invoking the will as a tripartite aspect of the trinitarian soul along with memory and understanding, I am of course invoking Augustine. It is part of Augustine's development of the concept of *libero arbitrio*, free choice, that willing is an achievement of temporal synthesis, as Wetzel puts it in *Augustine and the Limits of Virtue* (Cambridge: Cambridge University Press, 1992), 110. Our willing bears the impress of what we have been—and lack of integration in willing gives the past the power to disrupt the present. I shall return to some of these distinctions later on in the chapter. A superb archaeology of moral agency is undertaken by Thomas Pfau in *Minding the Modern: Human Agency, Intellectual Traditions, and Responsible Knowledge* (Notre Dame, IN: University of Notre Dame Press, 2013). It is part of the book's purview to show the etiolation of concepts of moral agency of great pertinence to my analysis of *Hamlet*. Pfau examines the slow erosion of a Christian/Platonic model where the human person arises from a productive alignment of will and intellect. "Agency here is not conceived epistemologically—that is, as involving (or lacking) some technical skill for solving situation-specific and ostensibly value neutral puzzles of what to *do*. Rather, it pivots on the far more complex and value-saturated mystery of what kind of person one seeks to *be*."

6. Susan Wolf's essay "Loving Attention: Lessons in Love from *The Philadelphia Story*" is a marvelous exposition of Iris Murdoch on a moral world informed by love and attention, rather than the deracinated, "naked" will and the choices it surveys. Reprinted in *The Variety of Values: Essays on Morality, Meaning, and Love* (Oxford: Oxford University Press, 2015), 163–80.

see that the fullness of ethical life involves not just doing, but also being; and not just these two but also loving (which is shorthand here for being moved by, being inspired by) what is constitutively good. It is a drastic reduction to think that we can capture the moral by focusing only on obligated action, as though it were of no ethical moment what you are and what you love. These are the essence of ethical life."[7] A narrow focus on choice renders other forms of ethical life harder to see.[8] "Let us not use methods in the struggle that we will be ashamed of." The tendency to tie moral life "too closely . . . exercised in the capacity to choose" is likely to make "other forms of moral activity invisible."[9]

Doing, Being, Loving. I've been saying that *Hamlet* criticism has been very preoccupied by a thinned-down version of ethics as "what ought to be done?" What of being? What of loving? *Hamlet* begins with all the hyperbolic trappings of the revenge plot—the Senecan ghost, the secret murder, the lack of justice in the centers of power, even the attention to theater itself is a stock part of revenge dramaturgy—and it turns them into an *ars moriendi*, a play exploring the metaphysical questions of life and death, the craft or art of dying. Questions of doing are opened out into questions of being such that these investigations become the very texture of the *Hamlet* universe. Peter Mercer puts this the following way: "We might . . . say that Shakespeare has created for his tragedy a world so inherently resistant to the fierce simplifications of such an action, so unresponsive to

7. Charles Taylor, "Iris Murdoch and Moral Philosophy," in *Iris Murdoch and the Search for Human Goodness*, ed. Maria Antonaccio and William Schweiker (Chicago: University of Chicago Press, 1996), 15.

8. A point reiterated by Cora Diamond, "We Are All Perpetually Moralists: Iris Murdoch, Fact, and Value," in *Iris Murdoch and the Search for Human*, 102. This pattern has clearly radically marked the history of *Hamlet* criticism.

9. Cora Diamond, "We Are All Perpetually Moralists: Iris Murdoch, Fact, and Value," in *Iris Murdoch and the Search for Human* Goodness, ed. Maria Antonaccio and William Schweiker (Chicago: University of Chicago Press, 1996), 102.

that unique extravagance of passion and rhetoric, a world, in the end, so acutely aware of the distinction between reality and art, that it is hard to see how any revenger could impose upon it the murderous artifice of his ritual of death. It is that world that Hamlet must first seek to understand."[10] Hamlet's first soliloquy is directly concerned with modes of being, rather than modes of doing, and Hamlet's consciousness permanently expands into questions about what a human life is, what leading it comes to: "What a piece of work is a man—how noble in reason; how infinite in faculties, in form and moving; how express and admirable in action; how like an angel in apprehension; how like a god; . . . And yet to me what is this quintessence of dust?" (2.2.269–74). These are questions that can only embarrass utilitarian and other post-Kantian modes of moral philosophy which wish to root moral significance alone in "terms of choices, principles, and factually describable situations within which principles are applied or fail to be applied."[11]

Yet if there is a Senecan ghost in *Hamlet*, it is quite transformed. The ghost of Hamlet's father is utterly different to Don Andrea, the ghost in Thomas Kyd's play *The Spanish Tragedy*, and from all other models of the Senecan ghost. For our ghost enjoins Hamlet not simply to revenge his foul and most unnatural murder, but to remember him. Most complexly of all, young Hamlet is asked not to taint his soul or harm his mother in the process of remembrance and revenge. And further the ghost of King Hamlet tells a story—a story he says is untellable ("I could a tale unfold . . ." [1.5.15] of the torment of his soul dying "[u]nhouseled, disappointed, unanaled" [1.5.77]), not having prepared to meet his maker. It is a ghost who enjoins harrowing pity and not mere fury, anger, and bewilderment, whose injunctions are

10. Peter Mercer, *Hamlet and the Acting of Revenge* (Iowa City: University of Iowa Press, 1987), 122.
11. "We are all perpetually moralists," 105.

mutually impossible, likely in fact to "lose the name of action", since it is not clear what united action could fulfill them all at once.

Before I explore the broad expansion of narrow conceptions of doing to modes of being and loving, and the implications for thinking about *Hamlet* both in terms of moral philosophy, and as moral philosophy, I need to explore *Hamlet* as a play that reconfigures our understanding of the ends of revenge tragedy, the narrative ending of the play, and Hamlet's famous confrontation with death.

My stepmother's family business was undertaking. This has always struck me as a strange yet deeply suitable word for the business of burying our loved ones. For an undertaking is a difficult task or project, something taken on, as surely any funeral is, and it is a kind of pledge, an undertaking owed to everyone in death.[12] Perhaps for the very reason that she was surrounded by the dead when she was young she wishes to have no ceremony at her own death. She is most emphatic on this point. It is a point I find troubling.

It is well known that Hamlet begins in a mourning garb made ostentatious by the fact that the court has so evidently "moved on," and somewhat swiftly, from any ceremonious rites owed to the dead, to celebrate a wedding so that, in Claudius' deeply muddled and offensive image, there should be "mirth in funeral and dirge in marriage" (1.2.12). The fact that we are creatures who mourn and seek to honor each particular death reveals that it is important to us to find each other irreplaceable in our singularity, and that we recognize such singleness together. In a funeral the individual man or woman is mourned. It is an honor to him or her, but it is also an honoring

---

12. The sense of this is beautifully explored in Graham Swift's novel *Last Orders* (London: Picador, 2010), and in Thomas Lynch's stunning essays in *The Undertaking: Life Studies in the Dismal Trade* (New York: Norton, 1997).

to us, of who we take ourselves to be. We celebrate a singular death but a common fate. We experience not distaste or disagreement, but horror, a sense that we and the dead have been violated when we see deaths not honored. So a mourning rite honors the dead and the grief of the chief mourners, and reveals a community bound by its common love. It is both common and particular. The deaths we mourn we mourn in common but their effect on us if we are to honor them is intimately particular. The fact that death is common—that it happens to everyone, that we share it, is nothing but a commonplace if that is not recognized. Yet it is precisely the commonness and the particularity that have become unmoored in act 1, scene 2 of *Hamlet*.

Gertrude asks why Hamlet seeks his noble father in the dust and with an obtusely bland reassurance says: "Thou knowst 'tis common all that lives must die, / Passing through nature to eternity" (1.2.73–73). Hamlet's response is sardonic: "Ay, madam, it is common" (1.2.74). The common as what we share—since she appears not to share his grief—is no more than a commonplace to her. But Gertrude misunderstands his response: "If it be, / Why seems it so particular with thee?" (1.2.75). And this prompts Hamlet's hyperbolical retreat to what he has within "which passes show" (1.2.85). Claudius too uses most blandly and superficially the language of the common. Since "your father lost a father, / That father lost lost his" (1.2.89–90), so all are bound in filial obligation "to do obsequious sorrow" (1.2.87–90). But, he suggests, Hamlet is persisting in "obstinate condolement" (1.2.92) which he then goes on to describe as unmanly, impious, and most incorrect to heaven. It is hard to imagine that Hamlet's grief is obstinate given how recent we must suppose his father's death to be. Claudius goes on to say "what we know must be, and is as common / As any the most vulgar thing to sense . . ." (1.2.98–99) and so it is peevish to take it to heart. That something commonly happens does not undermine the need to feel or respond to it, but for Claudius what is common is not what is shared but what is "the most vulgar thing to sense," ascribing a vulgarity to Hamlet that is all his own. Once again he invokes the death of fathers as "a common theme" and invokes the earliest death—that of Abel by Cain. This is perhaps not the best example he might have chosen under the circumstances.

Hamlet makes visible what Claudius wants to consign to oblivion, makes apparent that Claudius thinks on the dead king "together with remembrance of ourselves" (1.2.7). It is an act of oblivion rather than memorialization. It is syntactically brilliant, for the remembrance of himself, as we will come to know, has altogether obscured, covered over the mourned man. It is remembrance of himself that has led to the murder of King Hamlet in the first place. It is the commitment to the remembrance of himself which will lead him to suspect Hamlet, to spy on him, and later on, to dispatch him to England with a death warrant on his head. What is buried with old Hamlet is an entire past. In so misusing the idea of what is "common," it is all the particularities of Hamlet's grief that are obscured, a grief that is alone faithful not simply to his father, but to a better past. Hamlet senses a violation before he knows quite the extent of it, before he even sees the ghost and listens to his grievous tale.

Gertrude's moral idiocy turns out to be central: "Why seems it so particular with thee?" No mourning can take place without its particularly to you or me being felt. This meditation on the common and particular is reprised again in the last act of the play in two marked ways—first through the figure of Yorick, and then through Ophelia's poor corpse. For the trajectory of act 5, scene 1 in relation to both figures is to single out the known dead from the vast generalities, the massed and disintegrating bodies who can be recast according to Hamlet's own imagination. As Hamlet and Horatio enter the graveyard, they see the witty and tuneful gravedigger displacing all kinds of old skulls as he makes room for a new coffin. The question of who this new grave is for is thus playfully deferred for their death-talk. Hamlet speculates about the identity of the first two skulls unceremoniously flung on the stage. The first skull might be Cain, the first murderer, he speculates, or perhaps a politician, perhaps a courtier. And now Hamlet assigns words to the skull, imitating the courtier in which role he has cast the skull: "Good morrow, sweet lord, how dost thou, sweet lord?" (5.1.77–78). As Hamlet ponders the "fine revolution" of death that brings his imagined courtier to the chapless, knocked-about, worm-ridden state he's now in, a second skull lands next to him, as so much spray off the gravedigger's shovel. Once again Hamlet conjures up miniplays: perhaps this skull was once a lawyer, involved in complex land conveyancing, and he goes on to imagine the concrete details of lawyerly work, imagining a set of purposes now made pointless by the end to which he comes: "Is this the fine of his fines . . . to have his fine pate full of fine dirt?" (5.1.100–101).[13] Hamlet has surpassed himself in making four puns on fine. (A fine is a legal document by which entailed property is changed into freehold possession; it is fine as in elegant, praiseworthy, it is fine as in thin and refined, and it is *fin*—an end, evoking the deepest pun in the play, the one on ends and ends—end as telos or purpose, and end as death, the cessation of life.[14] Hamlet now decides to engage in conversation with the gravemaker rather than simply watch over his work. He asks him how long he's been at the trade of making graves. And his answer dates his employment in finding a final resting home for the living to the twin events of old King Hamlet's duel with Fortinbras, and to his very own birth. It is as if the jester's death has shadowed his own. Hamlet asks him how long it takes for a man's body to begin rotting and disintegrating? And as he gives his expertise on the subject—a tanner's body

13. The reference here is to the Folio. Q2's reference is to the buyer of the land, rather than the lawyer.
14. Michael Neill explores this moment in *Hamlet* in his fine chapter "'To Know My Stops': *Hamlet* and Narrative Abruption," in *Issues of Death: Mortality and Identity in English Renaissance Tragedy* (Oxford: Clarendon Press, 1990), 217.

outlasting that of other men—he picks out an exemplary skull, a skull he minutely dates to be twenty-three years old. At this point Hamlet wants to know "whose was it" (5.1.165). But he does not expect to be familiar with the one-time inhabiter of it. Now the anonymous bones tossed up from a sea of death, the countless and innumerable prior generations, are given a minute and particular history, a history that turns out to have been an intimate part of his own. This was a man Hamlet knew. "Alas, poor Yorick. I knew him, Horatio" (5.1.174). Imagine coming across the bones of one you knew. He can't cast this skull as a courtier, doctor, lawyer, can't ascribe to him any words that come into his head, but must contemplate a man whose life was once so particularly entwined with his. His imagination "abhors" it, and pushes him out of satirical distance into horror and repugnance.[15] His mind moves quickly out of particularities again, though, as he imagines even the most mighty of military commanders coming to just such a foul-smelling and ignoble end, and more, stopping a bung-hole. He has recast Yorick as Alexander, and then imagined Alexander himself as a piece of loam to stop a beer barrel.

But now this wordplay is interrupted by the "maim'd rites" (5.1.208) of a funeral cortège. Once again death's great and common generalities are to be interrupted by a particularly known and loved person. The gravedigger has told him he is digging a grave for a woman, not a man. We know it is Ophelia's grave, but Hamlet doesn't. That knowledge is deferred for several more lines as Hamlet deflects his intimacy with Yorick into further speculation about Alexander and the bung-hole. But once again this transformation from the common,

15. See here Peter Mercer's interesting comments about the kinship of revenge tragedy and satire in Mercer, *Hamlet and the Acting of Revenge*, 91. The satirist and the revenger are isolated and alone, and they inhabit a world dispossessed by vice—they are both truth seekers wishing to tear the mask of the hypocrisy that hides the moral corruption with which they are obsessed. Mercer points out that the satirist looks for the reform and repentance of his audience; the revenger the victim's suffering and death. Is Hamlet shocked out of his mood as satirist here by the intimate connection of Yorick with his own history?

the generality of death, to the particular dead person profoundly intertwined with his own history has to be made. Hamlet identifies Laertes declaiming to the churlish priests about the "maim'd rites" given to his suicidal sister. And it is in this way that Hamlet realizes that it is Ophelia who is dead, one who has been "particular to him." Quite how particular we are about to learn in Hamlet's astonishing declaration: "This is I, / Hamlet the Dane" (5.1.246–47), as he too steps into the new grave. He says he will fight with Laertes forever on "this theme." We have learned that the Queen wished Hamlet to marry Ophelia, so Polonius's advice to Ophelia has been pointless, her enforced return of Hamlet's "remembrances to her" wasteful and cruelly redundant. She now asks on what theme he wishes to fight Laertes and he bursts out: "I loved Ophelia" (5.1.258). In singling her out he singles himself out as a lover, one who loved, and was perhaps loved, though rebuffed. It is a world of possibility agonizingly lost, and now only realized through that loss.[16] It is as such an affirmation of a world worthy to be lived in, worthy to be loved.

In one memorable production I saw at Stratford in 2013, Ophelia's body was left on stage for the entirety of the rest of the play. The periphery of the stage was made of earth, which gradually encroached upon the boards, framed then by the brown encroaching dust, the promised oblivion of death. It was a deeply appropriate image of Ophelia's centrality in the play, for it is alone in her exquisitely sad and broken fragments that anyone at all is appropriately mourned: "And will 'a not come again?" (4.5.182). It is Ophelia who blesses her father buried "huggermugger": "God a' mercy on his soul.

---

16. Tzachi Zamir has noted in a recent essay that "Tragedy is the process whereby values and their meanings are crystallized through loss (p. 78)." I would add that such losses—to work in a tragic idiom—can never be general; that it is only through the most particular realizations of loss that mourning can bring into play forms of tragic recognition. That *Hamlet* is a play about mourning has been noted by many, whether registered through the loss of a concept of purgatory, or through individual practices of mourning.

/ And of all Christians' souls" (4.5.191–92). We might be reminded that Hamlet is torn between his fascination with the death of Priam, and with the grief of Hecuba.

In a fascinating meditation on *Hamlet*, Lionel Abel places the graveyard scene pivotally in relation to the dramaturgy of death. In every scene of the play, he claims, one character is attempting to cast and dramatize another. Hamlet's father's ghost gives Hamlet the role of remembrancer and revenger. Claudius casts Laertes in the role of avenger, and double-plots (belt and braces, rapier and poisoned cup) an end for Hamlet. Polonius spies on his own children, casts Ophelia in the role of lure to entrap Hamlet, but he misunderstands the plot. Hamlet, of course has been cast in a role he finds a "spite" and which he never does fulfill in the way the ghost has demanded. He recasts himself as the most literal playwright of them all, composing some lines to an old play to be performed in front of the court. In that play, as we've seen, Lucianus is at once Claudius and young Hamlet, and we see him trying on the part when his sword pauses over Claudius' praying head. Abel suggests it is when he recognizes Yorick that he sees the "truth of that dramatic script in which no one can refuse to act; death will make us all theatrical, no matter what we have done in life."[17] If the ultimate playwright is death, it will write an end for us that we cannot foresee, nor will we fully experience it, the rest being silence.

If *Hamlet* opens up these questions from doing to being, he also opens them up into loving. Hamlet's astonishing declaration in Ophelia's grave, "I loved Ophelia," "takes us beyond the questions of what we ought to do to what it is good to be, and then even beyond that, and related to that, to what can command our fullest love."[18]

---

17. Lionel Abel, *Metatheatre* (1963), republished in *Tragedy and Metatheatre: Essays on Dramatic Form*, edited by Martin Puchner (New York: Holmes & Meier, 2003), 123.
18. Charles Taylor, "Iris Murdoch and Moral Philosophy," 5.

I don't think we knew that he loved Ophelia. His world was not one conducive to the expression of love, and his poor love, Ophelia, is bullied into rejecting him on the falsest grounds, and on altogether wrong assumptions. Ophelia's madness, her drowning, is the truest indication of the price of such stupidity, and it is given to her, as I and many other critics have mentioned, to offer the most fitting funeral rites of the entire play.

In declaring his love, he declares himself: "It is I, Hamlet the Dane" discloses himself as a lover, a lover of Ophelia, but not alone Ophelia. Since the declaration is an affirmation of a world in which love is possible, it is an affirmation of a world which can command our love.

The possibilities opened up by this way of thinking help us make sense of the ending of the play. After the graveyard scene, Hamlet and Horatio engage in two extraordinary conversations. It is worth observing here that we are learning about Hamlet not now through his soliloquies (he stops soliloquizing after 4.4, "how all occasions do inform against me") but through his interactions with others. His antic disposition, his histrionic trying on of roles has obscured our understanding of him a courtier, soldier, and scholar. We can now learn about him through his engagements with others around him for he is no longer hiding. In these conversations with Horatio he tells him of the events on board the ship—both his discovery of his death warrant in Rosencrantz and Guildenstern's keeping, and his substitution of his for theirs, as well as the utterly fortuitous capture by pirates which allows him safely home. All this he says he did "Rashly— / And praise be rashness for it" (5.2.6–7). His deep plots have palled and it is through rashness that he saved his own life. He ascribes these events to a providence shaping our ends. This coheres with Lionel Abel's sense that our exits, in that famous dramatic metaphor, their timing, the way they happen—are not fully under our control. If this is merely a truism as a generality, it is lived, existentially and particularly as insight and self-understanding.

When Horatio advises Hamlet not to engage in the duel with Laertes, I often find that students call Hamlet's response fatalistic. "We defy augury. There is special providence in the fall of a sparrow. If it be, 'tis not to come. If it be not to come, it will be now. If it be not now, yet it will come. The readiness is all, since no man of aught he leaves knows what is't to leave betimes" (5.2.197–201).

It is my understanding that it is only from the point of view of the naked human will choosing that this can be seen in a fatalistic light. Hamlet is saying that his end will come. This is not so much fatalistic as true. His end is inevitable; but he cannot know or predict how it will come about. An acceptance of one's necessary ignorance in a contingent world is not the same as fatalism. He accepts the inexorable contingency of the world and what happens in it. The attitude of the will here has undergone a thoroughgoing transformation. He is not concertedly willing, plotting, designing the end of the King, but he is ready to face whatever comes his way, including his own death. We are no longer on the terrain of the oughts of action, but in the category of *response*. Hamlet at this point is not going to plot or plan but to be ready for whatever may come, not anticipating or knowing what that is or will be. Such an attitude might involve a trust in one's own resources. It more importantly involves a relinquishment of any fantasies of will rough-hewing our own ends or the ends of others. And here of course the complex pun on ends involves its meaning as both purpose—the teleology or end of action, the purpose toward which it tends, and ends as in the ends of life—one's own, or the other's on whom revenge sets its violent and histrionic designs. In the astonishing finale of the play there is a great sense of the mystery of the life beyond, the undiscovered country. Hamlet ends midsentence with his enigmatic phrase, "the rest is silence" (5.2.342) but he wishes Horatio to explain the circumstances of what has ensued in the carnage around him so that what he has done can be properly understood. There is an understanding here of a continuation of life that does not totally end in our deaths. Charles Taylor puts it this way: "The point of things is not exhausted by life, the fullness of life, even the goodness of life." Taylor is here attempting to describe death not merely as negation and undoing, but as "the affirmation of something which matters beyond life, on which life originally draws"[19] Opening to this possibility is involving yourself in a change of identity. It is that conversion which Hamlet has undergone at this stage in the play.

For what does Hamlet do at the end of the play? Under one description we could say this: he duels with Laertes bravely. He wins the first two bouts of fencing with Laertes. The Queen drinks to his health against the King's advice. (Very much depends on how Gertrude plays this line.) In the third bout they exchange daggers in the scuffle and they both hit each other, but since Hamlet now mistakenly has Laertes's poisoned dagger, he is poisoned. The Queen announces to Hamlet that she is poisoned and lets him know that the King is the poisoner. Laertes tells Hamlet that he is poisoned by the rapier and he tells Hamlet that the King is to blame for both the poisoned cup and the poisoned rapier. It is now and only now that Hamlet stabs the King with the poisoned dagger and forces him to drink the remaining poison from the chalice.

I'll pause there in the tumultuous and fast-moving action and reaction of the last scene. What has Hamlet done? His act could superficially be described as an act of revenge. And critics of Hamlet's delay can also breathe a sigh of relief to say "mission accomplished!" But might not this action just as easily be described as an act of self-defense, or/and a revenge of the mistaken death of the Queen who has gone out of her way to save Hamlet's life and not the King's face? His truth is out; it is public, and for that reason Hamlet has killed the King not in a private act of vengeance but as a tyrant who has

19. Taylor, "Iris Murdoch and Moral Philosophy," 20.

usurped his brother's throne and wife, and perverted the course of justice in such a way that it is now obvious to all that the entire court and kingdom have been living lies. Another way of describing this then is the following: he has succeeded in dealing with Claudius without becoming like him, without, that is, becoming evil.[20] He has, too, overcome the specter of his former self—the hatred expressed in the fifth and sixth soliloquies. He has not undertaken an act of secret murder—which would have been his act had he killed the King in prayer. We might also say that he has—despite the horrors of murderous lust that seem to have subsumed for him all possibilities of human erotic affection—succeeded in both loving and declaring his love. He has succeeded in seeing that both a human and a divine love are possible and so we can succeed in thinking him, with Horatio, a "sweet Prince" (5.2.343) and join the prayer that flights of angels may sing him to his rest.

Nigel Alexander has said that it is thus also Hamlet's triumph that he has rescued the mourned dead, made invisible through Claudius's "remembrance of himself," from oblivion. For Claudius's self-regarding will has subsumed both understanding and memory. But Hamlet's dramaturgy theatrically restores the past and brings it to bear on the present. Alexander says that: "The entire play acts as a theatre of memory which stamps upon the mind of the audience an impression of Hamlet's consciousness."[21] Thus even in the face of the great disintegrating anonymity of death, amid the sardonic gravediggers, ready to face the odds stacked against him, the prince can know that no matter the universality, the common-ness of ends, of death, how we play our particular parts is all important. The commonness of our fate does not absolve us of the responsibility for figuring out our own role in it.

20. Alexander, *Poison, Play, and Duel*, 73.
21. Alexander, *Poison, Play, and Duel*, 171.

We have seen that only under the most superficial description is Hamlet's act what his father's ghost envisaged. So we might also say of Hamlet's act at the end of the play, that it is his act, and not his father's. It is a signal achievement of identity, to play his role and not the one his father's ghost has given to him. He wants it to be described aright because he knows that it could come under many descriptions.

The great revenge cycle the *Oresteia* ended with the court of Athena ruling on Orestes's revenge on his mother, Clytemnestra. The Furies, those wild justicers who must answer the blood that has been split in revenge, are bound into the polity and the great trilogy ends in the foundation of law, as a supreme achievement of Greek polity, and Greek theater. Theater is indeed the place, as Paul Woodruff has brilliantly noticed, in which justice needs to be seen to be done.[22] In *Hamlet*'s last act, Shakespeare has "dramatized the power of conscience, understanding and love which holds out the slender possibility that the killing may be stopped and the cycle of revenge broken."[23]

Peter Mercer has suggested that Hamlet has achieved his act of revenge without becoming a revenger: "Hamlet is brought, finally, to the achievement of his revenge, but in a way which extraordinarily leaves him free of guilt."[24] It is in this sense that *Hamlet* is not a revenge tragedy at all. But perhaps we had rather adjust our sense of the possibilities of tragedy in the light of this extraordinary play. Only what can move us to wonder can be violated[25] and so it is Hamlet's sensitivity and attentiveness to the world around him to which we respond. Hamlet's ethics, if you like, can better be understood as

22. Paul Woodruff, *The Necessity of Theatre: The Art of Watching and Being Watched* (Oxford: Oxford University Press, 2010).

23. Alexander, *Poison, Play, and Duel*, 185.

24. Peter Mercer, *Hamlet and the Acting of Revenge* (Iowa City: University of Iowa Press, 1987), 247.

25. An idea beautifully explored in Christopher Cordner's work. See his *Ethical Encounter: The Depth of Moral Meaning*, Swansea Studies in Philosophy (Swansea: Palgrave Macmillan, 2002).

an exploration of what Stanley Cavell calls "the responsibilities of response," wherein he locates our morality.

In his brilliant chapter "Evil Done and Evil Suffered" in *Good and Evil: An Absolute Conception*, Raimond Gaita shows us how problematic certain conceptions of evil are in moral philosophy by virtue of a powerful thought experiment, the kind of experiment that Murdoch might have had in mind in her essay "Against Dryness."[26] He takes the example of the kind used by consequentialists: what if you could save ten people by shooting one? He claims that those who think that it is obvious that one should be shot to save ten have no sense of evil done or suffered. He imagines the response of one who is saved by virtue of the shooting of the one. I will give simply a short excerpt from his account:

> If he dies, I will live, because he died, and because there are nine others with me, each of the nine others will be able to say the same. Yet when he is dead, will I be able to console myself by saying that he died only one tenth for me? Though you think you must kill him not for me or for any of the others taken individually, when he is dead each of us must accept the fact that insofar as he was murdered for our sake, he died for us singly and individually. Each of us, in his singularity, is implicated in the evil of his murder . . . . If you must count, then let it be like this: one, one, one . . ., and when there is no more "one" to be said, content yourself with that and resist the temptation to say: And they total ten whereas there is only one over there.[27]

Raimond Gaita is trying to get at the artificial separation of the very idea of evil done and evil suffered, and at the moral idiocy of choice

26. Iris Murdoch, "Against Dryness," in *Existentialists and Mystics: Writings on Philosophy and Literature* (Harmondsworth: Penguin, 1997), 287–95. This essay was first published in *Encounter* in 1961.
27. Raimond Gaita, *Good and Evil: An Absolute Conception*, 2nd ed. (New York: Routledge, 2004), 68.

in certain examples. "My example," he suggests, "shows that the most important philosophical question is not 'What ought to be done?' The most important question is how to characterise the situation and to capture the evil in it."[28] What Gaita has done by virtue of his superbly perceptive writing is to get us to see the situation posed by the consequentialists in a different light. The situation now comes under an altogether new description and renders absurd the strict parameters as it is conceived in the moral philosopher's "dilemma," parameters that entirely dissolve reality. For in imagining and protecting the surveying eye/I, viewing a range of options in a world of possibilities, the real dimensions of self and world are vanishing from view.[29] Gaita's point—and it is surely Shakespeare's point too in Hamlet (also of course crucially explored in Macbeth)—is that what we do, our actions, come under myriad descriptions. These descriptions define us because they articulate the positions we are prepared to take and what we hold ourselves responsible for.[30] Gaita consistently helps us to see the inadequacies of the idea that moral agency involves a world of facts and attitudes we might take toward them. As Lars Hertzberg has said in a lucid commentary on Gaita's work: "As I read him, he considers the question of what I take to be the case and the way I respond to it to be inseparable aspects of the situation."[31] This is how vision, not choice, is a central dimension of moral agency

28. See Cavell, The Claim of Reason, part 3, pp. 247ff, for a brilliant critique of moral philosophy in terms of "what ought to be done."

29. Forsberg, Language Lost and Found, 171: "a loss of concepts is, at bottom, due to a lack, or a distorted form of self-understanding. This lack or these distortions are in turn related, but not reducible to misunderstandings of our language."

30. See Stanley Cavell's critique of Rawls (The Claim of Reason, 324) and his elucidation of specifically moral claims: "What you are said to do can have various descriptions; under some you will know that you are doing it, under others you will not, under some your act will seem unjust to you, under others not. What alternatives we can and must take are not fixed, but chosen; and thereby fix us."

31. Lars Hertzberg, "Gaita on Recognizing the Human," in Ethics, Philosophy and a Common Humanity, ed. Christopher Cordner (London: Routledge, 2010), 7.

and why the way we see the world is as revelatory of us as of the world we see, respond to, and describe in everyday life and in fiction.[32]

Shakespeare's astonishing regard to the particularities, the irreducible and unsurpassable contingencies of Hamlet's world, and his responses to it, invite us to think, in turn, of what makes this play so particular to us in our patterns of response, and to show how minutely aesthetic judgment and ethical judgment depend on such attentions.

WORKS CITED

Abel, Lionel. 2003. "Metatheatre" (1963). *Tragedy and Metatheatre: Essays on Dramatic Form*. Ed. Martin Puchner. New York: Holmes & Meier.

Alexander, Nigel. 1971. *Poison, Play, and Duel: A Study in Hamlet*. Lincoln: University of Nebraska Press.

Cavell, Stanley. 1999. *The Claim of Reason: Wittgenstein, Skepticism, Morality, and Tragedy*. 2nd ed. Oxford: Oxford University Press.

Cordner, Christopher. 2002. *Ethical Encounter: The Depth of Moral Meaning*. Swansea: Palgrave Macmillan.

Diamond, Cora. 1996. "We Are All Perpetually Moralists: Iris Murdoch, Facts, and Value." *Iris Murdoch and the Search for Human Goodness*. Ed. Maria Antonaccio and William Schweiker. Chicago: University of Chicago Press. 79–109.

Doty, Mark. 2010. *The Art of Description: Word into World*. St. Paul, MN: Graywolf.

Forsberg, Niklas. 2013. *Language Lost and Found: On Iris Murdoch and the Limits of Philosophical Discourse*. New York: Bloomsbury.

Gaita, Raimond. 2000. *A Common Humanity: Thinking about Love, and Truth and Justice*. New York: Routledge.

———. 2004. *Good and Evil: An Absolute Conception*. 2nd ed. New York: Routledge.

Hertzberg, Lars. 2010. "Gaita on Recognizing the Human." *Ethics, Philosophy and a Common Humanity*. Ed. Christopher Cordner. London: Routledge.

Kerrigan, John. 1996. *English Revenge Tragedy: Aeschylus to Armageddon*. Oxford: Oxford University Press.

Lynch, Thomas. 1997. *The Undertaking: Life Studies in the Dismal Trade*. New York: Norton.

32. Mark Doty, *The Art of Description: Word into World* (Minneapolis: Graywolf Press, 2010), 65: "Description is an ART to the degree it gives us not just the world but the inner life of the witness."

Mercer, Peter. 1987. *Hamlet and the Acting of Revenge*. Iowa City: University of Iowa Press.

Murdoch, Iris. 1970. *The Sovereignty of Good*. New York: Routledge and Kegan Paul.

———. 1997a. "Against Dryness" (1961). *Existentialists and Mystics: Writings on Philosophy and Literature*. Ed. Peter Conradi and George Steiner. Harmondsworth: Penguin. 287–95.

Murdoch, Iris. 1997b. "Vision and Choice in Morality" (1956). *Existentialists and Mystics: Writings on Philosophy and Literature*. Ed. Peter Conradi and George Steiner. Harmondsworth: Penguin. 76–115.

Neill, Michael. 1990. *Issues of Death: Mortality and Identity in English Renaissance Tragedy*. Oxford: Oxford University Press.

Pfau, Thomas. 2013. *Minding the Modern: Human Agency, Intellectual Tradition, and Responsible Knowledge*. Notre Dame, IN: University of Notre Dame Press.

Swift, Graham. 2010. *Last Orders*. London: Picador.

Tanner, Tony. 2010. *Prefaces to Shakespeare*. Cambridge: Belknap Press of Harvard University Press.

Taylor, Charles. 1996. "Iris Murdoch and Moral Philosophy." *Iris Murdoch and the Search for Human Goodness*. Ed. Maria Antonaccio and William Schweiker. Chicago: University of Chicago Press. 3–28.

Wetzel, James. 1992. *Augustine and the Limits of Virtue*. Cambridge: Cambridge University Press.

Wolf, Susan. 2015. "Loving Attention: Lessons in Love from *The Philadelphia Story*." *The Variety of Values: Essays on Morality, Meaning, and Love*. Oxford: Oxford University Press. 163–80.

Woodbridge, Linda. 2010. *English Revenge Drama: Money, Resistance, Equality*. Cambridge: Cambridge University Press, 2010.

Woodruff, Paul. 2010. *The Necessity of Theatre: The Art of Watching and Being Watched*. Oxford: Oxford University Press.

Zamir, Tzachi. 2016. "Ethics and Shakespearean Tragedy." *The Oxford Handbook of Shakespearean Tragedy*. Eds. Michael Neill and David Schalkwyck. Oxford: Oxford University Press. 71–88.

Chapter 9

Interpreting *Hamlet*

The Early German Reception

KRISTIN GJESDAL

It is nearly impossible for twenty-first-century readers to fully grasp the force with which Shakespearean drama hit German audiences, schooled in the combination of Aristotelianism and rationalism that we typically characterize as classicism. What was the theater world going to make of an oeuvre that broke just about every rule for tragedy, comedy, and stage performance, and yet seemed to exercise a power and fascination of undeniable magnitude? It most certainly did not happen overnight. And there were, to be sure, efforts to reject Shakespeare's work, to slander it and demonstrate, in print and on stage, the debilitating effects of his drama. There were attempts to tame it, to rein it in through Alexandrine translations, creative adaptations, and an unabashedly ideological editing of characters and lines. The efforts, though, were largely unsuccessful. A few decades after C. W. von Borck's 1741 translation of *Julius Caesar*, Shakespeare had taken the German readership by storm.[1]

---

1. Like Greek tragedy, Shakespeare's drama was not staged, but mainly read in Germany. This, though, changes toward the end of the eighteenth century and in the first decades of the

Shakespeare presented eighteenth-century audiences, critics, and philosophers with a work that completely overthrew the conventional understanding of drama—and, as part of this, also challenged their faith in universal genre definitions and transhistorical aesthetic criteria. In this form, the German Shakespeare debate left an important mark on aesthetics. It is the goal of this chapter to discuss the philosophical impact of Shakespeare's work in the period from Gotthold Ephraim Lessing's *Hamburg Dramaturgy* (1767–69), via Johann Gottfried Herder's work in the 1770s and 1780s, to August Wilhelm Schlegel's 1808 Vienna lectures on dramatic art. I will argue that throughout this debate we see a shift from a top-down and rule-oriented to a bottom-up and work-oriented aesthetic paradigm, and an insistence on the need to approach more general aesthetic questions by way of concrete analysis and exercises in interpretation. Hence, in addition to the widely shared sense that in the late eighteenth century Shakespeare becomes, as it were, an honorary German, I submit that in the years between 1770 and the early 1800s, German aesthetics becomes, in a significant way, Shakespearean. This is not only the case because the *content* of aesthetic thought was marked by Shakespeare's drama, but also—and this will be my focus in this chapter—that its *methodologies* were shaped in and through the encounter with Shakespeare. My point is not that drama theory and eighteenth-century discussions of Shakespeare are the *only* ways in which this work-oriented tradition in aesthetics can be grasped (sculpture, and the debate around Laocoön, would be an obvious contender). More modestly, I suggest that, in the period from the late 1760s to the early 1800s and beyond, the Shakespeare debate represents one possible—and indeed rather promising—way in which this strand of European aesthetics can be explored. If this

nineteenth century. See Simon Williams, *Shakespeare on the German Stage*, vol. I, *1586–1914* (Cambridge: Cambridge University Press, 1990), chapters 3 and 4.

hypothesis holds, then it follows that we should avoid thinking, as it is standardly done, that modern aesthetics starts with Kant's analysis of pure aesthetic judgment and only later, with Hegel, turns to more art-centered approaches. Instead, the subtlety and profundity of the German Shakespeare debate indicates that the art-centered approaches are there, right from the beginning and, as part of this, that philosophy of theater holds a prominent place in the formation of modern European aesthetics.

Resting at the heart of the German Shakespeare debate, *Hamlet* is a particularly well-suited test case for my argument. While the play had initially caught Lessing's attention in terms of its stage ideas and the play within the play, Herder would focus on Hamlet's modern psychology.[2] Schlegel, in turn, would declare Shakespeare's *Hamlet*, which he read as a proto-romantic contribution, a paragon of modern art. In all these cases—Hamlet as dramaturge, Hamlet's psychology, and *Hamlet* as a paragon of modern art—it is the phenomenon of interpretation (Hamlet's and ours) that rests at the center of attention. This should hardly surprise. Once we experience a debunking of classicist ideals and standards, the question is no longer what counts as art and what does not, but, rather, how best to critique and understand new art and keep alive the works that have been handed down by tradition.

INTERPRETING ACTORS (LESSING)

In aesthetic circles, Lessing's posthumous fame is largely due to his 1766 *Laocoön* and his wrestling with Winckelmann's theory of

---

2. It is worth noting that for all his changing attitudes to Shakespeare, Voltaire had already pinpointed *Hamlet* as a key text. For an overview of Voltaire's approach to Shakespeare, see Michèle Willems, "Voltaire," in Peter Holland and Adrian Poole (eds.), *Great Shakespeareans*, 18 vols., vol. III, *Voltaire, Goethe, Schlegel, Coleridge*, ed. Roger Paulin (London: Continuum, 2010), 5–43.

sculpture.[3] Lessing, though, formulates his critique of Winckelmann as a question about the relationship—wrongly conceived, he thinks, by Winckelmann and his peers—between sculpture and literature. Drawn to the quiet grandeur and noble simplicity of the ancients, Winckelmann had assumed a continuity between poetry and sculpture. Lessing, by contrast, insists on a principled difference in medium between poetry and sculpture, and thus also in their respective artistic goals. Poetry, he argues, operates in time. Its domain is action. Painting and sculpture, by contrast, are spatial arts.[4] Lessing thus links the media-specificity and relative (discursive) autonomy of sculpture and poetry: they are each in need of and deserving their own aesthetic models. In this sense, there is a smooth transition from his early discussions of poetry (his contributions to the *Literaturbriefe* in the late 1750s) to his engagement with sculpture (in *Laocoön*), and then back again to poetry in *Hamburg Dramaturgy*.[5]

Lessing's *Hamburg Dramaturgy* consists of 104 short review pieces covering the repertoire of the new national theater in Hamburg. With the reflective distance of the Enlightenment critic, the sensitivity of the poet, and the pride of the newly appointed dramaturge, Lessing discusses acting styles, choice of plays, and the role of the theater in the world of a burgeoning middle class and its ideal of cultural *Bildung*.

---

3. For a helpful overview of Lessing's critique of Winckelmann, see H. B. Nisbet, *Gotthold Ephraim Lessing: His Life, Works, and Thought* (Oxford: Oxford University Press, 2013), 303–33.

4. Gotthold Ephraim Lessing, *Laocoön: An Essay on the Limits of Painting and Poetry*, trans. Edward Allen McCormick (Baltimore: Johns Hopkins University Press, 1984), 78; *Werke und Briefe in Zwölf Bänden*, ed. Wilfried Barner et al. (Frankfurt am Main: Deutscher Klassiker Verlag, 1985–2003), V/2, 116.

5. Upon turning to the *Hamburg Dramaturgy*, Lessing had already discussed drama in a number of contexts: his *Beyträge zur Historie und Aufnahme des Theaters* (1750), *Theatralische Bibliothek* (1754–58), "Briefwechsel über das Trauerspiel mit Nicolai und Mendelssohn" (1756–57), and *Briefe, die neueste Litteratur betreffend* (1759–65). See Peter Höyng, "Lessing's Drama Theory: Discursive Writings on Drama, Performance, and Theater," in Barbara Fischer and Thomas C. Fox (eds.), *A Company to the Works of Gotthold Ephraim Lessing* (Rochester, NY: Camden House, 2005), 211–29.

In this context, the turn to Shakespeare is far from obvious. Unlike the other works he discusses, Lessing did not quite have the guts to stage Shakespeare in Hamburg.[6] In the secondary literature, it is often claimed that in *Hamburg Dramaturgy* Lessing's discussion does not engage Shakespeare's drama on its own terms, but makes it serve, rather, the external purpose of leveraging a criticism of classicist taste.[7] Seeking to modify this reading, I suggest that Lessing's discussion of Shakespeare—and, in particular, of *Hamlet*—is significant in that it breaks with his relatively conservative stage repertoire *and* in that it gives rise to a brief, but philosophically pregnant, discussion of poetry that goes significantly beyond his horizon in *Laocoön*.[8]

In *Hamburg Dramaturgy, Hamlet* is introduced by way of the play within the play. Picking up on Diderot's interest in acting and the actor,[9] Lessing points out that Hamlet advocates "[a] temperance that may give [the acting] a smoothness" (HD sec. 5; Lessing refers to *Hamlet*, 3.2.6–7). The polemical intent is obvious: To the extent that Hamlet represents Shakespeare's own voice, the call for "temperance" and "smoothness" corrects the image of Shakespearean drama as too rugged and undisciplined for the Franco-German stage. Stronger still, in Lessing's view, Hamlet's advice should be elevated to "a golden rule for all actors who care for sensible approbation."[10]

---

6. Williams, *Shakespeare on the German Stage*, vol. I, 10.

7. See for instance Nisbet, *Gotthold Ephraim Lessing*, 257.

8. For a discussion of Lessing's repertoire, see Nisbet, Gotthold Ephraim Lessing, 370. For the absence of Shakespeare in Hamburg and on the German stage, see Roger Paulin, *The Critical Reception of Shakespeare in Germany 1682–1914: Native Literature and Foreign Genius* (Hildesheim: Georg Olms, 2003), 92.

9. Lessing had translated Diderot, including *Entretiens sur le fils naturel*, into German. See Lessing, *Werke*, V/1 11–233. For a discussion of the significance of this point, see J. G. Robertson, *Lessing's Dramatic Theory: Being an Introduction to and Commentary on his Hamburgische Dramaturgie* (Cambridge: Cambridge University Press, 1939), 341.

10. Gotthold Ephraim Lessing, *Hamburg Dramaturgy*, trans. Helene Zimmern (New York: Dover, 1962); *Hamburgische Dramaturgie, Werke*, vol. VI, sec. 5. Further references to this work will be abbreviated HD and inserted, with reference to letter number, in the main text.

This Hamletian temperance should not, though, kill the passion of acting. The question, rather, is how the passion of acting—the "torrent, tempest, and whirlwind" (HD sec. 5; again Lessing is referring to 3.2.6–7)—can be achieved. In line with his defense, in *Laocoön*, of the intrinsic freedom of literary expression (over against the more restricted registers of plastic art), Lessing declares Shakespeare's right to exercise creative freedom *and*, by the same token, appeal to the actor to moderate her work so as to allow the text to stand forth as poetry. For Lessing, this needs to be so because acting is situated "midway between the plastic arts and poetry" (HD sec. 5). In terms of bodily language and voice, the actress is subject to demands of moderation. Her words, by contrast, can go beyond "the calm dignity that makes ancient sculpture so imposing" (HD sec. 5). Only when this tension—between words on paper and their being brought to life on stage—is properly navigated can the play achieve "a semblance of truth" and thus, in the particular case of *Hamlet*, make the play within the play, significantly named The Mousetrap, a litmus test of the new king's guilt in killing Hamlet's father.

Hamlet's interpretation of the play—his demand that the actors proceed with fitting care and moderation and his role, as Ophelia points out, as commentator and chorus (3.2.238)—is thus designed so as to confirm his interpretation of the world, or, rather, to confirm (or disconfirm) that his deepest fear, that his father was murdered by his brother, is not simply based in a subjective image of the world, but reflects the world as it is, plain and simple.[11] Only such certainty can give Hamlet the confidence he needs to revenge his father—i.e., to act beyond his dramaturgical modifications of The Mousetrap

11. In a certain sense, Hamlet's entire interpretation of the world—that the time is out of joint (1.5.186), that "this goodly frame the earth seems . . . a sterile promontory . . . a foul and pestilent congregation of vapors" (2.2.264–68)—only leads up to his interpretation of The Mousetrap. Thus Hamlet, during the performance, tells Ophelia that he, as the master dramaturge of stage and world, could "interpret between [her] and [her] love" if he only "could see the puppets dallying" (3.2.239–40).

(3.2.65–77). At stake is, in other words, a hope for an interpretation
of the play that, in triggering a certain reaction from the king, will
quell Hamlet's worry about the contingency of his own interpretation of the world and, by implication, his tormenting doubts—a play
(or, rather a play*ing*) in which "the action [is suited to] the word, the
word to the action," 3.2.17–18).

On the face of it, Lessing's insistence on the sculpturesque qualities of acting—which, in Hegel, will later be extended to the very
notion of a tragic hero[12]—seems to place him well within the camp of
a larger classicist (or at least classicist-friendly) culture. And as Lessing
had made it clear in *Laocoön*, he did indeed agree with Winckelmann's
conclusions about the primacy of the ancient Greeks. Where he differs
is mostly with respect to the *premises* from which these conclusions
are drawn, especially Winckelmann's methodology, which, Lessing
argues, moves from general principles to evidence individual cases,
rather than the other way around.[13] Yet Lessing's point, in *Hamburg
Dramaturgy*, goes beyond the merely methodological. Or, stronger
still, if we compare his discussion of the play within the play with his
discussion, soon after, of the domestic ghost scene, his arguments
point beyond his classicist inclinations. Lessing's interpretation of

12. Julia Peters offers a nice interpretation of this dimension of Hegel's work in her *Hegel on
Beauty* (London: Routledge, 2015), 39–62. Peters does not, however, realize that the
idea of the external expression of the inner, as we find it in Hegel's anthropology and
philosophy of sculpture, is already there in earlier philosophers such as Winckelmann,
Lessing, and Herder. For this aspect of Herder's work, see *Ueber Leibnizens Grundsätze
von der Natur und Gnade*, in *Sämmtliche Werke*, edited by Bernhard Ludwig Suphan et al.
(Berlin: Weidmannsche Verlag, 1877–), vol. XXXII, 225–27.
13. Winckelmann, on his side, will accuse Lessing, who aspires toward an inductive approach,
of not being sufficiently empirical in his approach to sculpture. See Nisbet, *Gotthold
Ephraim Lessing*, 303–33. See also Herder's discussion of Winckelmann and Lessing in
the first part of *Critical Forests* in Johann Gottfried Herder, *Selected Writings on Aesthetics*,
ed. and trans. Gregory Moore (Princeton, NJ: Princeton University Press, 2006), 51–177;
Werke in zehn Bänden, ed. Martin Bollacher et al. (Frankfurt am Main: Deutscher Klassiker
Verlag, 1985–98), vol. II, 57–245. Further references to these works will be abbreviated,
respectively, SWA and W and inserted into the main text.

the Mousetrap scene, of Hamlet's approach to acting, the world, and the relationship between them, pays homage to *Laocoön* and its discussion of artistic media. His analysis of the ghost scene, by contrast, engages the relationship between dramaturgical stage choices and the cultural-historical horizon of the audience. It is as if his work-oriented approach opens for a new appreciation of the modernity of modern theater.

In this context, it is no longer Winckelmann, but, rather, Voltaire who is the target of Lessing's criticism. When it comes to Voltaire's phi-losophy of history, Lessing is quite enthusiastic (he had, indeed, trans-lated Voltaire's work in this field). Voltaire, the tragedian, though, is an altogether different matter (HD sec. 10). The discussion of the ghost scene stages Shakespeare against Voltaire—or, better still, through the discussion of *Hamlet*, it stages Voltaire, as progressive philosopher of history, against Voltaire, as a conservative force in the (German) thea-ter.[14] The question at stake is the following: How best to dramatize the appearance of a ghost, such as the one in *Hamlet*, to an enlightened audience whose appreciation of "all spectral good manners" is long gone? Voltaire, Lessing points out, fails to recognize the historicity of the audience. He introduces, on stage, a ghost that cannot, under any circumstances, convince a modern spectatorship: it "steps out in broad daylight" and is "not even fit for a bugbear wherewith to frighten child-ren. It is only a disguised actor" (HD sec. 11). Shakespeare, as Lessing reads him, works his dramaturgy more cleverly, especially when the ghost appears to Hamlet in his mother's presence: "Shakespeare lets only Hamlet see the ghost, and in the scene where his mother is pres-ent, she neither sees nor hears it. All our attention is therefore fixed on him, and the more evidence of terror and horror we discover in this

14. For Voltaire's best known reading of Shakespeare, see *Philosophical Letters: Or, Letters Regarding the English Nation*, ed. John Leigh, trans Prudence L. Steiner (Indianapolis: Hackett, 2007); *Lettres philosophiques. Derniers écrits sur Dieu*, ed. Gerhardt Stenger (Paris: Flammarion, 2006), eighteenth letter. See Marvin Carlson, *Voltaire and the Theatre of the Eighteenth Century* (London: Greenwood Press, 1998), 81–97 and Michèle Willems, "Voltaire" (Willems nicely lays out how Voltaire's approach to Shakespeare changes over time).

fear-stricken soul, the more ready we are to hold the apparition that has awakened such agitation as that for which he holds it. The spectre operates on us, but through him rather than by itself" (HD sec. 11). Hence, in bringing in the historicity of the audience—and a distinctly nonclassicist emphasis on modern audiences needing modern plays and stagings[15]—the notion of moderation in acting is given a new twist. Moderation is a way in which a critical new spectatorship, that of the bourgeois theater, can be brought to "truthfulness."[16]

In re-evaluating the status of the audience, in placing it, as it were, in a central position of the theater (the actors bring a text to life by presenting it to an audience), Lessing, all the same, legitimizes the role of the dramaturge (as situated between actors and audience) *and* defends the position of a modern theater in a modern world. With this, he takes a significant step beyond a classicist outlook (be it in the form of Winckelmann's Platonism, Voltaire's drama, or, possibly, even his own position in *Laocoön*), thus opening the way for a new, philosophical reception of Hamlet (the character) as reflective of a distinctively modern mindset. A few years later, this is precisely the thread that Herder picks up in his *Fragments on Recent German Literature* (1767–68), his essay on Shakespeare (1772), and his journal contributions in the 1780s.

DRAMA IN HISTORY (HERDER)

With his concern for drama and his central role at the newly established national theater in Hamburg, Lessing had focused on Hamlet

---

15. "[A]ll antiquity believed in ghosts. Therefore, the poets of antiquity were quite right to avail themselves of this belief. If we encountered ghosts among them, it would be unreasonable to object to them according to our better knowledge. But does this accord the same permission to our modern poets who share our better knowledge? Certainly not" (HD sec. 11).

16. Truthfulness, though, is not the same as truth understood as factual (or historical) correctness. For a discussion of this point, see HD secs. 23–24.

as dramaturge and *Hamlet* as staged. Herder, in contrast, pays almost no attention to the craft of stage-setting. As he reads Shakespeare, *Hamlet* is first and foremost a work of dramatic poetry (as different from a play-text)[17] and it is as part of this broader field that it can and should be defended.

Herder's voice as an Enlightenment critic is sharpened through his engagement with Voltaire, Winckelmann, Lessing, and other Enlightenment figures. In fact, an early work such as *Fragments on Recent German Literature* (written just before Lessing's *Hamburg Dramaturgy*) took shape as a comment to the *Letters on Literature*, to which Lessing had been an instrumental contributor. At stake, for the young Herder, is in other words a criticism of criticism—including a criticism of the contemporary debate on Shakespeare. Herder supports Lessing's fight against French-style classicism and advises that German-speaking audiences look to England and not only to France for their aesthetic ideals.[18] Stronger still, he counsels German-language poets to synthesize the best of the English and French approaches (SEW 39; W I 83), but, risking a weakening of his own argument, quickly makes it clear that the example of Shakespeare (the English) is preferable to that of Voltaire (the French). And as if his somewhat eccentric juggling of cultural-poetical ideals were not enough, the very idea of originality through imitation is itself a bit of an aesthetic knot. Herder's position, though, is not as peculiar as it first appears to be. As he expresses his view in *On Recent German Literature*, contemporary poetry, including dramatic poetry, is stuck in a creative abyss. On the one hand, artists are often tempted by

---

17. I here follow Susan Feagin's distinction between drama as literature and as play-text and thank her for a rewarding semester of coteaching philosophy of theater at Temple University in the fall of 2015.
18. Johann Gottfried Herder, *Selected Early Works, 1764–1767*, ed. Ernest A. Menze and Karl Menges, trans. Ernest A. Menze with Michael Palma (University Park: Pennsylvania State University Press, 1992), 38; W I 81–82. Further references to the former will be abbreviated SEW.

passive imitation, be it of the ancients or the French (see, for example, SEW 112; W I 191). On the other hand, artists, going beyond the paradigm of imitation, turn from poetry to reflection *on* poetry, i.e., to aesthetics (which, in Herder's mind, the Germans master quite well, SEW 45; W I 90–91). In both cases, we are dealing with an anemic and rather miserable state of the arts. Shakespeare's work, Herder thinks, can point a way out of this impasse. As Herder puts it, an artist should not provide rules to be followed, but examples to inspire (SEW 145; W I 234).[19] Shakespeare did not imitate the ancients. And precisely the fact that Shakespeare did not imitate is what modern poets should take over. What started out as criticism of Francophile taste (it appreciates the wrong kind of art) thus funnels into a criticism of its implicit aesthetics (it has misunderstood what art is in the first place and, in particular, it has misunderstood art's relationship to its own history).[20]

In the 1760s, Herder is fairly close to Lessing. *Shakespeare* and his later work represent a freer approach. Herder, in the first book of *Critical Forests* (1769), had criticized both Winckelmann and Lessing. While he recognizes their different argumentative platforms (Winckelmann's inclination toward Platonism and Lessing's toward Aristotelianism), he does not accept their shared premise that, as he puts it, only the Greeks represent the beautiful (SWA 82–83; W II 109–10). Herder appreciates the shift from a (French) cultivation of Roman ideals to a (German) cultivation of the ancient Greeks, but does not see this as a genuine response to the more principled, philosophical issues he sets out to tackle, especially the challenge of historicity. In Herder's view, what needs to be addressed is the very idea that modern art can be understood by reference to ancient works and

---

19. Herder here anticipates a later Kantian position. See John Zammito, *The Genesis of Kant's Critique of Judgment* (Chicago: University of Chicago Press, 1992), 137–39 and 142.

20. Lessing's point about the historicity of the audience is, in other words, expanded so as to incorporate aesthetic production.

that, as a consequence, its modernity must be excused (since it does not fit with the classical ideals of beauty). As he puts it, "Shakespeare's boldest friends have mostly been content to *excuse,* to *defend* him from ... attacks; to weigh his beauties against his transgressions of the rules and see the former as compensation for the latter, to utter the absolve over the accused" (SWA 291; W II 498). Herder's question, in other words, is how Shakespeare's drama (or, more broadly, art) will look if we—contra Lessing—simply let go of the ideals of the ancients. How, he asks, can we best picture that which makes modern art modern? The Greeks and the moderns are, Herder emphasizes, fundamentally different; they are different in their arts and different in their outlooks on life.[21] Be it appreciative or critical, Shakespeare's work cannot be assessed with reference to Sophocles and the ancients: "Sophocles' drama and Shakespeare's drama are two things that in a certain respect have scarcely their name in common" (SWA 292; W II 500). In fact, as Herder views it, the only thing Shakespeare has in common with the Greeks, most notably Sophocles, is that he does for the English what Sophocles did for the Greeks: he produces works through which they understand themselves and their culture. So, as Herder sees it, "Shakespeare is Sophocles' brother precisely where he seems so dissimilar to him" (SWA 303; W II 515). How is it, then, that we have failed to see that precisely *in* breaking with the Greeks, Shakespeare has followed them? At this point, Herder is in line with Lessing and Enlightenment criticism. He turns to a discussion of prejudice, taste, and judgment, as they, in his view, feed into and shape our criteria for what counts as art in the first place. What started out with a focus on art (What art is good? What do we mean when we talk about art in the first place?), ends up with a focus on the critical audience (What would it take to develop a readership

---

21. Anticipating Nietzsche's later reading in *The Birth of Tragedy,* Herder relates this back to the way Greek drama originates in the chorus (SWA 292–93; W II 500–501).

that reflects on the often provincial ways in which we respond to the questions above and are thus in a position to better judgments?). For Herder, a move away from a Francophone taste is the first step needed. As he polemically puts it: "may God have mercy on the sportive Frenchman who arrives during Shakespeare's fifth act, thinking he will thereby be able to gulp down the quintessence of the play's feeling. That may be possible with some French dramas, because everything is versified and trotted out in scenes for merely theatrical effect; but with Shakespeare, he would come away empty-handed" (SWA 303; W II 515). Shakespearean drama remains at the center of Herder's discussion of normativity in aesthetics, although in the 1770s he does not, as Lessing had done, anchor his reflections in more detailed interpretations of any one play.[22]

In the early 1800s, Herder, in *Adrastea*, finally turns to a closer analysis of Shakespeare's drama. At this point Herder has, as it were, been through a number of critical-therapeutic exercises seeking to improve the interpretative skills of the modern audiences.[23] As part of his anticolonialist sentiments, he has discussed works that fall outside of the European canon, either in that they are non-European (Hebrew and Middle Eastern poetry, for example) or in that they are not considered high and valuable poetry (folk songs, Sami and Inuit poetry). Herder's turn to Shakespeare thus continues his efforts to sensitize a modern readership to poetry that falls outside the pale of established taste. Here the outlook of Shakespeare's drama is presented as that of a modern audience, whose faith in its own interpretations of art and its world is now freed from the checklist of classicist criteria. The modernity, we could say, of this audience requires an

22. In his Shakespeare essay, Herder refers to *Othello, Macbeth*, and *Hamlet*. He also discusses the increasing historical distance from Shakespeare's work (SWA 307; W II 520).
23. This is most clear in Herder's writing on the study of theology (W IX/1139–609) and his dialogue on Hebrew poetry. See *The Spirit of Hebrew Poetry*, trans. James Marsh, 2 vols. (Burlington: Edward Smith, 1833; W V 661–1309. Voltaire had already commented on

awareness of the fact that its judgments are based on a certain interpretation of the world *and* that this world, across time periods and
cultures, is diverse and changing. For Herder, there are no transcul-
tural criteria by which different cultures and paradigms of taste can
be hierarchically ranged or placed within a teleological narrative of
development.

If Greek poets wrote about individual heroes, Shakespeare wrote
about the world—he creates, in Herder's words, a whole world cycle
(*Weltzyklus*, W X 332). In the early 1770s, Herder had argued that
Shakespeare's drama displays the multiple, ever-changing shapes of
the world.[24] Now he emphasizes that the modern world is reflected
in the character of Hamlet. Like Lessing, Herder focuses on Hamlet's
encounter with the ghost and the suspicion that "the serpent that did
sting [his] father's life now wears his crown" (W X 333; Herder refers
to 1.5.38–39). Herder, though, does not ask whether the audience
believes or does not believe in ghosts. The question that interests him
is what prevents Hamlet from murdering the murderer (W X 333).
In Herder's reading, Hamlet does not lack in will. Nor does he lack in
strength and determination (one strike of his will kill Polonius). What
explains Hamlet's reluctance to act is, as Herder sees it, a combination
of his psychological disposition and his educational background:
pensive (*nachdenkend*), scholarly, and inclined to metaphysical speculation, he is indeed trained in Wittenberg (W X 333).[25] But not only
his father's murder (and murderer) is approached through a haze of
speculation. Ophelia is also perceived as through air most clouded

how an interest in English literature and an interest in Hebrew poetry went hand in hand.
See *Philosophical Letters; Lettres philosophiques*, eighteenth letter.

24. "If in Sophocles *a single* refined and musical language resounds as if in some ethereal realm,
then Shakespeare speaks the language of all peoples, and races of men; he is the interpreter
of Nature in all her tongues" (SWA 299; W II 509).

25. In this way, Herder applies his historicist credo that the meaning of a work should be
explained with reference to its original context, to the character of a play within the
(historical-cultural) context laid out in the work.

(*wie aus einer Geisterwelt*). To the young prince, his world and his future emerge as a burden. Speculating on Wittenberg's effect on Hamlet, Herder opposes German-style brooding to Laertes's gayer mindset as he returns from France (W X 334). For the melancholy Hamlet, the very thought of his father's ghost becomes a weakness (*Skrupel*, W X 334). Only the play within the play will quell his metaphysical quandaries and lead him to act (W X 335). However, for all his qualms, Hamlet is but a mirror of humanity—or, as Herder also puts it, of *sensus humanitatis* (W X 336).

In this way, what started as a celebration of Shakespeare over against an ahistorical cultivation of the ideals of the ancient Greeks developed via a praise for his ability to represent a modern world to a modern audience, and culminates in an image of what this modernity consists in: the world as mirrored in Hamlet's protophilosophical mind. The very symptom of Hamlet's misery, his failure to find meaning in the world, is but a symptom of the modern era. In its proclivity to speculative thought and abstraction, the modern mindset can no longer take for granted its ability to feel at home in the world. After a twenty-year period of Shakespearean reading, translation, and criticism, referring to the tragedies and the historical works, it is *Hamlet* that brings out the more existential dimensions of Herder's philosophy. This, as Herder now puts it (gesturing back to his old battles with Winckelmann), is the *stille Große* of modern art: the individual mind is immersed in the world, which, in turn, is mirrored in the mind of a singular individual. It is no small weight the young prince bears on his shoulders— nor a small weight we, as readers and interpreters of Shakespeare's drama, bear on ours. Lessing had seen dramatic poetry as painting of action in time. Herder, by contrast, points out that Shakespeare's *Hamlet* addresses, if not exactly a lack of action, then at least the thinking and deliberation that, for a metaphysically predisposed student from Wittenberg, goes into making up his mind so as to act. With his philosophical disposition, Hamlet (and his author) presents the

Germans, whose creativity is about to be killed by a propensity to abstract thought, with a mindset in which they recognize themselves far too well. Herder maintains the point that every Shakespeare play is different and exposes a different *Welt-, Zeit- und Lebensgeist*. But he also realizes that this multiplicity of perspectives and ways of being human is something that may throw us, like Hamlet, into an epistemic, metaphysical, and existential conundrum. Hence, whereas Herder, even in his late work, shares in Lessing's hopes for *Bildung* through dramatic poetry (or, for Lessing, staged theater), he nonetheless goes beyond Lessing in that he, first, leaves behind the normative ideals of the ancients (including Sophocles and Aristotle) and, second, upon turning to the modernity of Shakespearean drama, sees Shakespeare— and *Hamlet* in particular—as a mirror in which modern audiences can begin to grasp their existence as genuinely and profoundly modern.[26] Hence, for Herder, the (negative) criticism of the idea of aesthetic rules goes hand in hand with a (positive) account of an artwork's ability to reflect its own time. In the late analysis of *Hamlet*, these points merge in a subtle and sensitive analysis of the play's protagonist and his relating (or perhaps failure to relate) to his world.

INTERPRETING MODERNITY (SCHLEGEL)

Throughout the 1780s, Herder consolidates his reading of Shakespeare as a genuinely modern playwright and Hamlet as the prince of a modern mindset of interpretation. With the work of

---

26. This point is later taken over and further elaborated by Hegel. See G. W. F. Hegel, *Lectures on Fine Art*, 2 vols., trans. T. M. Knox (Oxford: Clarendon Press, 1975), vol. I 583–84 and vol. II 1226; *Vorlesungen über die Ästhetik*, 3 vols., *Werke in 20 Bänden*, ed. Eva Moldenhauer and Karl Markus Michel (Frankfurt am Main: Suhrkamp Verlag, 1970) vol. II 207–8 and III 559.

A. W. Schlegel, this point gets brought into the very heart of the German Shakespeare reception.

August Wilhelm Schlegel and his younger brother Friedrich were dedicated philosophers of literature. They both took an interest in Shakespeare. And they both saw Goethe (whose reading of Shakespeare was inspired by Herder) as the flag-carrier of modern drama. August Wilhelm would write on Shakespeare and Goethe in Schiller's periodical *Die Horen*. Yet it would be his lectures on dramatic art, given some ten years later, that would confirm his reputation as a philosopher in the Shakespearean spirit. In different ways, Lessing and Herder had fought to have Shakespeare's drama acknowledged and appreciated by a German audience. When Schlegel, in the early 1800s, lectured on dramatic arts, *Hamlet* had already been staged in Germany, albeit often in somewhat stunted versions.[27] Schlegel himself had translated Shakespeare and thus contributed to his (Shakespeare's) increasing fame and popularity.

In his 1796 essay on Goethe and Shakespeare, Schlegel turns to the newly published *Wilhelm Meister's Apprenticeship*, the second installment of Goethe's sequence.[28] The subtext of his essay is clear: If Goethe, a modern writer par excellence, is working in the vein of Shakespeare, then any (philosophical) attempt to understand modern literature must involve an attempt to understand Shakespeare—and, especially, *Hamlet*, which Schlegel characterizes as the most admirable *and* the most misunderstood of Shakespeare's plays.[29] In his discussion of the differences between painting and

---

27. See Roger Paulin, *The Critical Reception of Shakespeare in Germany*, 192.
28. Goethe's speech *Zum Shakespeares Tag* was posthumously published.
29. August Wilhelm Schlegel, *Etwas über William Shakespeare bey Gelegenheit Wilhelm Meisters*, in Friedrich Schlegel, *Die Horen*, vol. 6, no. 4-1796, 57–112 (http://www.zbk-online.de/texte/A1661.htm). The quote is from p. 63. Further references will be abbreviated EWS, followed by page number.

poetry, Lessing had emphasized the centrality of acting and dramatic action. For Schlegel, however, *Hamlet* is first and foremost a *Gedankenschauspiel* (and so, for that sake, is Goethe's *Faust*, EWS 69). Be it as painter or poet (Schlegel deliberately traverses Lessing's distinction [EWS 76]), Shakespeare creates (*bildet*) human beings and gives them life (EWS 67). As Schlegel reads the play, Hamlet's life is not so much one of will as one of cognition.[30] This stance, however, leads actors, in playing Hamlet, to challenge their acting styles. And while Shakespeare introduces foreign names, customs, characters, and acting styles on stage, *Hamlet* still strikes a familiar chord in the German-speaking audiences (EWS 69).

If Lessing had mourned the absence of a modern, German audience and Herder the absence of modern, German art, Schlegel bravely announces the era of a new romantic literature.[31] *Hamlet* is an early prototype of this literary spirit. This thought—that modern literature is Shakespearean (or even Hamletian)—is further developed in Schlegel's lectures on dramatic poetry, though Schlegel, in this context, goes beyond the question of what Shakespeare can teach modern artists and looks to what kind of reflection *Hamlet* evokes in modern critics and aestheticians.

Over the span of thirty lectures, Schlegel discusses the nature of drama, the goals and methods of aesthetics, and the relationship between art and theory. Seven of the lectures are dedicated to Shakespeare. As Schlegel now presents it, reinforcing but also expanding his previous points, *Hamlet* is a proto-romantic figure,

---

30. "[S]eine Erkenntniß [ist] seiner Willenskraft weit überlegen" (EWS 69).
31. As Friedrich Schlegel would put it in *Critical Fragments* (1797), "Whoever could manage to interpret Goethe's *Meister* properly would have expressed what is now happening in literature. He could, so far as literary criticism is concerned, retire forever." Friedrich Schlegel, *Lucinde and the Fragments*, trans. Peter Firchow (Minneapolis: University of Minnesota Press, 1971), 158; *Kritische Friedrich-Schlegel-Ausgabe*, ed. Ernst Behler et al., vol. II, ed. Hans Eichner (Munich: Ferdinand Schöning, 1967), 162 (no. 120). In the *Athenaeum Fragments*, we also read that "Shakespeare's universality is like the center of romantic art." This fragment is immediately followed by a turn to Shakespeare, in fragment no. 121.

and romantic art, that is, art in the Hamletian spirit, is reflective and philosophical.

Again Schlegel approaches *Hamlet* from a Goethean framework. Not only had Schlegel written on Shakespeare and Goethe in *Die Horen*, but his brother, Friedrich Schlegel, had also championed Goethe's work by famously remarking, "The French Revolution, Fichte's Philosophy, and Goethe's *Meister* are the greatest tendencies of the age."[32] From this point of view, it is a bit of an understatement when August Wilhelm remarks that Goethe's *Wilhelm Meister* is "more than an episode."[33] So is also Wilhelm Meister's dedication to *Hamlet* (as *Gedankenschauspiel*).[34] And if *Hamlet* is a reflective play, then it is, all the same, an invitation for poetry and philosophers, whose métier is that of reflectiveness, to join forces.

In the Vienna lectures, Schlegel is speaking with the concerns of the translator. Should *Hamlet* be conveyed in its entirety or in a shortened form? Should it be rendered in prose or poetry? What should the audience make of the diverse characters populating the Shakespearean stage?[35] Can a play such as *Hamlet* at all be characterized by reference to the traditional distinction between tragedy and comedy? Shakespeare, Schlegel suggests, wrote neither comedies nor tragedies. His plays, rather, emerge as romantic drama (*Schauspiele*).[36] From Schlegel's point of view, it is evident that Greek drama is no

---

32. Friedrich Schlegel, *Lucinde and the Fragments*, 190; *Athenäum Fragmente, Kritische Friedrich-Schlegel-Ausgabe*, vol. II, 198 (no. 116).
33. August Wilhelm Schlegel, *Sämtliche Werke*, ed. Edouard Böcking, 16 vols. (Hildesheim: Olms, 1972), vol. VII, 24. Further references will be abbreviated SW.
34. See SW VII 31. Schlegel here challenges Lessing's notion of drama, a subfield of poetry, as being concerned with action.
35. Schlegel points to the complexity of Shakespeare's characters and the diversity of characters on stage (*Sämtliche Werke* VII 42), a point already made by Herder. For a discussion of this point, see Paulin, *Voltaire, Goethe, Schlegel*, 112.
36. August Wilhelm Schlegel, *Lectures on Dramatic Art and Literature*, trans. John Black, http://www.gutenberg.org/ebooks/7148, 229; SW VI 158. Further references to the former will be abbreviated DAL, followed by page number.

longer an ideal for imitation (i.e., unlike Lessing and Herder, he need not argue this point, but can assume it as more or less a given). Anticipating Nietzsche's later proposition (and drawing, we could add, on Herder's earlier analysis), Schlegel notes that Greek culture dies when the Greeks begin to imitate the Greeks (DAL 228; SW VI 156). Modern drama need not obey the unity of time and; it need not obey the purity of genre. Romantic drama is impure—a hybrid. If Hamlet lives in a world of subjective interpretation, so, too, do the other characters. And they live and act their interpretations. As such, romantic drama reflects romantic existence: "Romantic poetry," in Schlegel's words, "is the expression of the secret attraction to a chaos which lies concealed in the very bosom of the ordered universe, and is perpetually striving after new and marvelous births; the life-giving spirit of primal love broods here anew on the face of the waters" (DAL 230; SW VI 161). If ancient drama is like a group of sculptures (again, we see a reference to Lessing), then a romantic play such as *Hamlet* is more like a painting in which just about every feature of the world can be brought in (DAL 231; SW VI 162). Whereas Herder had compared the polyphonic modes of Shakespearean drama to the multiple reflections of a ray of light in a drop of water, Schlegel speaks of its magic light (DAL 231; SW VI 162).

Along the lines of Lessing (his discussion of the ghost scene) and Herder (his discussion of Hamlet's mindset), Schlegel's question, though, is not only what kind of art romantic drama is, but also what kind of response this art elicits. Before Lessing and Herder, an early generation of critics had described Shakespeare in not very flattering terms as a child of nature. Schlegel here mentions Milton (DAL 233; SW VI 167), but also Hume and Voltaire, to whom Shakespeare emerged as a madman (DAL 234; SW VI 168).[37] A later generation of critics would appropriate this description (the child of nature), but

37. See, again, *Philosophical Letters; Lettres philosophiques*, eighteenth letter.

reverse the normative weighting and celebrate Shakespeare's style as particularly free and imaginative: Shakespeare is indeed a child of nature, but, once we abandon classicist rules and petty-minded standards, this is not a problem in need of a solution, but the very source of his greatness. Wishing to get beyond this kind of either-or thinking—*either* we have a natural genius *or* a well-trained rule-follower—Schlegel insists that Shakespeare, while writing in a free and natural way, still has a clear (aesthetically trained) sense of what he is doing (DAL 234, 241; SW VI 168, 183). This, Schlegel suggests, is evident once his work is placed within its own historical context, that of Elizabethan culture.

In order to understand Shakespeare we need, Schlegel insists, to look "into the sources from which [he] drew the materials of his plays, and also into the previous and contemporary state of the English stage, and other kindred subjects of inquiry" (DAL 233; SW VI 165–66). Shakespeare's drama must be understood with reference to his world. This also applies to the diversity of characters populating Shakespeare's drama. Schlegel points to the gravedigger scene and remarks on how it stages a collision of cultures (today we would perhaps say of classes), albeit one that is characteristic of life in Shakespeare's England (DAL 235; SW VI 170). We can, he further remarks, get to know a lot about Elizabethan England through Shakespeare—not because Shakespeare wrote drama that can be evaluated with reference to factual accuracy (a point Lessing had brought forth against Voltaire), but because it presents a particular outlook on life (DAL 236; SW VI 171). As Schlegel presents it, modernity represents a manifold of historical and culturally coded interpretations. And modern (romantic) drama shows us how these interpretations are lived out and what happens in their encounters and collisions. As Herder had done before him, Schlegel worries about the possible end of art. We moderns are unpoetical, he claims (DAL 241; SW VI 183). Being constitutively unpoetical, we are alienated and displaced.

We are, as he puts it, not at home in the world when we are at home, but only when we are *not* at home and thus actively and consciously inhabiting our alienation (DAL 241; SW VI 183). Shakespeare portrays characters that do not own themselves and their interpretations of themselves and the world, but rely on the interpretation (or recognition) of others.[38] In Schlegel's words, "Shakespeare makes each of his principal characters the glass in which the others are reflected, and by like means enables us to discover what could not be immediately revealed to us" (DAL 248; SW VI 197). In this way, the characters on stage are, in a certain respect, all acting—*and* the actors are acting their enactments. Along these lines, Hamlet's life is, for Schlegel, one of acting—indeed, there is, for him, a link between acting and action (DAL 248; SW VI 197). As a character of Shakespeare's drama, his role is acted, yet this acting includes the realization of a young man who acts mad (DAL 272; SW VI 249). In Schlegel's view, Hamlet "has no firm belief either in himself or in anything else" (DAL 273; SW VI 250). For, as he quotes Shakespeare, "[t]here is nothing either good or bad, but thinking makes it so" (DAL 273; SW VI 250).[39] A modern world is a world of interpretation—yet as critics and audiences, as *romantic* critics and audiences, we should respond to this by seeing the interpretations offered *and* the very emphasis on interpretation as a distinctly modern (romantic) phenomenon. In this sense, art, for Schlegel, has reached an end. Criticism has been brought to the foreground.

38. Schlegel here repeats a point anticipated by Herder. As Herder had argued, human beings do not possess immediate self-understanding. Nor do they have immediate access to the minds of others. They only have access to self-understanding as they express themselves. Immediate self-understanding would require a divine point of view (W II 572). This point is later repeated in Hegel's *Phenomenology of Spirit*. It is, however, Sartre who, in his work on theater, will return to the Schlegelian point about the interrelationship between acting (on stage) and play-acting (in life).

39. In this way, Schlegel continues, "the destiny of humanity is here exhibited as a gigantic Sphinx, which threatens to precipitate into the abyss of skepticism all who are unable to solve her dreadful enigmas" (DAL 273; SW VI 251).

Actors, he moans, have become rusty and national stages are like hospitals (DAL 355; SW VI 429).[40] Aesthetics, not art, is the force of the moderns (DAL 356; SW VI 431), and speculation, not creation, their expressive modus. In reminding us of the early days of modern art, in first presenting art as modern, Shakespeare should thus be treated like an "ancient": Shakespeare represents a genealogical beginning of our art and Hamlet an early champion of modernity. In this way, Schlegel completes the Hamletian drift of German aesthetics. After Schlegel, Hegel, Schopenhauer, Dilthey, and Nietzsche all keep reading and commenting on Shakespeare and *Hamlet*. Yet they do so with an awareness that modern (or, with Schlegel, romantic) art is in a certain sense produced in a Shakespearean spirit.

CONCLUSION

From Lessing, via Herder, to Schlegel, the early, philosophical *Hamlet* reception leaves us with the following: Seeking to interpret his world, being aware that his worldview represents an interpretation, *and*, finally, thinking about the very nature of interpretation, Hamlet, the character, has given us a new task. Not only do we need to ask, critically and philosophically, what we mean when we use general aesthetic categories such as "art," "drama," or "tragedy," but in order to answer this question, we also need to engage in the interpretation of specific works (such as *Hamlet*). Moreover, to the extent that we follow Lessing, Herder, and Schlegel, we need to take into account what interpretation, philosophically speaking, is in the first place. As the classicist mindset, with its clear-cut ideals and rule sets,

---

40. Again Schlegel relies on a distinctly Herderian metaphor. Herder had described how Lessing's position on fear and pity forces him to "bid farewell to the theater" since he now finds himself in the hospital ("Lebe wohl, Theater! so bin ich in der Lazarettstube," SWA 172; W II 101).

loses its authority, so also does the certainty that we, as audiences, critics, and interpreters, know what art is. And the very question "What is art?" does, in their views, evoke the question, "Who are we, in seeking to answer this question?" As it grows out of the encounter with Shakespeare, and especially *Hamlet*, the interest in interpretation does not invite the kind of anything-goes attitude that we sometimes associate with the reception of Sturm und Drang, and romantic philosophy, and hermeneutics in the 1980s and beyond.[41] What we find, rather, is an awareness of historicity, of the relationship between drama and historicity, spectatorship and historicity, interpretation and historicity that will remain a crucial feature in European aesthetics as it later takes shape in Hegel, Dilthey, and Nietzsche. While Shakespeare and *Hamlet* will figure prominently in later nineteenth-century thought, it is late eighteenth-century criticism, as philosophers were still trying to figure out whether Shakespearean drama could and should be counted as poetry, that lays the groundwork for this reception. From this point of view, the interest in Shakespeare and *Hamlet*, in the decades from Lessing's *Literaturbrief* to Schlegel's Vienna lectures, is not simply a passing, somewhat quaint testimony to Enlightenment taste and its romantic cousin, but a most decisive moment for the systematic formation of aesthetics and philosophy of drama in the European tradition.

WORKS CITED

Carlson, Marvin. 1998. *Voltaire and the Theatre of the Eighteenth Century*. London: Greenwood Press.

Hegel, G. W. F. 1970. *Werke in 20 Bänden*. Ed. Eva Moldenhauer and Karl Markus Michel. Frankfurt am Main: Suhrkamp Verlag.

41. See, for example, Philippe Lacoue-Labarthe and Jean-Luc Nancy, *The Literary Absolute: The Theory of Literature in German Romanticism* (Albany: SUNY Press, 1988); *L'Absolu littéraire. Théorie de la literature du romantisme allemande* (Paris: Éditions du Seuil, 1978).

Hegel, G. W. F. 1975. *Lectures on Fine Art.* 2 vols. Trans. T. M. Knox. Oxford: Clarendon Press.

Herder, Johann Gottfried. 1833. *The Spirit of Hebrew Poetry.* Trans. James Marsh. 2 vols. Burlington: Edward Smith.

———. 1877. *Sämmtliche Werke.* Ed. Bernhard Ludwig Suphan et al. Berlin: Weidmannsche Verlag.

———. 1985–98. *Werke in zehn Bänden.* Ed. Martin Bollacher et al. Frankfurt am Main: Deutscher Klassiker Verlag.

———. 1992. *Selected Early Works, 1764–1767.* Ed. Ernest A. Menze and Karl Menges. Trans. Ernest A. Menze with Michael Palma. University Park: Pennsylvania State University Press.

———. 2006. *Selected Writings on Aesthetics.* Trans. and ed. Gregory Moore. Princeton, NJ: Princeton University Press.

Höyng, Peter. 2005. "Lessing's Drama Theory: Discursive Writings on Drama, Performance, and Theater." *A Company to the Works of Gotthold Ephraim Lessing.* Ed. Barbara Fischer and Thomas C. Fox. Rochester, NY: Camden House. 211–29.

Lacoue-Labarthe, Philippe, and Jean-Luc Nancy. 1978. *L'Absolu littéraire. Théorie de la literature du romantisme allemande.* Paris: Éditions du Seuil.

———. 1988. *The Literary Absolute: The Theory of Literature in German Romanticism.* Trans. Philip Barnard and Cheryl Lester. Albany: SUNY Press.

Lessing, Gotthold Ephraim. 1962. *Hamburg Dramaturgy.* Trans. Helene Zimmern. New York: Dover.

———. 1984. *Laocoön: An Essay on the Limits of Painting and Poetry.* Trans. Edward Allen McCormick. Baltimore: Johns Hopkins University Press.

———. 1985–2003. *Werke und Briefe in Zwölf Bänden.* Ed. Wilfried Barner et al. Frankfurt: Deutscher Klassiker Verlag.

Nisbet, H. B. 2013. *Gotthold Ephraim Lessing: His Life, Works, and Thought.* Oxford: Oxford University Press.

Paulin, Roger. 2003. *The Critical Reception of Shakespeare in Germany, 1682–1914: Native Literature and Foreign Genius.* Hildesheim: Georg Olms.

Peters, Julia. 2015. *Hegel on Beauty.* London: Routledge.

Robertson, J. G. 1939. *Lessing's Dramatic Theory: Being an Introduction to and Commentary on his "Hamburgische Dramaturgie".* Cambridge: Cambridge University Press.

Schlegel, August Wilhelm. 1796. *Etwas über William Shakespeare bey Gelegenheit Wilhelm Meisters. Die Horen* 6.4: 57–112. (http://www.zbk-online.de/texte/A1661.htm).

———. 1972. *Sämtliche Werke.* ed. Edouard Böcking. 16 vols. Hildesheim: Olms.

———. 2004. *Lectures on Dramatic Art and Literature.* Trans. John Black. http://www.gutenberg.org/ebooks/7148.

Schlegel, Friedrich. 1967. *Kritische Friedrich-Schlegel-Ausgabe.* Ed. Ernst Behler et al. Munich: Ferdinand Schöning.

————. 1971. *Lucinde and the Fragments*. Trans. Peter Firschow. Minneapolis: University of Minnesota Press.

Voltaire. 2006. *Lettres philosophiques. Derniers écrits sur Dieu*. Ed. Gerhardt Stenger. Paris: Flammarion.

————. 2007. *Philosophical Letters: Or, Letters Regarding the English Nation*. Trans. Prudence L. Steiner. Ed. John Leigh. Indianapolis: Hackett.

Willems, Michèle. 2010. "Voltaire." *Great Shakespeareans*. Ed. Peter Holland and Adrian Poole. 18 vols. Vol. III, *Voltaire, Goethe, Schlegel, Coleridge*. Ed. Roger Paulin. London: Continuum. 5–43.

Williams, Simon. 1990. *Shakespeare on the German Stage*. Vol. I, *1586–1914*. Cambridge: Cambridge University Press.

Zammito, John. 1992. *The Genesis of Kant's Critique of Judgment*. Chicago: University of Chicago Press.

INDEX